The Mexican Revolution

NUMBER FORTY-FOUR

Walter Prescott Webb Memorial Lectures

The Mexican Revolution

CONFLICT AND CONSOLIDATION, 1910–1940

Edited by Douglas W. Richmond & Sam W. Haynes

Introduction by John Mason Hart

Contributors:

Nicholas Villanueva Jr.
Don M. Coerver
Miguel Ángel González-Quiroga
Linda B. Hall
Francisco E. Balderrama
Jürgen Buchenau
Stephen E. Lewis
Carlos Martínez Assad
Thomas Benjamin

Published for the University of Texas at Arlington
by Texas A&M University Press
College Station

First edition

This paper meets the requirements of ANSI/NISO Z39.48–1992
(Permanence of Paper).
Binding materials have been chosen for durability.

Library of Congress Cataloging-in-Publication Data

The Mexican Revolution : conflict and consolidation, 1910–1940 / edited by Douglas W. Richmond and Sam W. Haynes ; introduction by John Mason Hart ; contributors: Nicholas Villanueva Jr. . . . [et al.].—1st ed.

p. cm.—(Walter Prescott Webb memorial lectures ; 44)

Includes index.

ISBN-13: 978-1-60344-816-1 (cloth : alk. paper)

ISBN-10: 1-60344-816-0 (cloth : alk. paper)

ISBN-13: 978-1-60344-955-7 (ebook-c)

ISBN-10: 1-60344-955-8 (ebook-c)

1. Mexico—History—Revolution, 1910–1920—Influence. 2. Mexico—History—Revolution, 1910–1920—Political aspects. 3. Mexico—History—Revolution, 1910–1920 Social aspects. 4. Mexican-American Border Region—History—20th century. 5. Mexican-American Border Region—Ethnic relations—Political a spects—History—20th century. 6. Nationalism—Mexico—History—20th century. 7. Mexico—History—1910–1946. 8. Texas—History—1846–1950. I. Richmond, Douglas W., 1946- II. Haynes, Sam W. (Sam Walter), 1956- III. Villanueva, Nicholas. IV. Series: Walter Prescott Webb memorial lectures ; 44.

F1234.M584 2013

972.08'16—dc23

2012029169

Contents

Preface

The Mexican Revolution is one of the seminal chapters in the history of Mexico. More than any other single event, the revolution was responsible for creating the modern Mexican nation-state by contributing to a greater degree of democratization, land reform, anticlericalism, and other far-reaching changes in Mexican society. In addition, the civil war, which began in 1910 and lasted more than a decade, had a profound impact on formal and informal relations between the United States and Mexico. Resulting in the flight of hundreds of thousands of refugees, the rebellion prompted the first major northern migration of Mexican citizens. In so doing, it permanently changed the demographics of the American Southwest, energizing and shaping Latino culture in the United States.

In 2008, history professor Douglas W. Richmond of the University of Texas at Arlington conceived of the idea of making the Mexican Revolution the focus of the 2010 Walter Prescott Webb Memorial Lectures, held annually by his department. Richard Francaviglia, then serving as director of the Center for Greater Southwestern Studies at UT Arlington, also began planning a series of events to commemorate the centennial of the revolution. Although Dr. Francaviglia retired the following year, work on the program continued under new director Sam W. Haynes. In its final form, the program consisted of a workshop on the Mexican Revolution for secondary-school teachers, a major photographic exhibit on the events of 1910–1921, and a two-day series of lectures featuring scholars from the United States and Mexico. Cosponsored by the UT Arlington history department and the Center for Greater Southwestern Studies, the chapters in this volume were presentations made on March 10–11 as part of the 45th annual Walter Prescott Webb Memorial Lectures.

The historians featured in this anthology have written and researched extensively on twentieth-century Mexico. The introduction to the volume was written by John Mason Hart, the John and Rebecca Moores Professor of History at the University of Houston, widely regarded as one of the foremost authorities on the revolutionary period. In the first chapter, Nicholas Villanueva Jr., winner of the 2010 Webb-Smith Essay Competition, held in conjunction with the Webb Lectures, examines the case of León Martínez, an El Paso youth who was executed for the murder of an Anglo woman, thereby raising questions about the fate of ethnic Mexicans living in Texas during the early years of the Mexican Revolution. Don Coerver of Texas Christian

University discusses how US and Mexican officials along the border sought to deal with the outbreak of violence after 1910 and the extent to which they were successful in coordinating their efforts. Well-known Monterrey historian Miguel Ángel González-Quiroga examines the role of Monterrey during the conflict, emphasizing that many of its citizens preferred the goals of economic development and increased commercial relations with the United States to the goals of the revolution. Linda B. Hall of the University of New Mexico discusses the US government's response to the arrival of Mexican immigrants and its prosecution of those who were suspected of criminal activity. Francisco Balderrama, California State University at Los Angeles, explains how Mexican immigrants became a convenient scapegoat for communities in the Southwest, such as Los Angeles, which were suffering economic hardship during the Depression. This led to widespread repatriation drives, with the result that one million Mexicans were illegally returned to Mexico. Professor Jürgen Buchenau of the University of North Carolina at Charlotte analyzes several significant leaders from the state of Sonora who controlled Mexico from 1920 to 1934 by means of astute political maneuvering and decisive military campaigns while championing the working class, anticlericalism, and education. Stephen Lewis of California State University at Chico examines the marginal, ethnically diverse state of Chiapas, which fiercely resisted the land, labor, and educational reforms commonly associated with the revolution. The violence that broke out in Chiapas at the end of the twentieth century may be attributed at least in part, Lewis maintains, to the compromised nature of the revolution's reforms. Dr. Carlos Martínez Assad of the Universidad Nacional Autónoma de México examines the postrevolutionary return to centralism in the 1920s and 1930s, when President Lázaro Cárdenas initiated the process of limiting the power of regional leaders by consolidating the authority of the national government's political party, the Partido de la Revolución Mexicana. The final chapter in this anthology is by Thomas Benjamin, Central Michigan University, who presented the Webb Lectures' keynote address, "Whither the Mexican Revolution? The Revolution as Legacy and Project." In this fitting postscript, Benjamin examines the memory and the legacy of the revolution and considers how they can be used by those seeking a progressive transformation of Mexico in the twenty-first century.

The photographs in this volume have been selected from three separate collections, all of which were exhibited on campus during the Mexican Revolution centennial program at the Center for Greater Southwestern Studies. In the spring of 2010 the UT Arlington Library was the venue for "Mexico: The Revolution and Beyond," a touring exhibit of more than 90 images from the Archivo Casasola, one of the world's first news-photography agencies, on loan from the National Institute of Anthropology and History (INAH) in Mexico City. The Center for Greater Southwestern Studies also secured "La Tierra y su Gente: The Rio Grande Photographs of Robert Runyon," a collection of 32 images by Brownsville commercial photographer Robert Runyon from the archives of the Dolph Briscoe Center for American History, UT Austin. To complement these two exhibits, the Center for Greater Southwestern Studies, working with the staff of the Central Library's Special Collections, produced an exhibit of its own, "Images of Conflict, 1910–1921," a selection of 40 images of various aspects of the revolution, from the Porfiriato to the Obregón years. Together, these three exhibits—totaling 162 images—provided a unique and compelling visual chronicle of life in Mexico and along its border with the United States in the early decades of the twentieth century.

A great many people helped to make the 45th annual Walter Prescott Webb Memorial Lectures and the Mexican Revolution centennial program possible. The Webb volumes are supported by a generous endowment from C. B. Smith Sr., a former student of Walter Prescott Webb, and supplemented by the Rudolf Hermanns Endowment for the Liberal Arts. In addition, the centennial program received generous financial support from the Summerlee Foundation, Humanities Texas, and UT Arlington's College of Liberal Arts, the Graduate School, and the Office of the Provost. A great many people also worked to make the program a success. We would like to thank Department of History chair Robert Fairbanks, Webb Lectures committee chair Joyce Goldberg, and graduate student Merry Jett, who served as assistant to the Webb Lectures committee. Introductions for the featured speakers were delivered by Chris Conway (associate professor of modern languages, UT Arlington), Aaron Navarro (associate professor of history, University of North Texas), José Ángel Gutiérrez (professor of political science, UT Arlington), Monica Rankin (associate professor, School of Arts and Humanities, University of Texas at Dallas), and Ron Tyler (director, Amon Carter Museum). We also wish to thank the Mexican Consulate, Dallas, and particularly cultural affairs program officer Adolfo Ayuso Audry and Astrid Galván Segura, who were instrumental in bringing the traveling exhibit "Mexico: The Revolution and Beyond" to campus. A reception to mark the opening of the Casasola exhibit was sponsored by the Center for Mexican American Studies. We would also like to thank Gerald Saxon, dean of the library, who made the library's facilities available to the Center for Greater Southwestern Studies for the Mexican Revolution centennial program. Two members of the Special Collections staff, Cathy Spitzenberger and Brenda McClurkin, assisted Sam Haynes, director of the center, with the "Images of Conflict, 1910–1921" exhibit. Erin O'Malley, the library's Exhibits Coordinator, deserves special mention for her work in mounting all three photographic exhibits on the library's sixth floor. Chris Conway provided Spanish-language translations of the exhibit's promotional materials. We would also like to thank administrative staff members Elizabeth York, Beverly Ann Jennings, and Amanda Harris of the Center for Greater Southwestern Studies.

Finally, this book is dedicated to Jenkins Garrett, who passed away in 2009, one year before these lectures were held. Students of the American Southwest owe a special debt of gratitude to Mr. Garrett, who was an avid collector of historical materials relating to Texas and Mexico. A prominent Fort Worth attorney, philanthropist, and champion of higher education in North Texas, Mr. Garrett will be remembered at UT Arlington chiefly for his generous support of the Central Library's Special Collections, the Center for Greater Southwestern Studies, and the history department. Former UT Arlington president Wendell Nedderman summed up Mr. Garrett's contributions succinctly but accurately: "He was the greatest benefactor UT Arlington has ever had."

— Douglas W. Richmond and Sam W. Haynes

The Mexican Revolution

Introduction

The Mexican Revolution

John Mason Hart

This fine collection of essays provides an essential understanding of the twentieth century's first monumental social and political upheaval. The deeper nature of the revolution—the altering of class relationships, immigration and its influence on the border population, the survival strategies of the oligarchy, the fate of revolutionary peasants and workers, the depth and extent of nationalism, the nature of genderized outcomes, and the transformation of the Mexican regime—are all discussed here with vivid insights.

The Mexican Revolution resonates today as one of the fateful episodes in the nation's history, second only to the Spanish invasion of the early sixteenth century, in which the *conquistadores* and those who immediately followed defeated a complex of civilizations. The Spaniards brought new economies, technologies, ethnic relationships, language, and religion to the masses. That process, as it relates to the revolution, resulted in social and political inequalities that were contradicted by the higher ideals of the village padres, with their role in the creation of the *municipio libre* and its *asamblea popular*, and by the rise of secular intellectual pluralism in the eighteenth and nineteenth centuries.

The material conditions that led to the revolution became acute during the *porfiriato* (1876–1910), when the regime's notion of bifurcated development resulted in formal education for the few but continued illiteracy for the masses, as well as the construction of infrastructure to provide transportation for rural products in agriculture, mining, and timber, which were produced on a large scale, while leaving rural settlements with ages-old trails. This unequal system concentrated wealth in the hands of 7,200 hacienda owners and some 45,000 rancheros, less than 1 percent of the rural population, while leaving more than 11,000,000 rural workers underemployed, destitute, and oppressed by debt peonage and even slavery. At the same time, some 162 foreign capitalists came to control more than 80 percent of the nation's frontiers and coastlines and, with concentrated investments, 22 percent of the national surface, including virtually all of the strategic resources. The extent of their indirect control via mortgages, trading arrangements, and financial contracts is still not known.

The revolution resulted in the nationalization of more than 150 million acres of elite and foreign-held lands. By 1940 the Mexican oligarchy had lost most of its hold over agricultural and timberlands, and the foreigners had lost their entire presence on the frontier regions, most of their ownership of strategic resources, and even infrastructure. From rural Yucatán to Soconusco in Chiapas, to Zacatepec in Morelos, to Mante in Tamaulipas, to Madero in Chihuahua, and to Nacozari in Sonora, an amalgam of local and state elites, workers, and campesinos, in the form of pueblos and cooperatives, had occupied these parts of the nation's economy. Despite rollbacks and the reemergence of oligarchic control in more recent times, these organizations still exist and periodically still openly challenge the political authority emanating from Mexico City and the state capitals.

One of the great strengths of these chapters is the insight they provide for the border regions encompassing both the northern tier of Mexican states and the American Southwest. Nicholas Villanueva Jr. presents the display of racist public outrage involving the murder charges against León Martínez Jr. as a useful case study of the nature of unrest that took place in the United States as a result of the Mexican Revolution. That unrest ranged from protest marches in New York City to lynch mobs in Texas. The charges that Mexicans were a "savage race" derived from the history of "Indian wars" almost endlessly waged in the United States prior to the twentieth century. After all, the Mexicans were almost entirely mestizos, viewed as half Indians or semisavages.

Racism in Texas was part of our way of life at the time, and the fact that many Mexican rebels were anarchists only compounded the problem. The crimes committed on US soil against Mexicans contributed to the attacks against North Americans in Mexico. These events became wildly exaggerated. In fact, while tens of thousands fled Mexico and widespread property confiscations occurred, only 365 US citizens were killed in Mexico between 1910 and 1920. Meanwhile, demagogues fed public panic with sometimes outright fraudulent claims. Immediate and historical circumstances victimized Martínez.

Francisco Balderrama amplifies our understanding by analyzing the situation in Los Angeles, California. At the same time that anti-Mexican sentiment was exploding with such force, cities such as Los Angeles and San Antonio witnessed the arrival of multilayered contingents of immigrants. Professor Balderrama adeptly portrays that complexity. Notable elements of the Mexican elites arrived in San Antonio in 1911, as soon as Francisco Madero came to power. They were not alone, however, because a large number of middle- and working-class people not only came as refugees; some of them also came to stay. They founded a number of newspapers and journals, such as *La Opinión* in Los Angeles, and many more in San Antonio and even Laredo. These cities witnessed the publication of protest literature as well.

The Anglo majority in these locales, however, did not sufficiently appreciate the architecture, literature, costumes, music, cuisine, or language enough to tolerate these differences. Their prejudice, rather than abating, combined with economic tensions during the next two decades and led to mass expulsions during the 1930s. In addition, mobs of US soldiers, sailors, and marines attacked immigrants and Mexican Americans on the streets of East Los Angeles during the 1940s.

Professors Miguel González-Quiroga and Stephen E. Lewis eloquently present the situations in Monterrey and Chiapas during the revolt. Those two areas manifested relative stability throughout the era. Two major factors stand out in the case of Monterrey. First, the most powerful capitalists in the United States also played that role in Monterrey by utilizing their control over infrastructure development, the transportation of goods, and economic stability, all of which were crucial to the prosperity of the local elites.

William Rockefeller, president and chairman of Standard Oil Company, the world's largest oil corporation, and a key director of the world's largest bank, National City Bank of New York, joined forces with both James Stillman, president and chairman of National City Bank and who, as an investor, had pioneered the construction of the Tampico to Monterrey and the Brownsville to Monterrey railroads, and John Stewart, president and chairman of the New York Trust Company, created by Stillman and J. P. Morgan. Together they ensured financial stability in the New York banking community, jointly owned the Monterrey Belt Railroad, which served the warehousing facilities that surrounded the city. They demanded political stability.

Second, General and Governor Bernardo Reyes ruled the area with an iron fist on behalf of not just the US investors but also the Monterrey elites, who prided themselves on their business acumen and nonindigenous racial composition. During the early 1880s, then Colonel Reyes had gained national notoriety for leading the suppression of the Huastecan peasant uprising (1879–1884). He did so by applying a scorched-earth campaign that included the elimination of entire pueblos, leaving parts of the region underpopulated.

Reyes's tight rule over Monterrey and Nuevo León was followed by the seizure of power there by *carrancista* General Pablo González, one of the commanders of the revolution who opposed the nationalization of foreign-owned strategic resources and properties regardless of whether they were located on the frontiers or the coastlines. He received enormous quantities of military supplies through Brownsville. One merchant in that city owned unredeemed receipts totaling more than 600,000 dollars at the end of the revolution. Although urban and rural working-class nationalism was overwhelmingly important in much of the nation, little of this sentiment has been found thus far in Monterrey or its immediate environs.

Professor Lewis demonstrates some of the variances between Nuevo León and Chiapas. Before the inception of the fighting, an independent and repressive ruling class that enjoyed the luxury of prosperous agriculture rather than industry also characterized Chiapas. These individuals also benefited from foreign-controlled infrastructure, port management at Salina Cruz, and the Skiddy chemical interests of Hartford and New York, who dominated land holding along the border and the Chiapas-Guatemalan Railroad. In addition, the original City Bank—financed by the United States and by Pan American Railroad from Salina Cruz through Soconusco to Tapachula—controlled a complex of orchards that ran alongside the railroad lines on the Pacific Coast and provided export income and local market demand for more traditional hacienda products coming from the state's interior. The state elites successfully denied concessions to the rural indigenous population well beyond the normally defined 1940 perimeter used by historians for revolutionary programs.

Professors Linda B. Hall and Donald Coerver are recognized authorities on the border, especially during the revolutionary period. They relate the sometimes farcical but deadly serious political ramifications of the boundary region between 1910 and 1930. These considerations include the immigration issue, states rights, and the overt support of special interests in Arizona, New Mexico, and Texas for various revolutionary factions and figures to the south. Among these are the support for Álvaro Obregón Salido exhibited by Texas oilmen and the southwestern US governors and the reciprocity he showed to large-scale US land and strategic-resource holders via his Plan de Agua Prieta and the Bucareli Treaty.

The Texas oilmen's overt support of the Madero family prompted Houston's civic leaders to award the keys to the city to the president's brother, Raoul Madero. Shortly thereafter, however, in the midst of the revolutionary fighting, the Carranza regime was accused of involvement in lower-class Mexican-American unrest in the Rio Grande Valley.[1] Although I would not call the fledgling government of Mexico a "leviathan" in 1920, I agree with Hall that President Obregón did an impressive job of quelling the lower-class-led unrest and placing reformist programs clearly in the hands of loyal functionaries.

Professors Jürgen Buchenau and Carlos Martínez Assad are two of the leading authorities on Mexico's political history during the first half of the twentieth century. In his chapter Buchenau traces the reconciliation with the church and the formation of the nearly all-embracing Partido Nacional Revolucionario. One of Buchenau's strengths is his successful linkage of political narrative with the deep economic and cultural divides that characterized Mexico in the late 1920s and early 1930s. He points out that the party's strength rested on nationalism, the promises of agrarian reform, and social justice for workers. Buchenau demonstrates President Emilio Portes Gil's importance in furthering these processes by reconciling the church and the government, establishing a semblance of labor peace, and giving out more than 2.5 million acres of farmland to the pueblos. Mexico encompasses 450 million acres, so 2.5 million acres may appear insignificant, but, selectively done, this may have stabilized rural political loyalties.

Meanwhile, Martínez Assad demonstrates the acceleration of these programs under the centralizing political authority of the national government between 1920 and 1940, the nominal year used by most historians to delineate the culmination of revolutionary programs. During his presidential tenure (1934–1940), Lázaro Cárdenas created national organizations under the aegis of the government or the national political party. These groups, among others, included the National Confederation of Campesinos and the Confederation of Mexican Workers. Cárdenas's political successes included the elimination of village militias and of some twenty regional warlords. Because of his early popularity, which sprang from his support of agrarian reform and the legitimization of strikes, Cardenas enjoyed enormous power, which led to the modern system of presidential appointments and initiatives that evolved during the rest of the century.

Thomas Benjamin demonstrates his wide-reaching command of the historical literature on the revolution. His understanding of the social and cultural meaning of the revolution enables him to explain the psychological empowerment of the downtrodden campesinos, who participated in regionally based neo-*zapatista* uprisings in the states of Chiapas, Morelos, Chihuahua, and Guerrero during the rest of the century.

And, still beneath the surface of most histories and media reporting, the Mexican Revolution serves as a liberating ideal for the entire Third World. Indeed, contemporary Native American/Indian congresses held throughout the Americas invariably invoke *zapatista* and neo-*zapatista* examples as models of emulation.

This book goes a long way in presenting the diverse expertise available to the Mexican-history profession in 2012 and presents themes that will require further study in the years to come.

Notes

1. Arnoldo de León, in *War along the Border* (College Station: Texas A&M University Press, 2012), discusses Mexican American revolts in South Texas and their relationship to Carranza and other Mexican leaders.

CHAPTER 1

Decade of Disorder

The Execution of León Martínez Jr. and Mexican/Anglo Race Relations in Texas during the First Four Years of the Mexican Revolution

Nicholas Villanueva Jr.

> I listened again to this list with a profound interest at the mixture of names, for the names bear the marks of the several national stocks from which these men came. But they are not Irishmen or Germans or Frenchmen or Hebrews any more. They were not when they went to Veracruz; they were Americans, every one of them, and were no different in their Americanism because of the stock from which they came.[1]

On May 11, 1914, President Woodrow Wilson read this tribute to the nineteen servicemen who had been killed in action at the Mexican port of Veracruz weeks earlier. A memorial procession bearing the dead soldiers traveled through the streets of New York City. The parade of vehicles passed one million onlookers, and cities across the country conducted their own ceremonies of honor. In concluding statements Wilson announced, "We have gone down to Mexico . . . to serve mankind."[2]

In Pecos, Texas, on that very day, a ceremony of a different type occurred. Citizens came to the county seat to witness the execution of León Martínez Jr., a Mexican teenager, for the murder of Emma Brown, a young Anglo woman. Newspaper reporters across Texas had followed the case for nearly three years. Citizens had voiced concerns about the inferiority of Mexican migrants and the increasing number of undesirable aliens entering the country. A racial order that privileged Anglos over Mexicans had long existed in Texas, but new developments were threatening to further reduce the number of Mexicans. The presence of anarchists and "un-American activity" among some people of Mexican descent increased Anglo hatred during the decade of the Mexican Revolution. Anglos viewed these men and women as uncivilized and intellectually inferior. The influx of more migrants into Texas during this decade further intensified Anglo abhorrence of Mexicans, who became increasingly vulnerable to verbal and physical attacks. This case study of León Martínez Jr. provides a window into the life of one such ill-fated Mexican.

Wilson's speech identified the Irish and the Jewish soldiers as US citizens who had given their lives at Veracruz, and he welcomed them into the North American family. The status of Mexican immigrants, by contrast, remained uncertain. Large numbers of Mexican laborers came to the United States in the first two decades of the twentieth century and became more visible to Anglos in border states like Texas. During the 1910s, Mexican refugees fled to the United States, particularly Texas. When the United States verged on war with Mexico in 1914, US troops along the border clashed with rebels, and Texas Rangers, border patrolmen, and North American servicemen lost their lives. At odds with native-born Texans, Mexicans during these tumultuous years appeared dangerous, and many questioned their national allegiance.

After the murder of Emma Brown, Anglos considered Martínez a sexual predator of Anglo women, one who could not control himself because of his savage roots. The jury dehumanized Martínez Jr. and convicted him of murder. In the local papers, journalists portrayed Martínez as a brute. His father, deemed a Mexican radical, linked the family with anarchist factions of the revolution, which threatened people both in Texas and abroad. During the final weeks of Martínez's life, US and Mexican diplomatic relations became strained, and newspapers posted warnings in border towns that Mexican rebels posed a threat to the locals. This study of the Martínez case raises more questions about the fate of ethnic Mexicans living in Texas during the early years of the Mexican Revolution: Were Mexicans falsely accused of crimes? Did they receive equal treatment under the law? Was Martínez innocent but unable to receive a fair trial in this hostile environment? To Anglo Texans, Martínez appeared as an enemy, and over the course of three years his image worsened as the Mexican Revolution intensified.

The Murder of Emma Brown

Martínez was born in the state of Durango, Mexico, in 1896. His parents, León Sr. and Sidra, also had a younger son named Manuel. As a youth, Martínez Jr. attended El Paso public schools. His father spoke English and Spanish and reared his son in Texas, while Sidra and Manuel remained in Durango. Neither father nor son applied for naturalization papers. The Martínezes left El Paso when young León became old enough to work. They moved to Toyah, a West Texas town in Reeves County eighty miles north of the US and Mexico border. Toyah was "a typical railroad town composed almost entirely of saloons and restaurants . . . a rendezvous for gamblers . . . a town in which six-shooters, shot-guns and dirks [long, straight-bladed daggers] were standard equipment and carried ready for use at any time."[3] Martínez Sr. worked for a Spanish-language newspaper, and his son was employed in a neighboring town at the Saragossa Mercantile Company, owned by Floyd Crenshaw. The mercantile company hosted a warehouse, a US post office, a Western Union office, and a general store. An intelligent youth who spoke Spanish and English, Martínez Jr. worked in both the general store and the post office. His appearance was that of a lighter-skinned Mexican, not that of most Mexican migrants, who had darker complexions. The week before the murder, the young boy met twenty-six-year-old schoolteacher Emma Brown.

Brown had traveled from her home in Austin, Texas, to Saragossa in June 1911 to spend the summer with her sister, Mrs. H. C. Cooper.[4] On the afternoon of July 22, 1911, after picking up supplies from the Saragossa Mercantile Company, she traveled back to her sister's home, east of Saragossa. Her four-mile trip stretched alongside the limestone foothills of the Davis Mountains. Her path crossed a pasture belonging to "Stump" Robbins, a pioneer rancher of Reeves County, who later found her body. Beyond the pasture the path entered a valley with fields of grass four to five feet high. Travelers of this half-mile stretch were hardly visible from the surrounding area, and it was here that Brown's murder occurred.[5]

The physical evidence collected at the scene provided enough information to retell the events as follows. Hoofprints from the murderer's horse indicated that the attacker came toward her from the east, not from Saragossa. The tracks from her buggy reached almost to the top of the valley, where they collided with those of the single horse. An abrupt change in the direction the buggy took indicated that something or someone had startled the woman. The tracks ran back and forth throughout the hidden valley. Bullet holes punctured the rear of the buggy, and one had pierced Brown. After falling from her only means of escape, her attacker had stabbed her several times in the chest. Emma Brown died in that field, lying face up to the stars all night, until ranchers discovered her body the following morning.[6]

The discovery of the young woman's body shocked the townspeople and prompted an immediate search for the killer. Several people had seen an unusual individual having an intimate conversation with the young woman on the morning of the murder. That person was León Martínez Jr., who became the first and only suspect of this crime.[7] Martínez owned a pistol, had the use of his employer's horses, and, most damaging of all, was seen by shoppers at the general store speaking with Brown on the day of her murder. Someone alleged that the two were planning a private rendezvous.[8] Both legal and extralegal forces began hunting for Martínez. He was easy to find, as he did not run or hide. He continued his weekly routine, and on Sunday afternoon, the day after the murder, he saw his boss, Floyd Crenshaw, traveling toward town. Crenshaw stopped Martínez and informed him that a young woman had been found murdered several miles from Saragossa. When Crenshaw asked whether he knew anything about the murder, Martínez denied any knowledge of it. The boy continued on his way to a watermelon patch, and while he was eating a melon, a group of men surrounded him.

Pecos merchant Jim Mayfield led the posse, which grew in number as the evening progressed. The men demanded that the boy confess to the crime. When Martínez protested his innocence, the angry mob threatened to hang him if he did not confess. The distraught boy cried for his mother and father to help him, and Mayfield responded, "You are not worthy of it." Martínez confessed after the men promised not to hang him until Sheriff Brown arrived.[9] Upon his arrival, Brown took the boy to the Pecos jail, where he ordered Martínez to confess, failing which the sheriff would release him to the men waiting for him outside. As dawn approached, District Attorney Will P. Brady held up a written confession to the crowd outside the jail.[10] The events of that evening were not introduced at Martínez's trial as evidence, only the signed confession.[11]

Two conflicting stories developed from the written confession and an interview with an El Paso reporter. The first story came from Martínez's signed confession, made on the night of his arrest. It stated that on Saturday morning, the previous day, Martínez and Brown had met at Crenshaw's shop. He was working at the time, and the two had had a conversation in which the young Anglo woman had promised Martínez sex, an unusual move for a young lady of that time. Later that afternoon around 4:00 P.M., they met two miles outside of town. Martínez, the confession claimed, had asked her to keep her promise, but she refused his advances and shouted, "You son-of-a-bitch, I am going to have you arrested." He said that was not necessary and that he only wanted her to do what they had planned. She stood up in her buggy, told him she would kill him, and then reached for her hip. Alarmed by this, Martínez pulled his weapon out and shot her in the chest. He returned to Saragossa, ate supper, and went back to Crenshaw's shop to do his evening stocking.[12]

It is difficult to determine the validity of a confession by someone who was the target of a lynch mob one hundred years ago. Quite often an alleged criminal who was sought by a posse of men believed that a confession to the sheriff was the only option for safety. Since Martínez was a young boy, this might have been the case. Historian Paul J. Vanderwood provides a rich analysis of the making of a Mexican folk saint in Tijuana, Mexico, who may have suffered the same fate. In his account of the execution of Juan Soldado, Vanderwood states, "It was said that more than anything else he feared being turned over to the mob, of literally being torn apart, limb by limb, kicked and trampled, by enraged townspeople."[13] Only six months prior to Martínez's arrest, a young Mexican migrant worker was burned alive by a mob for allegedly killing a rancher's wife. This story made local, national, and international news because of subsequent riots in Mexican cities. Martínez knew that, if handed over to the mob, death would be certain.

The second story developed from an interview by an unnamed reporter who accompanied Sheriff J. F. Franks of Caldwell County, where Martínez was moved in late August 1911. In this interview Martínez stated, "It is not true that I am eighteen years old. I was born in 1896. I did not kill Emma Brown." He reported that he had first learned of the murder from a Mexican man shortly before the authorities arrived and arrested him. He knew Brown from the store and admitted to loading her buggy with her purchases. However, he argued that he could prove he was not with her that afternoon. If time permitted before his trial, he could have found witnesses who saw him at Crenshaw's shop all day. When the reporter asked Martínez how he felt about his death sentence, he replied, "Gee whiz, I felt bad." The interviewer commented that the accused was "small in stature, about four feet ten inches in height, weighs 116 pounds, and seems very youthful . . . smiles often, and answers readily all questions. He speaks English perfectly."[14] These two conflicting stories went unresolved, and the majority of Anglos preferred the confession over the interview.

Shortly before midnight on Sunday, Reeves County Court Judge S. J. Isaacks learned of the murder of Miss Brown and the arrest of the young Mexican boy. The county court had recessed, and Judge Isaacks was at his home in Midland, about one hundred miles east of Pecos. Sheriff Brown informed Isaacks that, because anger toward the murderer was growing, Isaacks needed to depart immediately. In the early morning hours Isaacks boarded a train for Pecos, where he arrived shortly after dawn. He went directly to the Oriental Hotel, which was owned by his friend F. W. Johnson and a gathering spot for the county's elite. Isaacks and Johnson met with the district attorney and two of the wealthiest men in Pecos, W. D. Cowan and B. R. Stein, vice presidents of the local bank and financiers of the newly chartered Pecos Valley Southern Railroad.[15] Their order of business was to discuss the "excited condition" and "threatening attitude of the citizenship" toward Martínez and to determine what would be in the best interest and promote the safety of the town.[16] They decided that Sheriff Brown should escort Martínez to a jail in Midland, where the latter would remain until the trial began. This was the only time in his official career that Isaacks sent a prisoner from his own county jail to another for protection.[17]

On Monday, July 24, 1911, Isaacks convened a special session of the court in Pecos. The order he issued stated that the unusual and urgent procedure was necessary because "a horrible murder had been committed." By the end of the day, he had summoned a grand jury and secured an indictment for murder. Isaacks notified Sheriff Brown that a murder trial would take place on Friday, July, 28 1911. Confined in the Midland jail, Martínez did not meet with his defense attorneys until hours before the trial. Two attorneys were selected by Isaacks to defend the Mexican boy: George Estes, a former district attorney from El Paso, Texas, and R. L. Parker, a former Reeves County judge and friend of Judge Isaacks. The trial began Friday morning, with Martínez entering a plea of not guilty. The prosecution read Martínez's signed confession but omitted the statement that indicated that the accused was only fifteen years old. Before noon on Saturday, July 29, 1911, the jury returned a guilty verdict and sentenced Martínez to death.[18]

Judge Isaacks gave the defense until 3:30 P.M. to prepare a motion for a new trial. Isaacks ordered Texas Rangers to escort Martínez back to the county jail in Midland while his attorneys went to Parker's office and prepared an appeal. Since the irate citizens wanted an execution, it is unclear what prompted Estes and Parker to appeal. The court documents have no record of a request by Martínez, but months later the boy stated that his father had asked for an appeal because there should have been a change of venue. Martínez's Anglo attorneys possibly believed they had to do everything in their power to defend their client; Parker was a former judge and Estes a former district attorney. The news that these men were attempting to save the convicted teen spread rapidly. Shortly before 3:30 P.M. Estes and Parker left for the courthouse to file an appeal with Judge Isaacks. Meanwhile, F. W. Johnson, Jim Mayfield, and Sheriff Brown met with Cowan and Stein at the bank to gather up a group of men whose purpose was to prevent an appeal. Johnson reported that from the front door of the bank he could see Parker and Estes going toward the courthouse. The angry men shouted for the attorneys to stop. The mob met them "one hundred and fifty feet from the court house door."[19] Fifty men, including several that had served on the jury, stood between Martínez's attorneys and the courthouse. Jim Mayfield, who had been present the night of the arrest and had also threatened to hang Martínez personally if he did not confess, was one of the many elite citizens of Reeves County challenging the attorneys.

The local justice of the peace, A. W. Hosie, stepped up onto a box and shouted that the crowd would not permit an appeal.[20] Hosie, born of Scots-Irish immigrants, had a reputation in Reeves County as roughneck fighter.[21] Parker became concerned about the safety of the people of Pecos. Months later he stated, "I felt that if they undertook to take the Mexican from the rangers, some of them [citizens and Rangers] would get killed . . . and we could not well scrap a whole county, or what looked like a whole county to us at the time."[22]

Estes was less concerned about the safety of the citizens than he was for his own life. As Johnson argued with Parker, four to five men were shouting their disapproval. Members of the mob began yelling that "they could hang three as easy as they could hang one."[23] Parker reassured the crowd that no appeal would be made and told them to return home. Defense attorney George Estes boarded a train for El Paso that very evening. Later he would go on record stating that he had feared for his life on that hot summer afternoon. Parker and Isaacks returned to Johnson's hotel, had a private, "whispered discussion," and decided not to appeal the decision. Both Estes and Parker were ambitious politicians. Further representation of the Mexican boy, they now worried, would damage their reputations. Parker served the county's elite for years. Oriental Hotel owner Johnson, one of the most vocal of the mob, advised Parker days later to leave Pecos.[24] Meanwhile, Judge Isaacks ordered that Martínez be hanged on September 1, 1911.

Mexican Migrants and Mexican Refugees

In Texas, Anglo Americans grouped working-class Mexican migrants—termed peons—with African Americans—near the bottom of the racial hierarchy. Derived from peonage, the word described a lower-class Mexican worker, subjugated by Anglo society, who did work that whites felt was beneath them. The jobs these unskilled workers performed included building the increasingly important railroads connecting the Eastern Seaboard to the mineral-rich Western frontier and implementing new irrigation technology for agriculture and mining. Millions of migrant workers did these dangerous jobs in the early years of the twentieth century, creating boomtowns in the West almost overnight. With the need to carry out this work, more and more Mexican immigrants entered Texas.

In Mexico, the upper class grouped people into three main categories: European in origin, mestizo, and Indian. At the top of the social hierarchy was the European stock, which usually had a Spanish heritage and remained mostly unmixed with Indians but represented less than 15 percent of the country by the turn of the century. Next, the mestizos were a mixture of Spanish and Indian blood. Constituting more than half of the population of Mexico, this was the largest group. Finally, 35 percent of the population was Indian.[25] When US employers sought laborers, a vast majority who came to work in mining and agriculture and on the railroads were mestizos.

Many of the Mexican railroad workers were skilled in this line of work. Under President Porfirio Díaz, Mexico transitioned into a modern nation with a network of interconnecting rail lines throughout the country that linked up with US lines in places like El Paso, Texas. In 1876 railroads were "negligible," but by 1910 they stretched across fifteen thousand miles of the Mexican countryside. North American recruiters traveled into Mexico by train in search of workers to fill unskilled labor positions in the United States. The return trip brought many of these would-be workers to El Paso, Texas, an epicenter of the Mexican migrant-labor explosion. Here Mexican migrants met with employers who offered them $1.50 per day in railroad and agricultural positions and more than $2.00 per day in mining, as opposed to the 12 cents per day they would earn on the Mexican haciendas.[26] Recruiters continued to travel the central rail lines into Mexico as far as Mexico City, although they were needed less as the northern migration became more popular among Mexicans.

Mexican workers arrived in increasing numbers each decade after 1890. Between 1900 and 1930, the population of Mexican-born people living in Texas increased from 71,062 to 262,672.[27] A majority of these migrant workers were young men both single and married, but married men often arrived without their families and sent their earnings back to Mexico, creating an imbalance of men and women in the border towns. Nativists and proponents of Mexican labor argued about the need for these workers. Defenders of Mexican labor contended that they were useful and that they could easily be sent home once the need for them was exhausted.[28]

After the outbreak of the 1910 Mexican Revolution, refugees joined migrant workers crossing the border into the United States. In the early years of the revolution many Mexicans living in the northern state of Chihuahua fled to towns such as El Paso, where they found a number of sympathetic citizens. As the revolution intensified, the Mexican population in Texas surged. Anglo Texans became irritated and restless, identifying this rapid rise in the population as the "Mexican problem," which had two characteristics. First, Anglos believed the quality of the Mexicans entering Texas declined during the 1910s. Those who came as laborers prior to the revolution were preferred because of their willingness to perform menial jobs. The refugees were less desirable, the Anglos believed, because the best of the Mexican workers were either already in the United States or had joined the Mexican armies.

Second, refugees arrived by the hundreds and then thousands, creating processing delays at the border and leaving entire Mexican towns deserted. Within a three-day period, the border town of Del Rio, Texas, saw an influx of more than two thousand Mexican citizens from Las Vacas, Mexico. Upon arrival, these homeless foreigners waited for US immigration officials to clear them for entrance.[29] The inspection included a physical examination for potentially life-threatening and, more important to the Texans, communicable diseases. The *El Paso Morning Times* reported that six thousand refugees were deported from the Eagle Pass immigration inspection site because smallpox had been discovered among them. This news made front-page headlines, but only three actual cases of smallpox had been detected among the refugees.[30] The combination of news reports of diseases among the refugees and the public opinion that those arriving during the Mexican Revolution were less desirable led more Texans to resent the growing presence of Mexicans in the country.

In El Paso, citizens did not believe the "Mexican problem" was temporary. Schools and business began to segregate by race. Anglos believed the large number of Mexican migrants depressed the wages of working-class whites, creating a financial problem for the Texans. Frustrated El Paso citizens believed that at least a thousand Mexican laborers who lived across the border in Ciudad Juárez and worked in El Paso during the day were stealing $1,500 per day in wages. They described the men, women, and children crossing the border each day as a "silent invasion . . . before El Paso is hardly astir and the workers return to their homes after dark."[31] Anglos resented the labor that Mexicans toiled at during the day and despised the "degenerate" behavior they saw in Mexican men at night.

Border-crossing sites such as El Paso were full of bars and saloons eager to get a cut of the Mexicans' wages. Gambling, prostitution, and alcohol abuse flourished, and the nativists blamed all of these ills on the presence of Mexican peons. As one nativist reporter for the *El Paso Morning Times* declared, "The lower class of Mexicans have no more control over their passions than an angry beast and in their ignorance they are just as unreasonable."[32] Often the newspapers warned of single Mexican men as predators who lured young Anglo women across the Rio Grande in the darkness of night. Their reports dwelled on the arrests of Mexican men for crimes of rape, abuse, and even the use of strong language toward Anglo women.[33] Anglo men responded with threats to punish those who violated the color line with legal or extralegal punishment. Between 1848 and 1928 there were 597 known lynching cases of people of Mexican descent in the United States; more than 47 percent occurred in Texas. Vigilantes identified alleged murder and theft as the most common reason for lynching Mexicans, but accusations of rape or courting white women were also common. Sometimes Mexicans were lynched "just because they were Mexican."[34]

In view of the ethnic violence between Anglos and Mexicans on the US side of the border, I term the years of the Mexican Revolution the "decade of disorder." Mob violence against Mexicans increased during this period as Anglo Texans addressed the "Mexican problem." I use this phrase in reference to Anglo frustration with the growing population of Mexican refugees and immigrants, as well as the perceived connection of these men and women with revolutionary violence along the border and raids on Texas property, which created an overall tension between Mexicans and Anglo Texans.

Martínez was arrested for the crime of murder, but on the night of his arrest an angry posse demanded his life for the death of Emma Brown. Martínez might have heard stories about Mexican men such as Antonio Rodríguez who were savagely attacked by lynch mobs. On November 3, 1910, the Texas press reported that Rodríguez had murdered the wife of a well-known rancher. After his capture, the police reported that Rodríguez had confessed to committing the crime because "she had talked mean" to him when he approached her for food.[35] Texas newspapers first reported the murder with an article that appeared to encourage vigilantism.[36] Shortly after his arrest, an Anglo mob seized Antonio Rodríguez from his Rock Springs, Texas, jail. The vigilantes broke down the jail doors and took Rodríguez in the middle of the night to a fire they had prepared. The men took turns beating him until he was near death, only to douse him with oil and set him on fire.[37] After the Rodríguez lynching, the local newspapers speculated about his mental state and why he murdered the Anglo woman rather than bring attention to the horrendous crime of burning him alive.[38]

When the news of Rodríguez's lynching reached his hometown of Guadalajara, Mexico, an international crisis developed. Mexicans wanted their president, Porfirio Díaz, to demand that the US government investigate the crime, arrest the men responsible for the slaying, and guarantee the safety of Mexicans living in the United States. Protests broke out throughout Mexico and quickly turned into anti-American riots. The Mexican press fueled the fire that burned within the angry protesters with details of the lynching. Most of the articles explicitly attacked the Taft administration for not pursuing the men responsible. Several days of riots produced numerous editorials with anti-American rhetoric. Some of these editorials held Texans directly responsible:

> The iron hoof of the Texas "Yankee," in his barbarous and savage sentiments of race-hatred, is not trampling upon the Negro, but the rottenness of its core has spread out so as to wound and even kill a Mexican by the

> iniquitous method of lynching. Lynching is not practiced by the blond "Yankee" except upon beings whom, for ethnic reasons, he considers his inferiors. When a Mexican is immolated, it is to be inferred that the social conscience of the state of Texas, in her loathsome scorn, compares the sons of Negroland with the descendants of Cuauhtémoc. Our race is in no way inferior to the Anglo-Saxon.[39]

During the first night of rioting in Mexico City, two Mexican students and a Mexican man were killed by Mexican police trying to maintain order; consequently, a "bitter feeling was aroused as the result of the killing of the three Mexicans and trouble was expected early this morning."[40] Following the killings, anger increased and continued to target North Americans. Ambassador Henry Lane Wilson learned that rioters in Mexico City were plotting an attempt on his life. In Guadalajara, students protested outside the US consulate, where they chanted "Death to gringos." The protest became violent after several anti-American speeches, and at the end of the day the crowd's wrath turned to the destruction of US-owned property: "They smashed the windows of the American bank, the Masonic hall in the quarters of the American Candy company, the West End Realty company and those [windows] in the offices of two American dentists."[41] A US fatality occurred when Houston, Mississippi, native James M. Reid exited a restaurant in Mexico City one week after the Rodríguez riots had subsided. Waiting outside the restaurant was a Mexican police officer who shot two bullets into Reid. When questioned about the motive for the killing, officer Sebastian Vardel answered, "I have killed the gringo because the gringos burned a Mexican."[42]

Texas newspapers published reports that Rodríguez had been insane and that justice had been served with the lynching.[43] In a special report, the *Waco Times Herald* stated the following:

> Acting Adjutant General Phelps today said that state authorities will take no action toward identifying and arresting members of the mob which burned at the stake an unknown Mexican recently at Rock Springs, Texas, after he had shot to death the wife of a prominent ranchman.[44]

The community was convinced of Rodríguez's guilt prior to his execution, and in Mexico the situation was about to change. The Mexican Revolution was on the horizon, and justice for Rodríguez ceased to be of concern once it began. However, for ethnic Mexicans living in Texas, the Rodríguez lynching could not be easily forgotten.

Any Mexican male, regardless of age, who committed a crime against Anglo

Texans could be subjected to extralegal violence. On June 19, 1911, in Thorndale, Texas, a month before the murder of Emma Brown, thirteen-year-old Antonio Gómez was tapping on the wood siding of a local shop. Angered by the noise, the merchant inside the store attacked the young boy. Young Antonio plunged his pocketknife into the attacker's chest, killing the merchant in the center of town. What then transpired was a brutal lynching. The crowd, identified as "Thorndale's finest," wrapped a chain around the youth's neck, dragged him by a horse, and then hanged him until he died.[45] After news reports calling this act "The Most Infamous of All Our Crimes" and shaming Thorndale citizens for killing a boy in this way, Thorndale officials rushed to change the facts surrounding the killing. They reported to the newspapers that the merchant confronted the Mexican boy by asking him politely to stop. Suddenly, the small boy jumped and stabbed the man below the collarbone, instantly killing him. More than one hundred people testified that they had witnessed the events in the latter version, and the accused men were found not guilty.[46] In this case and others, mobs superseded the legal system within hours of an alleged crime against an Anglo. Large crowds removed Mexicans who had been detained in jails. One wounded Mexican man was taken from his hospital bed, hanged, and burned.[47] The public defended these actions as saving the county time and money.

The racial order that existed in Texas stigmatized Mexican migrants as racially inferior and subjugated them as outcasts in their border towns. These laborers, who were living far away from their families, often lived together and created Mexican neighborhoods. To nativists they were enemies of the Texans' moral virtues. León Martínez did not find a friendly face in Reeves County, and more than two years would elapse before he was returned to Pecos for his execution. During his incarceration his family found Mexicans sympathetic to his case in El Paso, Waco, San Antonio, and cities throughout Mexico. These people and the organizations they belonged to raised the $50,000 necessary to pay for his legal representation.[48] To Mexicans his case was another version of the David-and-Goliath struggle they had fought for years during Díaz's rule in Mexico.

The Martínez Case and the Mexican Revolution

Newspapers reported that "A feeling of general satisfaction prevails throughout the county . . . that justice was meted out to him in a fair and impartial manner."[49] After sentencing on July 29, 1911, Texas Rangers escorted Martínez back to his cell in Midland to await his execution. On Sunday, the day after the trial, Dr. Homer L. Magee, minister of the First Christian Church in Pecos, told his parishioners that he was satisfied that justice was served. He believed that Martínez's actions could teach parents a lesson. Magee declared that home is where parents feed their children's bellies and minds: "A crime of this kind is not committed as a result of sudden emotion, but it is the natural outcome of the training, or lack of training, received in the home . . . Home is God's first ordained institution where the conscience is trained to discern between right and wrong."[50] Martínez Jr., like many Mexican boys, lived in homes where the fathers either were absent, seeking employment, or had their sons work in the railroad and mining towns with them. Nevertheless, the people of Reeves County felt relieved because they believed that justice had prevailed.

On August 6, 1911, District Attorney Brown received a telegram from Governor Colquitt, stating he would not interfere with the Martínez case.[51] Officials in Pecos tried to refute the stories posted in newspapers around the state that described Reeves County as a vigilante community. They wrote an editorial for the *El Paso Morning Times* that praised the people of Reeves County for being law-abiding citizens: "Almost anywhere else on the face of the earth a resentful and indignant people would have acted otherwise and have taken justice into their own hands without the law"; moreover, "there is no more peace-loving people in the southwest."[52] In truth, however, the citizens of Reeves County had growing fears that Martínez might escape execution. National newspapers were reporting that a child had been sentenced to death in Texas. The Janus-faced people of Reeves County sent a letter to Colquitt that urged him not to get involved, maintained that the citizens of Texas would lose faith in a legal system that should protect them, and asserted that any intervention would force them to settle future matters with "Judge Lynch." Attached to this letter was a petition claiming to have been signed by every citizen in Reeves County.[53]

Their concerns that Martínez's life might be spared became valid. The story about a boy facing execution made national news. Not only the *New York Times* but also newspapers in large and small communities around the country reported on the Martínez case. Letters arrived from as far away as New Jersey, questioning Colquitt about the Texas legal system and the pending execution of a minor.[54] Concerned North Americans and outraged Mexicans wrote letters to Colquitt, expressing outrage that Martínez's trial should never have taken place in Reeves County in view of the local residents' hostility toward the boy. Albert Anders, a father from Canyon Creek, Montana, requested that the governor investigate the case and stated, "To prove him innocent after his death will be too late." Ida C. Airhart of Lake Charles, Louisiana, argued that it would be a crime to hang someone so immature and asked Colquitt "to investigate and think of the matter in a Christian spirit." In addition, J. W.

Arrowsmith, president of a surgical supply company with offices in Chicago, San Francisco, and Toronto, was infuriated: "How the great state of Texas can 'string up' an infant is beyond my comprehension."[55]

These protests impelled Colquitt to reprieve the sentence, and on August 26, 1911, Colquitt delayed the execution by thirty days for further investigation into the case.[56] During that time, Martínez's family sought financial support for the boy and employed a legal team that filed an appeal with the Texas Criminal Court of Appeals. The supporters who came to the boy's aid created as much outrage in the media as the initial murder and actually intensified Martínez's problems with white Texans. A racial system revealed the boy's vulnerability in a West Texas county. His family's association with Mexican radicals, however, connected him with the Mexican Revolution and made him an enemy of the state.

One of the most influential and outspoken leaders of the Mexican Revolution was Ricardo Flores Magón. Born in 1873 of working-class Mexican parents, Magón became a journalist who opposed the dictatorship of Porfirio Díaz. His open opposition to Díaz led to several arrests and then to his flight from Mexico to Laredo, Texas, in 1904. A year later he founded the Mexican Liberal Party (PLM) while living in the United States. The PLM became a revolutionary group that sought new leadership for the people of Mexico. The group called for open elections in Mexico, land reform more favorable to the working class, better wages, and improved working conditions for the Mexican proletariat. In Texas the PLM attempted to organize Mexican and Mexican American laborers. The response by the Mexican communities in Texas varied. Some people of Mexican descent supported these efforts, whereas others distanced themselves. Supporters of the PLM criticized US foreign policy, Texas officials for their lack of concern for Mexicans killed along the border, and Wall Street's "domination of Mexican affairs."[57]

Texas became a popular location for exiles of this sort. In San Antonio, Magón reestablished *Regeneración*, a radical Mexican newspaper that emphasized giving Mexico's land back to the Mexican working class.[58] In November of 1910, Magón declared, "The Liberal Party works for the welfare of the poor classes of the Mexican people. It does not impose a candidate because it will be up to the will of the people to settle the question: Do the people want a master?" His *Regeneración* article "El Derecho de Propiedad" [The Right of Property] argued that one's right to property is as ancient as one's stupidity.[59] Magón's speeches condemned wealthy Anglos as thieves and as oppressors of working-class Mexicans. Over time he became a notorious anarchist who lived in exile in Texas, and his followers were known as *magonistas*.

The editors of *Regeneración* published Magón's speeches. Anglo Texans became suspicious of his intentions when these words circulated around the state:

> The expropriation of the land possessed by the rich should be realized during the present insurrection. We liberals will not be committing a crime by turning over the land to the working people because it belongs to them, the people; it is the land that their most distant ancestors lived on and watered with their sweat . . . That land belongs to all Mexicans by natural law. Some of them [Anglos] might have bought it, but where did they get the money to make the purchase if not from the work of the unskilled Mexican workers and laborers?[60]

The land he desired was Texas, and the thieves were Anglo Texans. Citizens along the border worried about a hostile attempt to reclaim this land. The *magonistas* were only one of several radical factions on both sides of the border to which the Mexican Revolution had given birth, and their members often pillaged Southwestern ranches for food, supplies, and weapons.

Anglos stigmatized working-class Mexicans in Texas. After the 1910 Mexican Revolution, whites questioned the Mexicans about their allegiance to anarchist factions. El Paso had the greatest population of Mexicans in Texas during the 1910s, and by the end of the decade an unprecedented number of Mexican nationals sought refuge in the United States.[61] An increase in Spanish-language newspapers circulated throughout the border towns, some simply reporting the news in Spanish and others fostering radical thought. Papers like *Regeneración* had subscribers in the United States, Mexico, and Cuba, but the largest distribution occurred in Texas. According to one 1915 issue, 41.9 percent of the papers were sent to Texas, 13.3 percent to California, 12.5 percent to Mexico, 4.9 percent to Cuba, 4.3 percent to Arizona, and 23.1 percent elsewhere.[62] Conservative Anglos condemned these papers and the writers and editors who produced them.

Anglo newspapers reported that León Martínez Sr. was a *magonista*. In addition, W. A. Hudson, shareholder of the Citizens Bank of Barstow, located seven miles east of Pecos, reported to the editors of the *El Paso Morning Times* that he knew that Martínez Sr. was a *magonista*. He declared that radical groups provided the "money and influence to save a guilty wretch."[63] Martínez Sr. worked for a Toyah, Texas, Spanish-language newspaper that printed articles in support of Magón. Toyah, a railroad town several miles east of Pecos, also became home to two members of the jury in the trial of Martínez Jr.: W. M. Hopper and A. J. Hart.[64] Hopper and Hart might have known of Martínez Sr. and his reputation as a *magonista*. The elder Martínez was even rumored to have worked for Magón's paper, *Regeneración*. He may have been an assistant editor, as some Anglo papers speculated, but evidence of this association does not exist. What is clear is that Martínez was literate in both English and Spanish.

Martínez Sr. wrote to the editors of Spanish-language newspapers in El Paso, San Antonio, and Waco in search of financial support for his son's defense. Lauro Aguirre, editor of one such El Paso newspaper and who knew both father and son, reported that he did not believe that Martínez Jr. was guilty of the crime.[65] Martínez Sr. demonstrated a strong proficiency in the English language in his letter to the secretary of the Texas Criminal Court of Appeals regarding payment for a transcript of his son's trial.[66] The elegant signature at the bottom of the letter is in cursive, not common among Mexican working-class men at the time.

Whether a Mexican was lower or middle class was inconsequential to most Anglos in 1912; Mexicans of both classes became suspected of insurrectionist activities. According to many Anglos, the working class carried out the crimes, while the middle class created revolutionary literature. The *El Paso Morning Times* reported a "call to arms of Mexicans in the United States to fight against Americans." The US Secret Service broke up an El Paso operation at a printing press and found more than five thousand copies of an alleged insurrectionary document. Newspapers printed front-page headlines that read "Anti-American Plot Exposed."[67] Such stories about Mexicans fueled the Anglos' resentment.

Residents of El Paso who were current with national events knew that restrictionists were debating the immigration issue. An El Paso editorial informed the public that the Root Amendment of the Dillingham Bill, favored by the Senate, would protect Texans against radical immigrant factions who sought to undermine US authorities and threaten the country's safety. If passed, it would rid the US of undesirable aliens:

> Members of the Senate Foreign Relations Committee and of the Texas congressional delegation conferred with President Taft and his cabinet with regard to the Mexican situation and the practice of Mexicans of coming into the United States territory as refugees but really to agitate and promote armed expeditions into a country from which they have fled . . . It provides a more adequate remedy, however, for existing conditions than does the present neutrality law and is actively supported by Governor Colquitt of Texas.[68]

The author of this editorial argued that if such a provision were in place, subversive plots would not have the numbers necessary to carry them out. This legislation would protect Texans from these radicals because most of the organizing occurred on US soil, mainly Texas.[69] The Mexicans' association with groups like the *magonistas* connected them with radicals and made the Anglos suspicious of their activities.

The Execution

On November 3, 1911, in Austin, the Texas Criminal Court of Appeals reviewed the murder trial of León Martínez Jr. The majority opinion ruled against a new trial. Three appellate judges reviewed the lower court's documents and issued conflicting opinions. Appellate court Judge A. J. Harper of El Paso wrote the twenty-page opinion that supported the lower court's decision. A dissenting opinion came from Judge W. H. Davidson, who argued that Martínez deserved a new trial outside Reeves County. The seventy-four-year-old judge had built a reputation as a crusader against injustice. In another dissenting opinion he sharply criticized the "necessity" defense for a lynching: "It was *necessity* that prompted Pontius Pilate to appease the cry of the howling Jewish mob to murder the innocent Christ."[70] Davidson chastised those in authority who made examples of individuals to appease the populace. He condemned Judge Harper for an opinion "intended for the admiration of the people." He told the outraged Anglos of Reeves County, "I have made it the rule of my judicial life, and shall continue to do so, to decide questions as I see them after as careful investigation as my capacity affords, without reference to what public opinion may be."[71]

Davidson argued that Martínez's conviction violated the due process of law provision in the Fourteenth Amendment of the Constitution. In fact, the Law of Nations and two treaties between the United States and Mexico should have guaranteed Martínez the rights inherent in the Fourteenth Amendment.[72] According to Davidson, the case violated the treaties for the following reasons: undue haste in the trial, denial of the right to be heard by counsel of his own choosing, the right to have a defender faithful to his defense, and the unjust discrimination against Martínez, which allowed the court to satisfy the local citizens.[73] Davidson's concluding statement declared that "The law is not designed to be a swift engine of oppression and vengeance, but it was and is designed to try men only after due hearing and fair trial. I cannot concur with my brethren."[74]

Davidson's dissenting opinion drew sharp criticism from Judge Harper. The two judges were polar opposites and openly clashed, friction that made national headlines from New York to Los Angeles. Letters to the editors of major Texas newspapers criticized both judges for their public debate. The *Dallas Morning News* reported, "The hurt to at least the dignity of the State would have been much less severe than that which results from this public exhibition of their spleen."[75] Glenmore Farm, Texas, resident Charles Metcalfe voiced his mixed opinion of the situation. His letter to the editor began with an argument to reform the process by means of which these judges were elected. He went on to assert that the people of Texas had lost respect for the courts and that this case damaged Texans' confidence in the law that was designed to protect them from criminals. His final comment was as follows: "The overshadowing elements of uncertainty as to so-called law drive the people to primal, savage action. The result is [that] individuals commit and avenge bloody wrongs."[76] The public debate continued over the summer. Taylor McRae, a Fort Worth resident, read the case transcripts published in the *Southwestern Reporter* on May 8, 1912. He urged reform of the courts as a result of this case while maintaining that he was not concerned with the guilt or innocence of Martínez, unlike many of those who criticized the case.[77] His comments drew a response from Judge Isaacks, who pointed out errors in McRae's timeline; he noted that the door was unlocked during the confession and that the murder was in Reeves, not Pecos, County (the Reeves County courthouse is located in the city of Pecos).[78] This trivial response avoided the question about Martínez's baptismal records, which would verify that Martínez was only fifteen on the day of the murder.

The unusual haste of the original trial denied the Martínez family the six days they needed to travel to Durango, Mexico, to retrieve their son's baptismal records and therefore violated his rights to a fair trial. Davidson's dissent provided Martínez's attorney the necessary document to take the case to the next level: the US Supreme Court, which set a hearing for October 14, 1913. In Texas, strong feelings about the case divided Anglos and people of Mexican descent. Texas had become so alienated that Texas Attorney General B. F. Looney petitioned the US Supreme Court to advance the case:

> That the matters involved herein are of great public importance to the State of Texas . . . there has arisen a great disturbance and clash between the citizens of Texas and the citizens of Mexico during the pending and past revolutions in Mexico, and such delay in the final determination of this case has exaggerated the tension existing between the citizens of the border counties of Texas and the citizens of Mexico residing within the borders in Texas from Mexico, and that for these reasons this case should be advanced upon the docket by this honorable court and brought to a speedy termination therein.[79]

A number of US businesses that flourished during Díaz's presidency often hired US citizens for skilled labor positions in Mexico. They lived in the interior of Mexico and thus fled to the United States when threats of violence increased. In 1913 the US government urged its citizens to return for their safety. One El Paso construction worker warned his fellow citizens in Mexico that the local laborers were "worked up" and that the middle-class Mexicans held the same hatred toward US citizens but were better able to control themselves. He believed the Mexican authorities were losing control of the working class and feared that the growing number of rebels had become too powerful to control. Their detestation of foreigners, especially US citizens, was life threatening.[80] Stories such as these were commonly published in local papers, damaging the Anglos' already tattered image of working-class Mexicans.

In Mexico, US families fled the country after threats of attack. In Zacatecas, Mexico, Mexican rebels attacked the family of John Hoffman, a mine superintendent, repeatedly firing shots at the family's home. Mrs. Hoffman and her daughter hid in the storeroom of a local shop until they were able to flee by carriage while being cursed at and stoned by angry Mexican men.[81] Another US refugee, Gladys King, gave details of a mass exodus of North American women and children from Torreón, Mexico. She had traveled with 134 Anglo refugees on a train northbound to the United States. Along the way she had observed a distant train wrecked by rebels and noted that every bridge was damaged. She remembered looking from the rear of the train and watching a band of armed men burn one of the bridges they had just crossed.[82] The wife of a US dairyman in Ciudad Juárez, Mrs. H. M. McClure, fled across the river to El Paso in February 1912 without any intention of returning. She described herself as a longtime resident of the Mexican town and stated that in all her years prior to 1912 she had never received verbal abuse or threats to her life. She told a story about a gun-wielding Mexican woman who had chased her home, where she barricaded herself inside until hostilities subsided.[83] As the stories became more violent, editors amplified the headlines and included every gruesome detail.

These reports purported to illustrate the uncivilized behavior of Mexican men and women during the revolution. Along the Rio Grande, Mexican boys seemed to be fighting their own Mexican revolution. Police often arrested these children for their reenactment of the uprising. Many were pretending to fight for Pancho Villa. The El Paso police claimed they were regularly rounding up Mexican boys living on the Texas side of the Rio Grande who were fighting Mexican boys on the other side. The young residents of El Paso's Mexican district known as Chihuahuita threw stones across the river at Juárez children and homes.[84] Eventually this combat earned the name "playing Juárez." As the revolution intensified, so did the play. Outside El Paso, two fifteen-year-old Mexican boys fought the revolution with stones, and one boy killed the

MEXICAN BOY WHO IS UNDER DEATH SENTENCE.

Leon Martinez.

He is in jail at Waco, having been convicted of the murder of Miss Emma Brown at Saragossa, Tex. The Court of Criminal Appeals has remanded his case. In the picture Martinez is shown holding a model of a Mexican ship, which he made.

Figure 1.1. León Martínez Jr. in jail, awaiting execution (from the Dallas Morning News, *"Mexican Boy Who Is under Death Sentence," April 7, 1912, p. 5).*

other with his rifle. Witnesses said they were "playing Juárez" and remarked how uncivilized Mexican boys were compared to Anglos.[85] While these boys fought their revolution along the banks of the Rio Grande, Martínez battled the legal forces that were determined to follow through with his execution (figure 1.1).

During his time in prison Martínez entertained himself by displaying an artistic and pleasing side. In his Waco prison cell, officials allowed family members to give him a guitar. Martínez had not played before, but he taught himself how and entertained both prisoners and guards.[86] One reporter from the *Dallas Morning News* photographed him with a Mexican warship he had constructed out of materials that included a cigar box. In the picture he appeared clean and well dressed. This photo circulated only in the *Dallas Morning News*. Papers in border towns like El Paso refused to publish an image that humanized their murderer.[87] Mexican images that were most popular among Texans were from the revolution, and a picture-postcard craze "captivated" the country.[88] One of the most striking images was of Mexican children who participated in the revolution. Many different revolutionary factions recruited children to work as spies and infiltrate enemy positions. Insurgents were recruited as orphans, while others volunteered because it was the best opportunity

Figure 1.2. Street urchins and men in the Mexican armies during the Mexican Revolution, ca. 1914. Courtesy of Byron C. Utecht Papers, Special Collections, The University of Texas at Arlington Library, Arlington, Texas.

to find food and shelter.[89] These images outnumbered the single photograph of Martínez.

Figures 1.1 and 1.2 show the contrast between Martínez Jr. and the young soldiers. Tied around Martínez's neck is a tie that complements his coat and pants. The soldiers are draped with ammunition and in their hands are rifles. Martínez, by contrast, is shown holding a toy boat he created in jail. One can only wonder whether blood stained either the hands of Martínez or those of the boys in figure 1.2. Citizens of Texas border towns possibly imagined Martínez as one of the disruptive youths playing war games along the river or as one of the boys fighting in the revolution.

El Paso residents had justifiable concerns since Ciudad Juárez had become a battlefield for many rebel groups. In February 1912, the *Times* reported that Juárez was under attack and that businesses were being looted. El Paso went on alert, and the *Times* provided news throughout the day. Beyond the morning edition of the paper, four subsequent front-page extras warned readers of breaking events. Following this event the local merchants voiced their frustrations that the Mexican Revolution was bad for business. Hotel and restaurant owners noticed that the trains entering El Paso carried fewer vacationers and salesmen and that those leaving the city were carrying Anglo women and children to northern and western cities. Further harming the town's image was yellow journalism in major cities. More concerned with sales than accurate reporting, the *El Paso Morning Times* reported, "El Paso in Hands of Villa Troops," alleging that four thousand Mexicans had captured the city.[90] Rumors spread that Pancho Villa would come and avenge Martínez's death if executed and destroy the town of Pecos.[91] Once again, the events of the Mexican Revolution became damaging to Martínez.

The US Supreme Court dismissed the case on the grounds that the Court lacked jurisdiction. Martínez's only hope now rested with Governor Colquitt, known to many for having pardoned more than sixteen hundred criminals during his four years in office. Colquitt's reprieves were symbolic. He chose the Thanksgiving and Christmas holidays to pardon large groups of criminals. Race had never deterred the governor. On June 19, Emancipation Day, he shocked the citizens of Texas by "pardoning thirty aged negro convicts."[92] Women quickly learned of his forgiving reputation. Mothers wrote to plead for their sons, and wives for their husbands. They emphasized that their dire living situation had pressured others in the community to help ease their financial strain.[93] The *Dallas Morning News* reported the governor's capricious decisions. One story reported that Colquitt was in his office Sunday morning reviewing requests for clemency when his wife phoned him and said that he must escort her to church. When he responded that he was reviewing the records of Carl Craven, a resident of Kaufman County, Mrs. Colquitt replied, "Pardon him by all means, and come with me to church." With a pen already in his hand, he signed the pardon to please his wife.[94] Not all of his pardons were this easy, but most were symbolic.

On Mexican Independence Day in his first year of office, Colquitt pardoned elderly Mexicans as he did African Americans on Emancipation Day.[95] Both actions aroused the ire of many Texans. Nevertheless, the next year he again pardoned black prisoners on Emancipation Day. Because of the Mexican Revolution, the opposition to his pardoning of Mexican prisoners had grown. Newspapers began exaggerating the numbers of Mexicans he pardoned from nine to six hundred in just one month. Colquitt responded, "There are not six hundred in the penitentiary."[96] The following year, Mexican Independence day passed without pardons for Mexican prisoners, so clemency for Martínez became highly unlikely.

Border violence intensified in the months prior to Martínez's execution date. Citizens of Texas criticized Colquitt for his inability to protect the state. In an attempt to explain why the governor was not more aggressive with the "Mexican problem," many people alleged that he lacked manliness. Men wrote letters offering their assistance to take up arms and defend Texas from Mexican insurgents. They addressed Colquitt as "Little Oscar" and defined his approach to the Mexican revolutionary groups as "Sissy Diplomacy."[97] Local law enforcement officials and the Texas Rangers were outnumbered. Sheriffs from border towns urged Colquitt to secure federal troops to police the border.[98] Colquitt ordered 2,200 troops from Fort Sam Houston in San Antonio to El Paso for protection.[99] President Wilson sent another 4,000 US troops to Galveston. When matters worsened, Colquitt ordered the commander of the Texas Rangers to "shoot straight if necessary."[100] The orders were followed, and violent border clashes increased.

Texas Rangers and US troops mobilized in El Paso, Brownsville, and Douglas. Four companies of the state militia went to Brownsville after two US businessmen in the neighboring Mexican town of Matamoros were kidnapped and held for a $20,000 ransom. Captain Head of the Texas Rangers sent a telegram to Colquitt requesting permission to cross the river in order to retrieve the hostages. Colquitt refused the request and received more public criticism for his lack of aggression in dealing with the Mexican situation.[101] At Douglas in March 1913, two separate fights broke out, and six Mexicans were killed. Neither side took responsibility for the initial fight.[102] A major US and Mexican conflict seemed imminent. In February 1913 Victoriano Huerta became dictator of Mexico. Mexico's new leader encountered enemies among Villa's men and the *magonistas* and found few allies in Woodrow Wilson's administration. Denouncing Huerta as a despot, Wilson cut diplomatic relations with the self-proclaimed president of Mexico.[103] With Wilson planning to take down Huerta, and the governor of Texas busy appeasing a populace agitated by Mexicans, León Martínez had no chance of a pardon or even a sentence commutation.

In early 1913 US military efforts to monitor the Mexican port cities of Acapulco, Mazatlán, and Veracruz began as officials in Washington expressed their concern that weapons from Europe might arrive there.[104] Later that spring in Veracruz a minor misunderstanding broke out between Mexican soldiers and US sailors because of a Mexican officer's decision to arrest a group of seamen. As both sides denied any wrongdoing, Wilson and Huerta sparred in the newspapers, and the situation became known as the "Tampico Affair." Wilson demanded a twenty-one-gun salute to the US flag by Huerta's soldiers. When the deadline passed without compliance by the soldiers, the Atlantic fleet attacked Veracruz and occupied the city, resulting in the deaths of more than fifty Mexican troops, hundreds of Mexican citizens, and nineteen US servicemen.[105] With death and devastation in Mexico adding to the turbulent situation, as well as public mourning of the loss of US soldiers, Texans finally got the "justice" they had been demanding for three years for Emma Brown's murder.

On the fateful day of the boy's execution, US newspapers coast to coast recognized the courage of the fallen US soldiers at Veracruz. The Huerta government received little respect from Wilson's officials. One last plea for Martínez came from Juan Raino, Spain's ambassador in Washington. Speaking on behalf of Mexico, he requested that the governor, as an act of humanity, commute the sentence to life in prison because of Martínez's "tender age."[106] Colquitt denied the request, however, and Martínez was returned to Reeves County for his execution. The night before his death he condemned the court: "My conviction is the result of race prejudice upon the part of the jurors. I feel perfectly well and have absolutely no fears for the future. We all must die, you as well as I."[107] His only request was to wear the Mexican colors when he was hanged.[108] He quoted Saint John in his final statement: "Come unto me, all ye that labor, and I will give ye rest . . . God so loved the world that he gave his only begotten son."[109] On May 11, 1914, standing in view of an Anglo crowd, he announced that he was innocent.[110] He maintained the calm demeanor that he had become known for over the past three years among the reporters who met with him. In an ironic twist, the executioner was newly elected Sheriff Tom Harrison, not his predecessor, Sheriff Brown, the vocal opponent of Martínez who urged the court officers not to appeal the original case. Harrison is said to have lost thirty pounds within a month as he struggled with his court-ordered duty.[111] As several people in Reeves County watched, Harrison sprang the trap at noon, and fourteen minutes later Martínez was pronounced dead.

León Martínez represented the "Mexican problem" to the people of Texas. A member of an ethnic group who arrived in large numbers in Texas, Martínez suffered from being categorized as racially inferior to Anglo Texans. During the years of the Mexican Revolution, Mexican refugees fleeing into Texas exacerbated the Anglos' resentment. New developments involving the growing number of Mexican radicals in Texas and allegations of revolutionary plots further damaged the Mexicans' reputation and made them even more vulnerable in white Texas communities. This period was damaging to the people of a country that had once ruled the southwestern region of the United States. Many were caught between two worlds: Mexico, engaged in a civil war, and the United States, fostering ethnic hostilities against their neighbors to the south.

León Martínez Jr. lived in an Anglo world that determined his guilt without closely examining the evidence. If he was truly guilty, then Martínez paid the ultimate price for taking the life of Emma Brown. The burden of proof falls on the district attorney, not the defense, and not this historian. A forced confession by a discriminating mob on the night of his arrest, as well as the haste in securing a guilty verdict within a week of the crime suggests that Martínez was vulnerable to the Anglo/Mexican social disorder in West Texas. Violent death threats made to his attorneys prevented an appeal and illustrate the power of this community to persuade the authorities to acquiesce to its demands. Far worse were the actions of the state's highest judges and politicians, who concerned themselves with elections and pandered to the majority rather than determining what was "just" for a Mexican living in Texas.

The years of the Mexican Revolution were injurious to the people of Mexican descent who were living in Texas. Nevertheless, on the day that President Wilson was honoring the soldiers who had died at Veracruz, a Mexican boy had his life snuffed out at a public execution even though a swirl of stories about the crime, his apprehension, and trial, created more questions than answers. For those Mexicans who were living in Mexico and the United States, the decade of the 1910s was one of fear and confusion. In towns along the US and Mexican border, ethnic Mexicans, both US citizens and otherwise, were profiled by a prejudiced society and became targets of unwarranted searches, unjust legal decisions, and one of the most heinous acts of violence—lynching. It is important that we learn from our past and not forget the human rights that were violated during the decade of disorder. As W. E. B. DuBois once said, "We must remember because if the world forgets evil, evil is reborn."

Notes

1. *Washington Post*, "Honor Navy's Dead," May 12, 1914, p. 2.
2. Ibid.
3. Alton Hughes, *Pecos: A History of the Pioneer West* (Seagraves, Tex.: Pioneer, 1978), 94.
4. *Laredo Times*, "Miss Emma Brown Slain in Pecos," July 30, 1911, p. 1.
5. *El Paso Morning Times*, "Martinez to Hang Today," May 11, 1914, 1–2.
6. Ibid.
7. Ex Parte Martinez, no. 1457, "Opinion," 1.
8. Ibid., "Dissenting Opinion," 14.
9. Ibid., 29.
10. Ex Parte Martinez, no. 1457, "Opinion," 3.
11. Ibid., "Dissenting Opinion," 30.
12. Ex Parte Martinez, no. 1457, "Opinion," 14.
13. Paul J. Vanderwood, *Juan Soldado: Rapist, Murderer, Martyr, Saint* (Durham: Duke University Press, 2004), 48.
14. *El Paso Morning Times*, "Alleged Murder in Abilene Jail," Aug. 31, 1911, 1.
15. *Galveston Daily News*, "Irrigation Hope of Trans-Pecos Section," Jan. 7, 1912, 12.
16. Ex Parte Martinez, no. 1457, "Dissenting Opinion," 1.
17. Ibid., 5.
18. Ibid., 4.
19. Ibid.

20. Ibid., 6–7.
21. Hughes, *Pecos*, 340–41.
22. Ex Parte Martinez, no. 1457, "Dissenting Opinion," 8.
23. Ibid., 5.
24. Ibid., 7.
25. Charles Curtis Cumberland, *Mexican Revolution: Genesis under Madero* (Austin: University of Texas Press, 1952), 3–5.
26. George J. Sánchez, *Becoming Mexican American: Ethnicity, Culture, and Identity in Chicano Los Angeles, 1900–1945* (New York: Oxford University Press, 1993), 19.
27. The latter number (262,672) might be an underestimate of 30%, according to most historians; ibid., 57.
28. Patricia Nelson Limerick, *The Legacy of Conquest: The Unbroken Past of the American West* (New York: Norton, 1987), 247–48.
29. *Dallas Morning News*, "Mexican Town Deserted," Oct. 10, 1913, 2.
30. *El Paso Morning Times*, "Deport 6000 Refugees," Oct. 10, 1913, 1.
31. Ibid., "Alien Labor Hits El Paso Hard Blow," Nov. 24, 1911, 1.
32. Ibid., "Show Hatred for Americans: Peon Class Worked Up to Threatening Attitude," Sept. 14, 1911, 1.
33. Ibid., "American Women Being Insulted," Feb. 18, 1912, 1; "Red Flag Rebels Violate Woman: Wife of American Ranchman Criminally Assaulted Five Times in Succession," Mar. 12, 1912, 1.
34. William D. Carrigan and Clive Webb, "The Lynching of Persons of Mexican Origin or Descent in the United States, 1848 to 1928," *Journal of Social History* 37 (2003): 413.
35. Ibid., 2.
36. *Waco Times Herald*, "Armed Men Hunting for Mexican," Nov. 3, 1910, 8.
37. *New York Times*, "Why Rodriguez Was Burned," Nov. 11, 1910, 2.
38. Ibid., 8.
39. *El Debate*, "Dollaria," Nov. 5, 1910, 1.
40. Ibid.
41. *Waco Times Herald*, "Bull Fights Forbidden," Nov. 3, 1910, 3.
42. *Waco Times Herald*, "Was Shot to Death by Policeman," Nov. 25, 1910, 1.
43. Ibid., "Mexican Crazy or a Fugitive," Nov. 18, 1910, 2.
44. Ibid., "Mexican Murdered Woman: State Probably Will Not Investigate Lynching at Rock Springs," Nov. 10, 1910, 1.
45. *Dallas Morning News*, June 21, 1911, 8; June 25, 1911, 8.
46. *Dallas Morning News*, June 25, 1911, 8; Nov. 7, 1911, 11; Jan. 3, 1912, 7.
47. *El Paso Morning Times*, "Mexican Murderer Removed," Aug. 1, 1911, 4.
48. Ex Parte Martinez, no. 1457, "Dissenting Opinion," 68.
49. *El Paso Morning Times*, "Mexican Murderer Removed," Aug. 1, 1911, 4.

50. Ibid.
51. *El Paso Morning Times*, "Governor Colquitt Will Not Interfere," Aug. 7, 1911, 2.
52. Ibid., "People of Reeves County," Aug. 2, 1911, 5.
53. Ex Parte Martinez, no. 1457, "Dissenting Opinion," 9.
54. Texas State Archives, box 140, folder 1–31, 1912.
55. Ibid., "A," Oct. 16–Nov. 8, 1911; folder 12, "A" Aug. 5–Sept. 20, 1911; folder 10.
56. *Dallas Morning News*, "Oppose Commutation of Sentence," Sept. 3, 1911, 15.
57. Robert C. Overfelt, "Mexican Revolution," *Handbook of Texas Online* (http://www.tshaonline.org/handbook/online/articles/pqmhe), accessed May 19, 2012. Published by the Texas State Historical Association.
58. Linda B. Hall and Don M. Coerver, *Revolution on the Border: The United States and Mexico, 1910–1920* (Albuquerque: University of New Mexico Press, 1988), 17.
59. Ricardo Flores Magón, *Regeneración*, "El Derecho de Propiedad," Mar. 18, 1911, 1.
60. Ibid., 1.
61. Hall and Coerver, *Revolution on the Border*, 130.
62. James A. Sandos, *Rebellion in the Borderlands: Anarchism and the Plan of San Diego*, 1904–1923 (Norman: University of Oklahoma Press, 1992), 59.
63. *El Paso Morning Times*, "Pecos Attorney on the Martinez Case," Sept. 12, 1911, 1.
64. Ibid., "Father of Murderer Asks for Justice," July 27, 1911, 1.
65. Ibid., "Mexican Given Death Sentence," July 30, 1911, 1.
66. This could have been translated and typed for him, but even if that were the case, he was nonetheless literate in the Spanish language.
67. *El Paso Morning Times*, "Anti-American Plot Exposed," Feb. 25, 1912, 1.
68. Ibid., "Rid Country of Undesirable Aliens," May 8, 1912, 6.
69. Ibid.
70. "Tyranny or Necessity?" *Virginia Law Review* 18 (1912): 72–73.
71. *Dallas Morning News*, "Clash of Opinions in Martinez Case," Mar. 28, 1912, 1.
72. The following two treaties between the United States of America and the Republic of Mexico guarantee any Mexican citizen due process of law according to the Fourteenth Amendment of the US Constitution: Mar. 24, 1908, art. III (US document no. 5, 61st Congress, Second Session, 1909–1910, vol. 47, which is the same as vol. 1, 1205, of Treaties and Conventions,) and the Treaty of Guadalupe Hidalgo (idem, 1107, arts. I and XXVI).
73. Ex Parte Martinez, no. 1457, "Dissenting Opinion," 52.
74. Ibid., 63.
75. *Dallas Morning News*, Mar. 29, 1912, 8.
76. Ibid., "Martinez Case and Recall of Judges," Apr. 14, 1912, 6.
77. Ibid., "Should Make Slow Haste about Courts," June 18, 1912, 13.
78. Ibid., "Judge S. J. Isaacks Replies to M'Rae," June 23, 1912, 5.

79. Ibid., "Supreme Court Will Hear Martinez Case," May 13, 1913, 11.
80. *El Paso Morning Times*, "Show Hatred for Americans," Sept. 14, 1911, 1.
81. *San Antonio Light*, "Americans Were Hooted," Apr. 19, 1911, 5.
82. *El Paso Morning Times*, "American Women Being Insulted," Feb. 18, 1912, 1, 7.
83. Ibid., 1.
84. Ibid., "Mexican Juveniles in War," Aug. 20, 1911, 4.
85. Ibid., "Mexican Boy Held for Killing Another," Apr. 26, 1912, 4.
86. *Wichita Falls Daily Times*, "Condemned Mexican Boy Learning to Play Guitar," Feb. 26, 1914, 1.
87. *Dallas Morning News*, "Mexican Boy Who Is under Death Sentence," Apr. 7, 1912, 5.
88. Paul J. Vanderwood and Frank N. Samponaro, *Border Fury: A Picture Postcard Record of Mexico's Revolution and US War Preparedness, 1910–1917* (Albuquerque: University of New Mexico Press, 1988), vii.
89. Ibid., 164–65.
90. *El Paso Morning Times*, "El Paso in Hands of Villa Troops," Apr. 24, 1914, 2.
91. Hughes, *Pecos*, 195.
92. *Dallas Morning News*, "Commendation for Colquitt," June 26, 1911, 5.
93. Ibid., "Colquitt Pardons Negros [sic]," June 18, 1912, 7.
94. Ibid., "Governor Issues Pardon," Mar. 28, 1911, 13.
95. Ibid., "Colquitt Pardons Negros [sic]," June 18, 1912, 7.
96. Ibid., "Colquitt Answers Ramsey's Challenge," July 21, 1912, 10.
97. Texas State Archives, box 140, folder 1–31, 1912.
98. Ibid.
99. *El Paso Morning Times*, "2200 Troops Are Now in El Paso," Feb. 28, 1912, 1.
100. Ibid., "Texas Governor Wires Ranger Captain to Shoot Straight If It Is Necessary," Jan. 31, 1913, 1.
101. Ibid., "Clash Possible at Brownsville," Feb. 25, 1913, 1.
102. Ibid., "American and Mexican Troops Clash on Border near Douglas," Mar. 3, 1913, 1; "Another Fight near Douglas," Mar. 5, 1913, 1.
103. *El Paso Morning Times*, "Breach Has Come between the United States and Mexico," Apr. 20, 1914, 1.
104. Ibid., "US Warships to Mexican Waters Result of Washington Conference," Feb. 11, 1913, 1.
105. Ibid., "Mexican Loss Two Hundred," Apr. 22, 1914, 1.
106. *Dallas Morning News*, "Ask Leniency for Martinez," May 10, 1914, 11.
107. *El Paso Morning Times*, "Martinez to Hang Today," May 11, 1914, 1.
108. Ibid., "Martinez Case before Court," Nov. 4, 1911, 2.
109. Ibid., "Martinez to Hang Today," May 11, 1914, 1.
110. Ibid.
111. Hughes, *Pecos*, 195.

CHAPTER 2

"Wire Me before Shooting"

Federalism in (In)action—The Texas-Mexico Border during the Revolution, 1910–1920

Don M. Coerver

The Rio Grande region has a long history of rustling, smuggling, banditry, and revolutionary activity. By the early twentieth century, however, Mexico had experienced a lengthy period of relative stability under Porfirio Díaz while, on the Texas side of the river, the area seemed to be leaving behind its troubled past and pursuing economic development. Officials at the local, state, and federal levels in both Texas and Mexico were ill prepared for the unprecedented violence and disorder that the Mexican Revolution would bring to the border area from 1910 to 1920. With much of the revolutionary activity centered in northern Mexico near the international boundary, officials struggled throughout the period to keep the revolution from spilling over the border.

The US system of federalism guaranteed that there would be a wide variety of agents and agencies involved in law enforcement along the border. At the local level, mayors, sheriffs, and city councils all had varying law-enforcement responsibilities. Under state law at the time, mayors and sheriffs even had the power to call up the local unit of the Texas National Guard. At the state level, governors had a particularly active role to play. The governors during this period—Oscar B. Colquitt (1911–1915), James E. Ferguson (1915–1917), and William P. Hobby (1917–1921)—faced a wide variety of political, military, and financial problems. Colquitt, in particular, would be actively involved in maintaining law and order. He took office in January 1911, just as the impact of the Mexican Revolution was about to be felt along the Rio Grande. In dealing with the situation, governors could call out the Texas National Guard or utilize the Texas Rangers.[1] It cost less to use the Texas Rangers, but in January 1911, the entire Ranger force consisted of twelve men—two officers and ten enlisted personnel.[2] In his 1910 campaign for the governorship, Colquitt had talked about the possibility of reducing even that small force.

An array of federal agents and agencies also played a role in law enforcement on the border. The Department of State had overall responsibility for US-Mexican relations, of which border policy was one aspect. The War Department was actively involved in law enforcement on the border, especially enforcement of the neutrality laws, although it did not technically have law-enforcement responsibilities. The Department of Justice was responsible for implementing federal laws and also served as an intelligence-gathering agency using its recently formed Bureau of Investigation. Immigration issues were the responsibility of the Department of Commerce and Labor. The Treasury Department was also active along the border, going beyond its fiscal activities to engage in intelligence gathering.

The two presidents during the period—William Howard Taft (1909–1913) and Woodrow Wilson (1913–1921)—also engaged in actions that generated jurisdictional disputes and communications problems. Taft ordered a major concentration of military forces in South Texas without previously informing his secretary of state. Later, he entered into a formal agreement with Colquitt for state enforcement of federal neutrality laws, leading the governor to assume incorrectly that federal officials would reciprocate and assist in enforcing state laws. Wilson confused the lines of communication by frequently bypassing the State Department in favor of using his personal representatives in developing and implementing his Mexican policy. Washington directed army commanders in the field not to inform state officials about what specific instructions they had in case a border incident threatened lives and property in Texas. Commanders operated until March 1916 under orders not to cross the international boundary without prior approval from Washington. However, US troops could return fire across the border.[3]

An important feature of the border area that would be affected by the revolution was the series of twin cities along the Rio Grande. These border twins stretched from Brownsville-Matamoros to El Paso-Ciudad Juárez; the latter was the most important of the twin cities.[4] For the Mexican federal government and assorted revolutionary groups, Juárez held a number of attractions. Control of the customs house provided an important source of revenue. As the most important port of entry on the international boundary, Juárez was a major avenue for the movement of war materials from the United States into northern Mexico. Possession of Juárez had an important psychological value and provided a high profile for groups seeking international recognition. The city also served as a potential escape hatch for defeated revolutionaries or federal soldiers seeking exile in El Paso. The Mexican and Mexican-American populations of El Paso were often an important source of support for revolutionaries in Juárez. El Paso's Fort Bliss would influence and be influenced by revolutionary developments in Juárez. El Paso became a frequent base for revolutionary exiles plotting their political comebacks and a fertile ground for recruiting would-be revolutionaries. John Reed, in his classic account of the revolution, *Insurgent Mexico*, observed the following: "El Paso, Texas, is the Supreme Lodge of the Ancient Order of Conspirators of the World. The personnel changes from year to year; but its purpose is always the same—to destroy the existing government of Mexico."[5] Control of Juárez changed on seven different occasions between 1911 and 1919. Authorities on both sides of the border worried about Ciudad Juárez regardless of who held it.

After the start of the revolution on November 18, 1910, Juárez soon became a target for the revolutionaries. As early as February 1911, there were reports that revolutionary forces under Pascual Orozco would soon attack the federal stronghold. In response to a request from Sheriff Peyton Edwards of El Paso, Governor Colquitt called up the local unit of the Texas National Guard—unnecessarily, as it turned out.[6] State and local officials got a preview of what might happen at El Paso-Juárez after an incident at another set of border twins, Douglas, Arizona, and Agua Prieta, Sonora. A rebel attack on Agua Prieta on April 13 resulted in two killed and eleven wounded in Douglas.

As the likelihood of a struggle over Juárez increased, officials at all levels became increasingly concerned over what might happen in El Paso. The Madero movement enjoyed considerable support among the Mexican and Mexican-American communities in El Paso. Authorities feared that Madero supporters might cross the boundary and join in the fighting in the event of a rebel attack on Juárez. A further complication was the possibility that Texans might attack Juárez if there were casualties on the US side, as had taken place in Douglas, Arizona. Ironically, army troops at Fort Bliss were not authorized to cross the international boundary if shells fell on the US side, but they did have orders to use force to prevent Texans from crossing the river to attack Juárez.[7] Officials also worried about the growing enthusiasm for treating the revolution as a spectator sport. When rebels threatened to attack Juárez in February 1911, El Paso police and troops from Fort Bliss had to be used to keep the curious away from the banks of the river. With a battle over Juárez looming in early May 1911, the *El Paso Morning Times* encouraged its readers to do a little revolution watching, observing cheerily that the "insurrectos are still with us in great numbers" at Juárez.[8]

As rebel forces isolated Juárez as a preliminary to an attack, Francisco Madero became increasingly nervous that an attack on Juárez would lead to death and destruction in El Paso and intervention by US forces. Consequently, he

Figure 2.1. Francisco Madero and his wife encamped west of El Paso, 1910. Courtesy of The University of Texas at Arlington Library Special Collections.

ordered his troops to break off the siege and move south. With victory close at hand, dissident forces under Pascual Orozco and Pancho Villa were unwilling to withdraw and instead launched an unauthorized attack on May 8, 1911. Shells began falling almost immediately in El Paso, ultimately killing six and wounding fifteen. The response by US Army forces at El Paso was to warn both the rebels and the Mexican federals to avoid firing into El Paso and to keep spectators away from the river. The army followed its orders not to cross the international boundary and did not even fire into Juárez as the soldiers were authorized to do. Governor Colquitt was outraged that the only US military response was to restrain the residents of El Paso. Fortunately for all parties concerned, the first battle for Juárez was brief, with the Mexican federals surrendering on May 10, 1911, after just two days of fighting.[9]

Although the fighting was brief, this first battle for Juárez was to have a long-term impact, especially on Governor Colquitt, who would apply what he saw as the "lessons of Juárez" to future crises along the Texas-Mexico border. From Colquitt's viewpoint, the events at Juárez confirmed his suspicions that officials at Washington did not fully appreciate the seriousness of the security situation on the border. Colquitt concluded that a repetition of the type of incident that had taken place at Juárez must be avoided at all cost, even if the state of Texas had to take military action to prevent casualties on the Texas side. Convinced that the federal government lacked a border policy, Colquitt was willing to develop one of his own to guide state activity.

Although Colquitt wanted to improve border security, he was also mindful of the dismal condition of state finances. The governor concluded that the most cost-effective method of protecting the border was to obtain federal funding for an expanded Ranger force, which in turn would help enforce federal neutrality laws. Colquitt met with President Taft in September 1911 and reached an agreement for an expanded, federally funded Ranger force that would—in addition to its state duties—also enforce the US neutrality laws. The Rangers rapidly expanded to forty-two personnel; when federal funding stopped at the end of January 1912, the force just as quickly contracted to twenty-one Rangers.[10] Ironically, the Rangers downsized just in time for the latest crisis at Juárez.

On January 31, 1912, the federal garrison at Juárez revolted against the Madero government. Although there was some loss of life in Juárez, there were no casualties in El Paso. Forces loyal to Madero, particularly renowned artillery officer, General Felipe Angeles (figure 2.2), did not attempt to retake the city, but a minor incident soon demonstrated the volatile nature of the El Paso-Juárez area. US Army Lieutenant Ben W. Fields, recently arrived in El Paso, had orders to take a detail of men to guard one of the international bridges. The detail would take part of the trip by special streetcar and then march the last part of the journey on foot. Fields determined correctly that the entire trip could be taken by streetcar, not realizing that the streetcar would loop through Juárez before returning to the US side, where the guard post was located. Fields led his group of nineteen armed men approximately one hundred yards into Juárez before being confronted by a group of armed customs officials. Word quickly spread of the North American "invasion." The mayor of Juárez showed up, "brandishing a large pistol," followed by an angry and armed mob ready to do battle with the gringo invaders. Local authorities quickly released the soldiers and returned them immediately to the US side.

The incident, however, was not concluded. Angry Mexicans in El Paso started street demonstrations against what they considered the lenient treatment of the US soldiers, leading officials to call out the El Paso unit of the Texas National Guard. While the mayor of El Paso called for more army troops, Sheriff Peyton Edwards announced that he was forming a posse of five hundred "responsible citizens" to deal with the deteriorating situation. Edwards got all of his volunteers in twenty-four hours, a move that unnerved both state and federal officials.[11]

The revolt at Juárez would soon morph into a more dangerous situation. In March 1912, Pascual Orozco—the general who had helped to put Madero in the presidency in 1911—revolted against the Madero government. The rebels who had revolted earlier at Juárez came out in favor of Orozco, sparking new fears of a conflict over the city. El Paso's mayor, C. E. Kelly, wrote to President

Figure 2.2. General Felipe Angeles directing artillery assault. Courtesy of The University of Texas at Arlington Library Special Collections.

Figure 2.3. Yaqui Indians who fought for Madero. Courtesy of The University of Texas at Arlington Library Special Collections.

Taft that US Army troops had been used primarily to "prevent American citizens from defending themselves." Taking a page from the hard-line approach of Governor Colquitt, Kelly informed Taft: "I do not propose to maintain order in the City of Juárez, but I do intend to protect life and property in the corporate limits of El Paso, Texas."[12]

The crisis lingered throughout the summer of 1912, with state authorities escalating their involvement. In June Governor Colquitt dispatched Adjutant General Henry Hutchings, head of the Texas National Guard, to El Paso to monitor the situation firsthand. Colquitt also directed Hutchings to prepare the Texas National Guard's only artillery unit, stationed at Dallas, for possible action at El Paso. The usually frugal governor even told Hutchings to order the Dallas battery to El Paso on a special train if necessary. On June 18 Colquitt cautioned Hutchings to "wire me before you take any final action or do any shooting." The following day, with financial concerns again in the forefront, the governor wired his adjutant general: "Do nothing that incurs expense until you fully investigate and report to me."[13]

The El Paso-Juárez area increasingly became the center of Colquitt's emerging border policy. On June 29 Colquitt postponed the scheduled summer maneuvers of the Texas National Guard, citing the "unsettled conditions on the border [at El Paso] that may require early mobilization of a large portion of state forces." The National Guard unit at El Paso began drilling three times a week instead of the customary once a week; ambulances and other military equipment were sent to El Paso. Captain F. A. Logan, commander of the National Guard artillery unit in Dallas, also traveled to El Paso to scout out gun positions and to determine the distances to different targets in Juárez. Adjutant General Hutchings informed the governor that the people of El Paso were looking to state authorities, not federal, for protection—a situation that might lead to "possible federal complications."[14] All of this military activity by the state of Texas once again proved unnecessary. Orozco's rebellion was eclipsed as a result of economic pressure from the United States, which imposed an embargo on trade between Juárez and El Paso. Military pressure from Mexican federal forces under General Victoriano Huerta removed Orozco as an immediate threat. Huerta drove Orozco's forces north toward the border. The Mexican federals retook Juárez on August 16, 1912, without any loss of life in El Paso.[15]

A change of administration in Washington held out the possibility of smoother federal-state-local relations with regard to border policy. In March 1913 Democrat Woodrow Wilson replaced Republican William Howard Taft. Although Colquitt had not been a particularly enthusiastic supporter of Wilson, he realized the importance of trying to influence federal policy as early as possible. Colquitt believed that much of the trouble along the border resulted from the failure of a small number of federal officials to deal sternly with the Madero revolt in 1910–1911. According to the governor, some of these officials had even accepted bribes from Madero. To correct this situation, Colquitt asked President-elect Wilson to appoint federal officials along the border who were

Figure 2.4. Palacio Nacional, Mexico City. Courtesy of The University of Texas at Arlington Library Special Collections.

"in sympathy and harmony with the State Government of Texas in its efforts to preserve law, order, and neutrality on the border."[16] Colquitt soon found out that little sympathy or harmony could be had, as Taft's "patient nonintervention" gave way to Woodrow Wilson's "watchful waiting" on the Rio Grande.[17] Federal-state cooperation on a border policy became further complicated by the murder of Madero by his former defender, Victoriano Huerta, who soon confronted a variety of revolutionary opponents.

The governor's hope that a Democratic administration in Washington would mean a tougher and better-coordinated border policy soon collided with the political, diplomatic, and military realities of the Texas-Mexico border. Colquitt became engaged in a dispute with US federal authorities over the passage of Mexican troops through Texas. The troops, supporters of Huerta, had been driven out of Sonora into Arizona. Subsequently, they were transported to El Paso, where they were supposed to be permitted to cross over into Juárez. In telegrams to Secretary of State William Jennings Bryan, Colquitt objected to the movement as a violation of "the rights of the State of Texas," as well as on practical grounds: "We have enough troubles of our own along the Texas border without the introduction of other factors of trouble from neighboring states." The governor threatened to have the Texas Rangers "arrest" the Mexican troops if they tried to cross from El Paso to Juárez.[18] Colquitt finally prevailed in his confrontation. The Mexican troops remained at Fort Bliss until US federal officials moved them to California.[19]

Colquitt's goal of taking a more aggressive stand on the border continued to encounter financial issues until the end of his term in January 1915. When asked whether he would call a special session of the state legislature to get more funding for border protection, the governor undiplomatically replied: "I would rather have war with Mexico than a [special] session of the Texas legislature."[20] Colquitt continued to be reluctant to use the Texas National Guard on the border due to the expense involved. From 1913 to 1914, units of the Guard mobilized six times to deal with border troubles, with the governor calling them out only two of the six times. On the other four occasions, mayors and sheriffs called out the Guard. On a per-capita basis, Texas ranked seventh among national guards in financing received from the federal government but forty-sixth in state spending on its National Guard. For the 1913–1914 biennium, state spending averaged about eleven dollars per National Guard member.[21] Use of the Texas National Guard also became uncertain as a result of federal threats to reduce funding after reports that Texas National Guard equipment that had been ordered destroyed had instead been sold to Mexican revolutionaries by Guard personnel.[22]

Colquitt's relations with the Wilson administration became increasingly rocky as the governor quickly lost patience with Wilson's "watchful waiting." In an appearance before the Texas Cattle Raiser's Association in March 1914, Colquitt set aside his prepared speech on the Livestock Sanitary Commission and quarantine regulations in favor of a highly charged presentation on Wilson's Mexican policy and states' rights. Dismissing Wilson's Mexican policy as "namby-pamby," the governor offered his take on states' rights: "I am for Texas first. The Governor of the State of Texas is superior to the President of the United States in matters entrusted to his care and keeping." After several sarcastic remarks directed at Secretary of State "Billy" Bryan, Colquitt leveled some criticism at a number of his fellow Texas politicians: "Congressmen and Senators have become cowards for political pelf and patronage. Not a one, thus far, has had the nerve to stand up and defend Texas." Colquitt concluded that he might "retire from office, but I'll never kiss anybody's toe at Washington." The Cattle Raisers Association went on record as supporting the governor's "vigorous policy" but did not include the criticism of national authorities.[23] When the federal government tried to pacify the governor by sending two additional infantry regiments to the border, Colquitt responded: "Give me 100 Texas Rangers, and I can do more toward keeping law and order in Texas than 10,000 US troops."[24] Colquitt continued his running argument with the Wilson administration until the closing days of his governorship. In late December 1914, Colquitt publicly dismissed the Wilson administration as "the greatest failure in the history of the presidency." Describing Wilson's foreign policy as "imbecilic," the governor concluded that the Wilson-Bryan Mexican policy was an "egregious failure."[25]

Federal-state relations were considerably less vitriolic under Colquitt's successor, James Ferguson, but the general environment deteriorated substantially. The same month that Ferguson took office—January 1915—the possibility of new violence along the Texas-Mexico border emerged with the "Plan of San Diego," a revolutionary manifesto supposedly written in the South Texas town of San Diego. The plan called for a combination revolution–race war that would liberate Texas, New Mexico, Arizona, California, and Colorado from US control and create an independent republic that might later seek annexation by Mexico. The plan called for the revolution to begin on February 20, 1915. When February 20 arrived, there was a slightly altered version of the plan but no revolt. Both state and federal authorities dismissed the plan as rhetoric rather than revolution, one more border pronouncement that could be safely ignored.

This attitude changed quickly when raids began in connection with the plan in July 1915. Although the raids were confined to the lower Rio Grande Valley, they caused alarm throughout the Texas-Mexico border region. Federal officials initially misread the raids as simply extreme examples of the banditry that had existed along the Rio Grande for generations and maintained that the attacks were originating on the Texas side of the border. Army leaders concluded that it was the responsibility of state authorities to deal with the problem. Agreeing that the problem should be left up to state authorities, Ferguson expanded the Ranger force despite federal refusal to aid in the financing. As the frequency and intensity of the assaults increased, both state and federal authorities identified an international character to the violence that originated on the Mexican side of the Rio Grande in an area controlled by forces loyal to Venustiano Carranza. When the United States extended diplomatic recognition to Carranza in October 1915, the raids abruptly ended, confirming the Carranza connection.[26]

Governor Ferguson attempted to cultivate both Carranza and Wilson. Ferguson met with Carranza on the border on November 23, 1915. The two agreed to promptly return bandits attempting to cross the Rio Grande to authorities on the other side "without going into details to fix the cause of the trouble or assign responsibility." Carranza also announced that he was changing the commander of the Mexican forces in the area along the river where the Plan of San Diego raids had been originating. The new commander was to be General Alfredo Ricaut, Carranza's nephew.[27] Ferguson later remarked of Carranza: "General Carranza is a man of the safe and sane type, a man of intellect and one that I am sure will be able to handle the [border] situation."[28] In December 1915 Governor Ferguson—in contrast to Governor Colquitt—agreed to the movement of Carranza's forces through Texas in order to attack troops supporting Pancho Villa. Ferguson gave his permission despite objections by El Paso officials and businessmen.[29]

The governor also made the rounds in Washington, D.C. In December 1915 Ferguson traveled to Washington to try to obtain the Democratic National

Convention for Dallas and to consult with officials on the Mexican situation. Ferguson met with Secretary of War Lindley Garrison about the status of the Texas National Guard. The Wilson administration had reduced federal funding for the Guard from more than $108,000 to $9,000 annually when it was determined that, as mentioned earlier, National Guard equipment that was supposed to be destroyed had instead been sold to Mexican revolutionaries. The Guard received a major boost when the federal government announced that federal funding would be made available to finance two additional artillery units, at a cost of $100,000 per unit. Ferguson also met with Wilson and Secretary of State Robert Lansing to discuss the Mexican situation. The governor assured Wilson and Lansing that Carranza was fully capable of handling the situation along the Texas-Mexico border. Ferguson came away from the meeting convinced that the Mexican situation was "now better understood in Washington."[30]

While Ferguson was lobbying in Washington, a new group of exiled revolutionaries was involved in a plot that would bring two familiar faces back to the border: Victoriano Huerta and Pascual Orozco. After his overthrow, Huerta had gone into exile in Spain, where German agents soon contacted him. Germany considered Huerta a useful tool, whose return to power could be a formidable distraction for the United States. For his part, Huerta was plotting a return to power and could use the military and financial aid that Germany was offering. Both Huerta and Orozco understood the convenience of joining forces in their attempt to regain their former control. Huerta arrived in New York City on April 12, 1915. Ignoring the well-known hostility of the Wilson administration, Huerta did little to conceal his intentions. After cheerfully informing reporters that he was on a "pleasure trip," Huerta held a series of meetings with German agents and former Mexican army officers. It proved a productive stay for Huerta. The German financial commitment to his conspiracy would eventually total almost $12,000,000.[31]

Pascual Orozco's fortunes had declined since July 1914. He immediately rebelled against Carranza's government but had to flee to Texas, where he made connections with a group of insurrectionary exiles known as the "El Paso group," taking over the leadership of the conspirators. Before the Orozco rebellion could take place, it merged with the expanding Huerta conspiracy. In early May 1915, Orozco met with Huerta in New York. The two leaders finalized plans for the revolt, including its starting date: June 28. Orozco agreed to precede Huerta to El Paso in order to make the final preparations for the uprising.[32] Zachary Cobb, the US customs collector at El Paso and a border veteran, warned Secretary of State Bryan that the Huerta conspirators were planning an attack on Juárez.[33]

On June 24—just four days before the revolt was supposed to begin—Huerta departed from New York with an announced destination of San Francisco. At Kansas City, Huerta switched to an El Paso–bound train. Rather than attract attention by getting off at El Paso, Huerta elected to meet Orozco at nearby Newman, New Mexico. The maneuver failed miserably. When Huerta alighted from the train, Orozco was there to greet him; so were Justice Department officials, federal marshals, local law-enforcement officers, and even a detachment of cavalry.[34] Officials took Huerta and Orozco to El Paso, where they were charged with violations of the neutrality laws. Huerta quickly acquired some high-powered legal assistance: successful criminal lawyer—and also mayor of El Paso—Tom Lea Jr. With large, pro-Huerta crowds gathering at the federal building, Lea requested that federal officials move the prisoners to Fort Bliss, a request that the court approved. Both Orozco and Huerta posted bond, permitting them to continue to meet with other rebel exiles.[35]

Huerta's legal problems took a new twist when General Fidel Avila, *villista* governor of Chihuahua, requested from Governor Ferguson the arrest and extradition of Huerta on a murder charge. The Carranza government filed a similar request. Ferguson could have dealt with extradition on his own but decided to consult with Washington before taking any action. Secretary of State Lansing advised against extradition, citing among several considerations the fact that the United States did not diplomatically recognize either faction. Following the State Department's recommendation, Ferguson declined to extradite Huerta.[36]

The legal situations of Orozco and Huerta changed dramatically on July 3, when Orozco eluded his extensive surveillance team and jumped bail. Federal authorities reacted by canceling Huerta's bond and arresting him once more. Huerta declined to post bond in exchange for the federal government's agreeing to move him from jail back to Fort Bliss. Following his escape, Orozco remained in the El Paso area on the US side of the border. On August 30, 1915, Orozco and four of his supporters found themselves pursued by a diverse collection of officials that comprised local law-enforcement officers, the Texas Rangers, US federal marshals, and US Army cavalry. In the shootout that followed on the US side of the border, Orozco and his four companions were killed, whereas his pursuers suffered no casualties. The lopsided nature of the results led many of the Orozco and Huerta supporters to claim that Orozco had been "assassinated." The official government version of the event insisted that Orozco and the other four men had died in a "fair fight," killed by various officials acting in "self-defense."[37] The diverse nature of the posse that did him in—local, state, and federal officers—spoke volumes about the nature of law and order on the Texas-Mexico border. Although local officers and Texas Rangers were involved, Orozco was not being sought for violation of any local or state laws.

With Huerta in federal custody and Orozco dead, one of the highest-profile, best-financed, and well-organized border conspiracies had failed. Huerta, a well-known heavy drinker, experienced a rapid decline in health. Following two operations, Huerta died on January 13, 1916, from gall bladder and liver problems. Some of Huerta's supporters charged that the operations had been deliberately botched to kill the general. The day before his death, a federal grand jury in San Antonio indicted him for violating the federal neutrality laws, accusing him of being involved in a "conspiracy to begin and set on foot a military expedition" against the government of Mexico.[38] In a classic example of law and order on the Rio Grande, the US Department of Justice accused Huerta of trying to overthrow the Carranza regime at the same time that the US Department of State claimed that there was no government of Mexico.

As Huerta and Orozco disappeared from the border, a familiar face reappeared—Pancho Villa. In October 1915, US recognition of the Carranza government produced an increasingly anti-US attitude on the part of Villa. Adding to Villa's anger was US cooperation with Carranza. After Wilson permitted the rail movement of Carranza's troops through Texas in order to attack Villa's forces at various places along the border, Villa's declining military fortunes forced him to abandon Juárez in December 1915.[39] This series of events became the prelude to two major incidents—the Santa Ysabel massacre and Villa's attack on Columbus, New Mexico.

Villa's military defeats had reduced him to a regional role. Unfortunately for Carranza and Wilson, the region where Villa was still a force to be reckoned with was the border region centered on the state of Chihuahua. This was also an area of considerable mining activity, an industry that the Carranza administration was eager to rejuvenate. In the fall of 1915, the US government had urged US mining employees to leave the area. By December 1915 Carranza's officials were urging them to return, assuring them that Carranza's forces controlled the area. In early January 1916, General Álvaro Obregón—the key figure behind the defeat of Villa—sent additional troops into the region to remove any lingering fears that the US miners might have had. On January 16, a group of North American and Mexican employees of the Cusi Mining Company were returning to renew their operations when a band of Villa's raiders stopped their train near Santa Ysabel, Chihuahua. The *villistas* took the North Americans off the train and systematically executed all but one of them, who escaped by pretending to be dead.[40]

The news of the Santa Ysabel massacre created a sensation along the border, especially in El Paso, with its ties to the mining industry in northern Mexico.

Mexicans and Mexican Americans became the targets of indiscriminate attacks by both US civilians and even some soldiers. As the situation spiraled out of control, local officials called up the police reserves. Mayor Tom Lea ordered the arrest of prominent *villista* sympathizers on grounds of vagrancy violations, while El Paso police captain W. D. Green promised that "every Villa leader in El Paso will be run out of town." Fears of Texans crossing into Juárez to attack Mexicans circulated with reports that civilians and even soldiers in Juárez were planning to cross into El Paso to support local Mexicans and Mexican Americans. The situation appeared so threatening that the commander at Fort Bliss, General John Pershing, sent troops into El Paso to maintain order. Army forces cordoned off the Mexican area of town and searched it for weapons. Residents in the neighborhood were not permitted to leave without the army's permission.[41] Although the Wilson administration refused to intervene militarily, it did warn Carranza that the massacre had caused "intense excitement" in the United States and that only "prompt and vigorous efforts" to capture the raiders would allay it.[42]

Unfortunately for the citizens of the border region, Villa had even more "excitement" in store for them. On March 9 a force of about 500 *villistas* attacked Columbus, New Mexico, despite the presence of 350 troops of the US 13th Cavalry. The raiders killed seventeen North Americans and burned much of the town before being driven off by the US Army. Elements of the 13th Cavalry violated the long-standing prohibition on US forces crossing the international boundary and engaged in "hot pursuit" of the raiders into Mexico. Unable to ignore such a flagrant attack on US soil, the Wilson administration announced that a "punitive expedition" under Gen. John Pershing would be organized to capture Villa and disperse his followers. Organized as a provisional division, the Pershing expedition had an initial strength of more than five thousand and crossed over into Chihuahua on March 15, far too late to engage in "hot pursuit" of Villa. Carranza considered the Pershing expedition an invasion of Mexican territory but did not offer any military resistance to its movement. He did, however, refuse to cooperate with Pershing's force; most notably he declined to allow the United States to use the railroads, which figured prominently in US logistical thinking.[43]

It was not long before the expedition led to an expansion and escalation of military activity. Under the Plan of San Diego, Carranza renewed raids into South Texas, which sparked "little punitive expeditions" into Mexico by US forces. The ban on US forces crossing the Rio Grande had been lifted, and army troops began engaging in "hot pursuit" of raiders and bandits. Army Chief of Staff, General Hugh Scott, met with General Alvaro Obregón in Juárez and El Paso from April 28 to May 11, 1916, in an effort to reach a peaceful settlement of the situation.

The negotiations broke down over what was to become a familiar problem. Mexico wanted the United States to promise to remove the Pershing expedition before serious negotiations could take place, while the United States maintained that the expedition would stay until an agreement could be reached.[44] As the situation along the border and in northern Mexico grew more serious, Washington considered the possibility of federalizing the Texas National Guard. On May 1, Governor Ferguson received notice from Secretary of War Newton Baker to "take such steps as could be taken without publicity to expedite action if a call-up should become necessary." On May 9 Baker federalized the National Guard units of Texas, New Mexico, and Arizona, citing the need to prevent "further aggression upon the territory of the United States from Mexico and to properly protect the frontier." Governor Ferguson responded by ordering the Texas National Guard to report for federal duty at San Antonio. More than 3,500 members of the Guard reported to San Antonio for federal service. Although short on funds as usual, Ferguson also expanded the Ranger force to 40 and sent them all to the border.[45] On June 18, 1916, the federal government called up the National Guard units of the remaining states; by July 31, 112,000 National Guardsmen were serving on the border. This massive military buildup had a major impact on Fort Bliss, which played a central role in supporting both the National Guard units on the border and the regular army forces on the border and in northern Mexico. At the peak of operations for the Pershing expedition, 40,000 soldiers were stationed at Fort Bliss.[46]

The application of federalism on the border did not involve exclusively military activities and law-enforcement problems. Officials at all levels of government on both sides of the border swung into action as a result of efforts by El Paso mayor Tom Lea to quarantine and disinfect travelers from Juárez to El Paso. Lea became convinced that lice-ridden immigrants from Mexico would spread typhus into El Paso. The mayor even wore silk underwear because he had been informed by a doctor that lice would not stick to silk. Lea urged federal officials to establish a "quarantine camp" where Mexican immigrants would be held for up to two weeks to ensure that they were free of typhus before being allowed to enter El Paso. While federal authorities did not agree to the idea of a quarantine camp, US Customs did finance the construction of a disinfection plant next to one of the international bridges. Immigrants from the interior of Mexico or "second-class" residents of Juárez wishing to cross over to El Paso had to have their clothes and baggage steamed and fumigated, submit to a personal examination, and take a kerosene and vinegar "bath" if they were found to have lice. After being disinfected, the immigrants received a certificate that was good for a week's travel between Juárez and El Paso. After a week, the process had to be repeated.[47]

When the disinfection plant went into operation in January 1917, it soon produced an international incident. On January 28 a group of women refused to be disinfected and blocked streetcar traffic on the international bridge. They then tried to march on the disinfection plant, leading to a confrontation with US immigration and public-health officials. At the request of local officials, both US and Mexican troops were called to the bridge to restore order. The disturbance became so pronounced that the Juárez racetrack had to close, something that had usually been avoided even with threats of revolutionary attacks. The rioting renewed on January 29, although streetcar traffic was still interrupted. The El Paso Chamber of Commerce held a special meeting to discuss the economic implications of the situation. At the meeting, the US officials softened their stance by indicating that they would permit Mexican immigrants to enter El Paso without requiring them to be disinfected or to show a certificate. These authorities also said that they would accept certificates of disinfection issued by Mexican officials.[48] The uproar over disinfection was a good indicator of how revolution on the border was hardening both class and ethnic lines.

The status of the Pershing expedition in Mexico and the National Guard units on the border received greater scrutiny by US officials. The intervention had accomplished its most important goal: the dispersal of Villa's forces so they no longer threatened the border. The other major goal of capturing Villa seemed increasingly unlikely. There was also a powerful financial motive to end the intervention; the expedition and the federalization of the National Guard were costing the federal government about $15 million per month. The demobilization process started with the withdrawal of the National Guard units from the border beginning in the fall of 1916. On January 27, 1917, the expedition began a phased withdrawal from Mexico; after almost eleven months in Mexico, the last of the expedition's troops returned to US soil on February 5.[49] The demobilization and withdrawal had taken place without any concessions by the Carranza administration. The largest US intervention of the 1910–1920 period did not end with peace restored to the border or good relations renewed with the Mexican government.

Entry of the United States into World War I in April 1917 had a powerful impact on the operations of all levels of government along the border. Action at the state level would be in the hands of a new governor, William P. Hobby, who became governor in September 1917 following the impeachment and removal of Ferguson. As a result of the war, the Rangers underwent the greatest expansion in their history. This expansion included an increase in the regular Ranger force, as well as the creation of a new category of Rangers, the Loyalty Rangers. When Hobby took office in September 1917, there were 73 regular Rangers; by February 1918 that number had increased to 165. The Loyalty Rangers exercised the same warrant of authority that regular Rangers did, but they had a special characteristic that the governor liked: They received no compensation. The Loyalty Rangers were responsible for enforcing all state laws and also functioned as a secret-service organization for the state. The Loyalty Rangers would consist of three persons picked from each county and would normally serve only in their own county. Their main duty was to support local law enforcement. The principal responsibility of the regular Rangers remained what it had been for some time: protection of the border. Even with a substantial expansion in the Rangers, they were still spread thin along the border; one company of fourteen men, for example, was responsible for covering some ninety miles of the Rio Grande. The Rangers had to cooperate with a wide variety of federal agencies: army intelligence, immigration, customs, and the Department of Justice. As in the past, they were also enforcing federal laws, ranging from the Mann Act to draft evasion.[50]

The Texas-Mexico border continued to be a center of US military activity even after the withdrawal of the Pershing expedition and the various National Guards. The Texas National Guard had been mustered out of federal service in March 1917, called back to federal service in April, and mobilized again in August. Despite the demands of the war in Europe, the Wilson administration kept approximately thirty thousand troops along the border, with most of them along the Rio Grande. The War Department considered border service as a "training situation" for army troops. The US Army continued its policy of hot pursuit of bandits and raiders across the boundary, sparking frequent complaints from the Carranza administration. In response to these protests, in May 1918 Secretary of War Newton Baker issued new orders to his commanders along the border: US troops were not to shoot at persons on the Mexican side of the boundary unless they had been fired upon first. Troops could return fire only if necessary for self-defense. Pursuit of raiders into Mexico was not to take place except to recover captives and only then if it appeared that Mexican forces were unable to retrieve them. Pursuit could not go more than twenty miles beyond the boundary, and the nearest Mexican commander had to be notified of the pursuit. Special agreements could be made between local Mexican and US commanders for cooperation, but Baker indicated that the War Department did not want to enter into an "international agreement relating to pursuit of raiding parties."[51]

With the end of the war in Europe, the border once again became the principal area of interest for the US military. It also remained the main area of concern for a diminished Texas Ranger force. At the end of the war, the regular Ranger force numbered 161. Legislation passed in March 1919 restricted the maximum strength of the Rangers to 75. The Loyalty Rangers numbered approximately 800 in late 1918, and Hobby abolished them in February 1919.[52] Local, state, and federal officials were increasingly concerned about the security situation on the border. The Carranza administration faced mounting domestic opposition as maneuvering for the Mexican presidential elections of 1920 had begun. Carranza could not run for reelection and had refused to endorse his most obvious successor, Álvaro Obregón. Even more unsettling was the military comeback of Pancho Villa in northern Mexico in the spring of 1919. Villa had already taken the mining center of Parral in southern Chihuahua, and authorities on both sides of the Rio Grande worried that he would try to take Juárez, which had changed hands seven times since the start of the revolution in 1910. In the event of an attack on Juárez, it was unlikely that Villa would be concerned about the possibility of civilian casualties or property damage in El Paso. Without intervention by US forces, there were legitimate fears of a repeat of the disastrous events of May 1911 in El Paso, which had not only caused problems for US-Mexican relations but also complicated federal-state relations on the US side for years.

As it turned out, the US government was prepared to take action to prevent the recurrence of the 1911 scenario. Secretary of War Newton Baker issued a general order authorizing army troops to enter Mexico in defense of US lives and property. There were also specific orders concerning an attack on Juárez. If Villa's forces fired on El Paso, then US troops could cross into Juárez and disperse them. While the US Army was bringing in 1,675 additional troops from Columbus, New Mexico, to El Paso, Governor Hobby refused the Carranza administration's request to bring troops through Texas to reinforce Juárez. Villa launched his attack on Juárez on June 15, 1919. His troops attempted to direct their attack to avoid firing into El Paso; despite this effort, shells began to fall almost immediately on the US side, causing several casualties. The initial response on the Texas side was to send additional army troops to the international bridges and to call out the entire El Paso police force.[53] Villa's forces soon controlled most of Juárez.

Operating under the new orders from the War Department, US authorities began planning a major response to the situation across the river. General James Erwin, army commander at El Paso, informed General Federico González, commander of Carranza's troops at Juárez, that US forces would be crossing into Juárez to end the shooting into El Paso. González responded not by protesting the intervention but rather by withdrawing his remaining forces to Fort Hidalgo, in the hills overlooking Juárez. On the evening of June 15, US troops crossed the international boundary. Comprising cavalry, infantry, and even artillery, this force of thirty-six hundred quickly drove off Villa's forces and returned to El Paso the next day. Army casualties included two killed and ten wounded; civilian casualties in El Paso were two killed and four wounded. Villa's casualties were estimated at one hundred.[54] González later claimed that US military involvement was unnecessary as his troops had "defended the town most bravely." The general did not have much of an opinion beyond that, indicating that "this is a matter for my superior officers and for my president to consider. I am not in a position to impose my own views upon the situation."[55] In his official report, González claimed that he had ordered US troops to get out of Juárez in twenty minutes, earning a congratulatory telegram from President Carranza.[56]

The intervention at Juárez in June 1919 was the last major US military action along the border in the bloody 1910–1920 period. It also, however, indicated a much more aggressive US policy in the region. The Wilson administration sent additional troops and equipment to the area, including twenty-six tanks and eighteen aircraft. As of June 1919, twenty-four army posts were operational in Texas, with Brownsville and El Paso accommodating the two largest army ordnance depots in the United States. The Wilson administration made it clear that the days of "watchful waiting" had passed. Secretary of War Baker left little doubt about the limits of the new policy: "If Villa or Carranza cut any capers along the border, our troops will go after them into Mexico. The War Department has adopted and will carry out a firm and decisive policy hereafter regarding border affairs."[57] The Department of State also sounded a harder line, warning the Carranza administration that "its continued inability or unwillingness to afford adequate protection for American citizens may force the United States to adopt a radical change in its policy with regard to Mexico."[58] In a memorably undiplomatic statement to the Mexican ambassador to the United States, Secretary of State Lansing said that he was "hoping against hope that sense and decency would finally penetrate the thick skull of President Carranza. He seems as obstinate, as impervious to reason, and as hostile to Americans as he has ever been."[59]

Carranza's domestic opponents had also run out of patience with the president. When he attempted to impose his successor for the presidency, a revolt broke out in April 1920 on behalf of General Obregón. In May Juárez went over to the revolutionaries without a struggle; that same month a group of rebels assassinated Carranza as he was trying to flee from Mexico City to Veracruz. If the rebel takeover of Juárez in May 1920 evoked any memories of the revolutionary takeover in May 1911, few comments emerged. The main figures in 1911—Francisco Madero, Pascual Orozco, and Pancho Villa—were going or already gone from the revolutionary scene. Violence claimed Madero in 1913 and Pascual Orozco in 1915. In 1920 Villa reached an agreement with the Obregón group, under which he retired in return for a hacienda and certain financial benefits. This golden parachute did Villa little good, however. He died in a hail of bullets in 1923.

The curious mixture of federalism and revolution on the border between 1910 and 1920 came to an appropriately contradictory conclusion. In October 1920, President-elect Obregón received a warm reception when he arrived in El Paso, where some ten thousand people turned out to greet him. At a banquet the next day, Governor Hobby called for US recognition of the Obregón regime. Obregón then traveled to the state fair in Dallas, where the Mexican exhibit had as its theme closer relations between Texas and Mexico. In December 1920, Hobby attended Obregón's inauguration as an honored guest but without the blessing of the Wilson administration, which did not recognize the new government. The final irony came when Governor Hobby laid a memorial wreath at the monument to the military cadets who had died defending Chapultepec against US troops in the Mexican-American War.[60] Although much had changed on the Texas-Mexico border between 1910 and 1920, at least one thing had endured: the problem of harmonizing local, state, and federal action in dealing with border issues in a revolutionary environment. Adjutant General Henry Hutchings summarized the situation very well. Following a raid by local, state, and federal officials that broke up a revolutionary conspiracy, a reporter asked Hutchings about state officials enforcing federal laws. Hutchings replied: "I don't know anything, and I am not positive about that."[61]

Notes

1. Texas, Adjutant General, *Biennial Report of the Adjutant General of Texas, 1911–1912*, 3–8.
2. Texas, House of Representatives, *Texas House Journal*, Thirty-Fourth Legislature, Regular Session, Jan. 12, 1915, 48–49.
3. Don M. Coerver and Linda B. Hall, *Texas and the Mexican Revolution: A Study in State and National Border Policy, 1910–1920* (San Antonio: Trinity University Press, 1984), 3–6.
4. Milo Kearney and Anthony Knopp, *Border Cuates: A History of the US-Mexican Twin Cities* (Austin: Eakin, 1995), 151–93.
5. Quoted in David Dorado Romo, *Ringside Seat to a Revolution: An Underground Cultural History of El Paso and Juárez, 1893–1923* (El Paso: Cinco Puntos, 2005), 110.
6. *San Antonio Express*, Feb. 3, 1911, 1; Feb. 4, 1911, 4; Feb. 10, 1911, 1. Hereafter cited as *SAE*. February 7 was "ladies' day" at the popular Juárez racetrack; that morning the *El Paso Morning Times* ran a headline proclaiming "Orozco at Gates of Juárez." *El Paso Morning Times*, Feb. 7, 1911, 4. Hereafter cited as *EPMT*.
7. *Washington Post*, Apr. 22, 1911, 1.

8. *EPMT*, Feb. 6, 1911, 1; May 6, 1911, 1.
9. Casualty figures for El Paso are in City Clerk of El Paso to Col. E. Z. Steever [army commander at El Paso], May 12, 1911, in Acting Secretary of War to Secretary of State, May 22, 1911, *Records of the Department of State relating to the Internal Affairs of Mexico, 1910–1929*, National Archives Microfilm Publication, microcopy no. 274, file no. 812.00/854. Hereafter cited as *RDS-IA*, followed by the file number.
10. Charles H. Harris III and Louis R. Sadler, *The Texas Rangers and the Mexican Revolution: The Bloodiest Decade, 1910–1920* (Albuquerque: University of New Mexico Press, 2004), 76, 88.
11. Secretary of War to Secretary of State, Feb. 16, 1912, *RDS-IA*, 812.00/2807; *EPMT*, Feb. 16, 1912, 1–2; Feb. 17, 1912, 1; Feb. 25, 1912, 1; Feb. 26, 1912, 1; *SAE*, Feb. 16, 1912, 3; Feb. 17, 1912, 2.
12. Kelly to Taft, Mar. 11, 1912, Texas State Archives, Governor's Papers: Oscar Branch Colquitt, Adjutant General's Department.
13. Colquitt to Hutchings, June 18 and 19, 1912, Texas State Archives, Adjutant General: General Correspondence.
14. Texas, Adjutant General, *Biennial Report of the Adjutant General of Texas, 1911–1912*, 192, 194. Logan to Hutchings, July 1, 1912; Hutchings to Colquitt, July 7, 1912, Texas State Archives, Governor's Papers: Oscar Branch Colquitt, Adjutant General's Department; *EPMT*, July 2, 1912, 1–2.
15. Michael C. Meyer, *Mexican Rebel: Pascual Orozco and the Mexican Revolution, 1910–1915* (Lincoln: University of Nebraska Press, 1967), 80–87. Ironically, Orozco and Huerta later wound up as conspirators, a conspiracy that would lead to Orozco's death.
16. Colquitt to Wilson, Dec. 27, 1912, Colquitt Papers: University of Texas.
17. The phrase "watchful waiting," which came to be associated with Wilson's Mexican policy, was the combination of two terms used by Wilson in a message to Congress in August 1913. Wilson said that he would "wait" and "vigilantly watch" revolutionary developments in Mexico. See US Department of State, *Papers relating to the Foreign Relations of the United States, 1913* (Washington, D.C.: USGPO, 1914), 820–27. Hereafter cited as *FR*, followed by year.
18. Colquitt to Bryan, Apr. 26, 1913, and Apr. 30, 1913, Texas State Archives, Governor's Papers: Oscar Branch Colquitt, Telegrams.
19. *EPMT*, Aug. 20, 1913, 1.
20. *SAE*, Apr. 25, 1914, 5.
21. Texas, Adjutant General, *Biennial Report of the Adjutant General of Texas, 1913–1914*, 6–7.
22. *EPMT*, May 14, 1915, 2.
23. *SAE*, Mar. 11, 1914, 1, 13; Mar. 12, 1914, 1–2.
24. *EPMT*, Mar. 13, 1914, 2. Colquitt was not critical of army officials, with whom he maintained consistently good relations. He was emphasizing that Rangers were peace officers who could make arrests which US troops could not do.

25. *SAE*, Dec. 27, 1914, 1.
26. Coerver and Hall, *Texas and the Mexican Revolution*, 85–93.
27. *EPMT*, Nov. 24, 1915, 1; SAE, Nov. 24, 1915, 1–2.
28. *SAE*, Dec. 4, 1915, 1.
29. Wroe to Secretary of State, Dec. 9, 13, and 15, 1915, Texas State Archives, Governor's Papers: James E. Ferguson, Letter Press. Hereafter cited as TSA, GP: JEF; *EPMT*, Dec. 18, 1915, 1.
30. *SAE*, Dec. 4, 1915, 1; Dec. 15, 1915, 2; Dec. 21, 1915, 3. The Wilson administration later restored the normal funding level for the Texas National Guard.
31. Michael C. Meyer, "The Mexican-German Conspiracy of 1915," *Americas* 23 (July 1966): 76–89.
32. Meyer, *Mexican Rebel*, 115–27.
33. Cobb to Secretary of State, June 7, 1915, *RDS-IA*, 812.00/15155.
34. Cobb to Secretary of State, June 27, 1915, United States, *FR*, 1915, 828–29.
35. Cobb to Secretary of State, June 30, 1915, FR, 1915, 830; *SAE*, June 29, 1915, 1.
36. Ferguson to Secretary of State, June 30, 1915; July 7, 1915, TSA, GP: JEF; Confidential Agent of the Constitutionalist Government of Mexico to Secretary of State, July 1, 1915, *FR*, 1915, 830–32.
37. Cobb to Secretary of State, Aug. 30 and 31, Sept. 2 and 4, 1915, *RDS-IA*, 812.00/15971, 15982, 16008, and 16016. Stone to Bureau of Investigation, Aug. 31, 1915, United States, National Archives, Federal Bureau of Investigation, Record Group 65, Mexican File, file number 232–162. Harris and Sadler maintain that there were former and future—but no current—Rangers in the posse. The Rangers had been involved in the search for—but not the shootout with—Orozco. See *Texas Rangers and the Mexican Revolution*, 298–99.
38. The United States v. Victoriano Huerta et al., District Court, Western District of Texas, no. 2185, National Archives and Records Administration, Southwest Region, Fort Worth.
39. Wroe to Secretary of State, Dec. 9, 13, and 15, 1915, TSA, GP: JEF; *EPMT*, Dec. 18, 1915, 1.
40. The report of the Santa Ysabel massacre, including the account of its only survivor, Thomas Holmes, is in Cobb to Secretary of State, Jan. 12, 1916, and Cobb to Secretary of State, no. 2, Jan. 12, 1916, *FR*, 1916, 652. Cobb, customs collector at El Paso, had warned the State Department that US recognition of the Carranza regime might lead to reprisals by Villa.
41. *EPMT*, Jan. 14, 1916, 1; *SAE*, Jan. 14, 1916, 1–2.
42. Warning in Secretary of State to Special Agent Silliman, Jan. 13, 1916, *FR*, 1916, 656.
43. Linda B. Hall and Don M. Coerver, *Revolution on the Border: The United States and Mexico, 1910–1920* (Albuquerque: University of New Mexico Press, 1988), 59–66.
44. Generals Scott and Funston to Secretary of War, May 8, 1916, *FR*, 1916, 543–44. In his report Scott recommended the immediate call-up of the national guards of Texas, New Mexico, and Arizona—a move that took place the next day.

45. Texas, Adjutant General, *Biennial Report, 1915–1916*, 4–11, 118; RDS-IA, 812.00/181441/2.
46. US War Department, *Annual Report, 1916*, vol. 1, 10–15, 193.
47. Romo, *Ringside Seat to a Revolution*, 223–43.
48. *EPMT*, Jan. 29, 1917, 1; Jan. 30, 1917, 1. An earlier effort at disinfection in El Paso had produced even worse results. On Mar. 5, 1916, city health officials were disinfecting prisoners at the city jail with a mixture of gasoline, coal oil, and vinegar. An explosion and fire took place, which led to the deaths of twenty-seven prisoners, including nineteen Mexicans. See Romo, *Ringside Seat to a Revolution*, 226–28.
49. US War Department, *Annual Report, 1917*, vol. 1, 9–10, 141, 197–98. Hall and Coerver, *Revolution on the Border*, 76–77.
50. Harris and Sadler, *Texas Rangers and the Mexican Revolution*, 322–29, 341–42, 362–65.
51. Secretary of War to Secretary of State, May 11, 1918, *RDS-IA*, 812.00/21981. The Wilson administration had tried to obtain just such an international agreement following the raid by Villa's forces on Columbus in March 1916. Texas, Adjutant General, *Biennial Report of the Adjutant General, 1917–1918*, 8, 61–63.
52. Harris and Sadler, *Texas Rangers and the Mexican Revolution*, 427, 462–70
53. *EPMT*, June 15, 1919, 1, 7; SAE, June 11, 1919, 1–2; June 13, 1919, 1–2; June 14, 1919, 2.
54. *RDS-IA*, 812.00/22572, 22817, 22822, 22826.
55. *EPMT*, June 16, 1919, 1.
56. *SAE*, June 28, 1919, 2.
57. *EPMT*, Aug. 17, 1919, 1–2; SAE, June 26, 1919, 1; June 27, 1919, 1–2.
58. Phillips to Summerlin, July 21, 1919, *Records of the Department of State relating to Political Relations between the United States and Mexico, 1910–1929*, 711.12/216. Hereafter cited as *RDS-PR*.
59. Lansing memorandum, Nov. 28, 1919, *RDS-PR*, 711.12/229.
60. *SAE*, Oct. 7, 1920, 1; Oct. 8, 1920, 1; Oct. 10, 1920, 1; Oct. 17, 1920, 1; Dec. 1, 1920, 1; Dec. 3, 1920, 1.
61. *SAE*, Nov. 19, 1911, 10. Governor Colquitt once found himself in the position of requesting federal assistance in helping state officials to enforce federal laws. See Adjutant General to Duncan, Nov. 12, 1911, *RDS-IA*, 812.00/2533.

CHAPTER 3

The Rhetoric and Reality of Nationalism

Monterrey in the Revolution

Miguel Ángel González-Quiroga

Introduction

Monterrey, northeast Mexico's most important city and one of the Huerta government's few remaining bastions, was under siege by Constitutionalist forces on April 21, 1914, when news reached the city that US marines had landed at Veracruz. A patriotic, anti-US response was immediately set in motion. General Wilfredo Massieu, commander of the federal forces in the city, appealed to the rebels to cease hostilities and form a united front against the North American invaders, a plea that was rejected by General Pablo González, head of the Constitutionalist troops, who demanded immediate and unconditional surrender. The state governor, Salomé Botello, and the mayor of Monterrey, Ramón Treviño, both Huerta supporters, made inflammatory speeches exhorting the people to unite to defend the nation. Shouts of "death to the gringos" could be heard throughout the city. An eyewitness to these events declared that "marching bands and an immense multitude roamed the streets . . . proclaiming that the nation was in peril."[1]

Prodded by the military authorities, the crowd began tearing down the US flags that adorned the houses of the very substantial North American community and inevitably arrived at the consulate of the United States. The flag was ordered down and heaped in a pile with other US flags and desecrated in the middle of the street while Consul General Philip Hanna was taken prisoner. But in the very heart of this patriotic outburst, another story was unfolding. Some of the members of the unruly crowd were uncomfortable with the consul's treatment because, according to the eyewitness, Hanna with his family "had lived among us for some time and . . . had won our love . . . because of his kindness and humanitarianism."[2] Many among the crowd probably recalled his tireless efforts to bring relief to thousands of poor and homeless Mexicans during the great flood of 1909, which killed thousands and devastated Monterrey. As the consul general was led away the crowd was further moved by the words of a young girl (probably one of Hanna's nieces): "What is this about? We have always loved the Mexicans very much."[3]

Hanna was taken to the prison, where he was met at the entrance by the old warden, who berated the consul's captors: "This is no place for General Hanna. He is one of my dearest friends, as he is the friend of every Mexican. I will not receive him in this penitentiary." Hanna was taken to the palace of the state government, where he was locked up in the reception hall until freed shortly thereafter by the Constitutionalist rebels, who had taken the city.[4]

This episode offers several lessons. First, there is a clear connection between what was happening in the streets of Monterrey and the events in Veracruz and even farther away, in the centers of power in Washington, D.C., and Mexico City, where decisions that affected the two countries were made. Thus, any discussion about what transpired in Monterrey during the revolution must consider the broader national and international context. Second, the incident reveals particular groups' use of nationalist rhetoric to further their interests. The *huertista* authorities of Monterrey attacked the two most visible symbols of the North American presence: the flag and the consul general. However, they did so more because they wished to neutralize the rebels at the city gates and less from a sudden love of country. When this failed, they attempted to mobilize and unite the people to repel the Constitutionalists. They also used nationalism not in support of the revolution but to prop up Victoriano Huerta's counterrevolution.[5] The incident makes plain a third lesson: The nationalist rhetoric, at least with respect to the assault on the US diplomatic representative, did not convince everyone.

This chapter deals with the issue of nationalism and the way it was expressed in Monterrey during the revolutionary period (1910–1920). However, first it is essential to briefly discuss the nature of nationalism and its relation to the Mexican Revolution.

No one can deny that nationalism is one of the most powerful forces in the modern world. This doctrine glorifies the nation, a concept defined as an "imagined community" by Benedict Anderson and which has won broad acceptance from scholars. It is imagined, according to Anderson, "because the members of even the smallest nation will never know most of their fellow-members, meet them, or even hear of them, yet in the minds of each lives the image of their communion." This concept transcends social classes because, "regardless of the actual inequality and exploitation that may prevail in each,

Figure 3.1. The US consul in Monterrey, Philip Hanna. Courtesy of The University of Nevada Las Vegas Libraries, Special Collections.

the nation is always conceived as a deep, horizontal comradeship. Ultimately it is this fraternity that makes it possible . . . for so many millions of people, not so much to kill, as willingly to die for such limited imaginings."[6]

Nationalism has always been considered a crucial component of the Mexican Revolution, and no doubt the brand of revolutionary nationalism that emerged from the armed conflict and from the *cardenista* expropriation of the oil industry in 1938 has played a significant role in Mexican national politics and external relations to this very day.[7] There are two prevailing views with regard to the function of nationalism in the Mexican Revolution. John M. Hart argues that it played a crucial role:

> Economically and politically estranged pequeña burguesía, provincial and local elites, urban and industrial workers, and peasants joined forces in a nationalistic uprising. . . . This cross-section of society unified around nationalism to regain control of the nation's basic resources and economic infrastructure from foreign domination.[8]

Ramón Eduardo Ruíz also detected an abiding nationalism, especially in the northern states of Sonora, Chihuahua, and Coahuila, which were more dependent on the US economy and whose lands and economic enterprises were heavily monopolized by North Americans. Those who were affected attributed this to the system of privileges established by the Porfirian government, so that "[f]rom the beginning, the battle against the Old Regime and foreign domination were one and the same." Ruíz concludes that although nationalism was not solely responsible for the outbreak of the revolution, without it "no combination of events or ideas adequately explains why untold numbers of middle-class and wealthy Mexicans gambled their lives and fortunes on armed rebellion."[9]

Alan Knight adheres to a different position: "The revolution was not, least of all in terms of its basic origins and popular manifestations, a nationalist, or anti-American, or anti-imperialist revolution." With respect to the massive US interests in Mexico, Knight argues that during the armed phase of the conflict, they "suffered chiefly indirectly and incidentally, not because of focused popular xenophobia; the latter existed, but rarely vented itself on Americans." He makes a distinction between the patriotic fervor of the population and its attitude toward North American economic interests: "While political patriotic sentiment appealed to a broad constituency, economic nationalism was the vehicle of a small, elite minority whose ideas displayed clear Porfirian as well as wider Latin American parallels."[10]

To avoid confusion, it is necessary to clarify a basic point. The foreign presence during the *porfiriato* involved several nations, but due to historical reasons and because of the overwhelming preeminence of its investments and, later, its incessant meddling in the revolution, the United States became the principal target of patriotic outbursts. This chapter, then, focuses on anti-Americanism as a source of revolutionary nationalism. The foreign domination Hart refers to involves mainly the United States. Before the revolution, more than one-fourth of Mexico's land, some 130 million acres, was in the hands of North Americans. Various sources estimate the sum of US investments at $1–1.5 billion. From one-fourth to one-half of US investments worldwide were in Mexico.[11] Moisés González Navarro states that North American investments "were the most constant, the most extensive, the most 'colonial' and the ones that generated the most mistrust."[12]

One of Knight's arguments is that the size of the investments was not a crucial element in generating a nationalistic response. The important point is whether those investments were perceived to be exploitative or whether they entered into competition with those of Mexican nationals. He further asserts that "Mexican and foreign enterprises were more often complementary and reinforcing, and the Mexican response to foreign investment—which brought jobs, money, orders—was more often collaborationist than hostile."[13]

There were many causes of anti-Americanism during the revolution, and some would have an effect on events and attitudes in Monterrey. Many consular officials believed that envy of US wealth and power became a major source of anti-US sentiment. Another came from North American colonists who "appropriated land without providing the jobs and higher wages which were often associated with American real estate investment."[14] Competition between Mexicans and North Americans for skilled jobs often generated a nationalistic response on the part of Mexicans. This fueled the conflict at Cananea in 1906 and became a major issue in the railroad dispute of 1912, when North Americans went on strike to prevent skilled Mexican workers from taking their jobs. Some believed that Germans motivated anti-US sentiments because they maintained a large presence in Mexican cities like Monterrey and wanted to see the United States mired in trouble in Mexico.[15]

Particular events often set off explosions of anti-US nationalism. One such incident occurred when a Texas mob burned Antonio Rodríguez, a Mexican national, at the stake in November 1910. Violent protests erupted in Guadalajara, Mexico City, and other parts of Mexico when the nationalist press widely disseminated and condemned the incident.[16] However, without a doubt, the most important cause of impassioned anti-Americanism during the revolution originated in the decisions made in Washington. The decision to place an embargo on the sale of arms to a given faction; the decision to recognize or withhold recognition from a particular government; and the decision to invade Mexico, as during the occupation of Veracruz in April 1914 or the Pershing expedition in March 1916, all generated a vigorous anti-US response.[17]

Alan Knight has argued that a general antipathy toward North Americans did not exist. A voice from the past agrees with him. Philip Hanna, who as consul general supervised most of the consular districts in northern Mexico, wrote in 1911 that "the Mexican people are generally friendly to Americans unless there is some occasion for unfriendliness."[18] Nonetheless, other scholars and most of the US consular representatives who wrote about the subject in 1911 agree that anti-US sentiment was widespread.[19] Another way of describing the antipathy toward North Americans is that it was latent and on occasion became aroused into frenzied activity. This apparent episodic nature is captured in a phrase by González Navarro: "[A]nti-American sentiment can be considered as an endemic disease with epidemic revivals."[20] Knight argues that xenophobia resulted from short-term factors "relating to US-Mexican relations, rather than by any grand process of social conditioning, foreign capitalist penetration, nationalist resentment and the like."[21]

There is a diversity of views on the subject,[22] but this last statement by Knight seems to describe best what transpired in Monterrey during the revolution. It is my belief that a strong nationalist response fueled by anti-US sentiment did not develop in Monterrey and its surrounding region during the revolutionary period of 1910 to 1920. Various factors contributed to this, including Monterrey's exceptionalism within Mexican society; the position of its people toward the revolution; the attitude and actions of the principal US diplomatic representative in the city; and assorted issues associated with economic matters that I refer to later as the economic imperative.

Restrictions of space do not permit a full discussion of other issues. The proximity of the border, for example, allowed many of the inhabitants of Nuevo León to look to Texas for their salvation. Political exiles of the different factions found safe haven at one time or another by crossing the border. Many rural and urban workers, who lost their jobs because of rebel raids on ranches and haciendas or the closing of factories, went to Texas to find work and provide for their families, something they had been doing for decades but now in far greater numbers. Even if these Mexicans felt prejudice toward the United States, they were forced to embrace that country for powerful reasons of survival. It is clear that the migration of people from one nation to another in search of work constitutes a threat to nationalism, as Avishai Margalit has pointed out.[23]

Another issue, which is not so much a factor but a reflection of nationalist attitudes in Monterrey, is the treatment given to North Americans during the years of turmoil. As in other parts of Mexico, US citizens caught up in the revolution suffered the theft or destruction of their property. However, there is little evidence of a generalized hostility toward North Americans and much less of constant threats to their physical presence. Ignacio Pesqueira, a Constitutionalist leader from Sonora, rejected press reports of an "underlying hostility toward Americans." He stated emphatically that "not one American citizen has lost his life because of his nationality."[24] This is clearly an exaggeration, but Alan Knight argues that "a balanced review of the evidence (one that does not seize upon a few dramatic instances) reveals that Americans often went unmolested during the Revolution, and that other foreign groups bore the brunt of whatever xenophobia there was." For that reason, North Americans probably suffered less than Mexican property owners.[25]

This coincides with reports Hanna sent to the State Department. In April 1913, he wrote that US citizens had been "as well treated as the subjects and citizens of other foreign countries and in many cases are better treated than the natives." On another occasion, he stated that there was "evidently a special effort being put forth by both the federals and the revolutionists to protect at least the lives of Americans and in most cases protect their property."[26] Later, in the wake of the Pershing expedition in early 1916, Hanna wrote: "The excitement which existed here and in many parts of Mexico following the Columbus massacre and the entrance of American troops has completely died out . . . Americans were never better treated here than now."[27]

Monterrey's Exceptionalism

To fully understand these attitudes and the general acceptance of North Americans, one must also understand the historical and prerevolutionary context of Monterrey. Located at the base of the imposing Sierra Madre Mountains, Monterrey, the capital of Nuevo León, went through an astonishing transformation in the three decades prior to the revolution. It grew from a population of 35,000 in 1880 to 80,000 in 1910 and from a regional commercial hub mired in economic crisis to a booming industrial center with multiple railroad lines extending in every direction, connecting the city to the United States and the international economy. Public services, operated by foreign firms, included a modern water and drainage system, electric lights, and streetcars powered by electricity. Monterrey possessed textile mills, glass and brick factories, the nation's largest brewery, various smelters, and the Fundidora de Fierro y Acero de Monterrey, Latin America's first integrated steel mill. These enterprises converted Monterrey into Mexico's principal industrial center, producing 13.5 percent of the nation's industrial products, more than Mexico City and the state of Mexico, which had rates of 11.7 and 11.2 percent, respectively. Monterrey's strategic location near the mines of Coahuila, Zacatecas, and San Luis Potosí particularly suited the city for its smelting and steel-making operations.[28]

Modernization did not touch all of the city or its surrounding region. Only 13 percent of Monterrey's residents had access to potable water in 1917. A large poor and working-class sector without clean water became easy prey to diseases. The barrios of the poorer class "concentrated the majority of the population. . . . These were characterized by a deplorable hygiene, high rates of prostitution, alcoholism and crime."[29]

The rural areas were also left out of the modernizing project. Nuevo León differed from most of the rest of the country in that land tenure did not become centered on the haciendas but on *comunidades*, "peasant communities of self-sufficient producers."[30] The dominant system of land tenure in Mexico, the hacienda, was also present in Nuevo León, but according to Juan Mora-Torres, it "differed from the ordinary Porfirian hacienda in three ways: it was smaller and had lower amounts of capital invested and lower production capacities." Nevertheless, it was important "as the main source of food production and the largest employer of labor. By 1910 thirty thousand *jornaleros* toiled on haciendas, a labor force far greater than Monterrey's industrial proletariat." Although more research on Monterrey's hinterland is needed, Mora-Torres concludes that "rural society was more or less egalitarian: the great majority were poor, but had land."[31] It cannot be denied that rural workers were exploited in Nuevo León, as in the rest of the nation. However, when the revolution came, many chose to march to Texas instead of marching to war.

A local capitalist group that adapted with ease to the needs of the international economy generated the industrial surge of Monterrey. It had largely accumulated its wealth through trade with the United States and had taken full advantage of a combination of favorable factors, including the proximity of the vast North American market, the "Porfirian peace," and the stimulus provided by the favorable economic policies of the national and state governments. Unified by marriages and multiple business associations, this regional oligarchy, which included powerful family names such as Calderón, Milmo, Garza, Sada, Muguerza, Madero, Hernández, Rivero, and Zambrano, numbered no more than one hundred and became a dominant force in the economic, political, and social life of the region.[32]

Moreover, local capital financed most of the major manufacturing enterprises in Monterrey. Isidro Vizcaya estimates that Mexican capital made up 80 percent of the industrial investments.[33] A German industrialist is quoted as saying, "The preponderance of the United States is much greater in Mexico City than in Monterrey. Banks, smelters, manufacturing plants and commerce are virtually in the hands of Mexicans, so there is no doubt that the American element is clearly in the minority."[34] In his book *The Great Rebellion*, Ramón Eduardo Ruíz reviews the revolutionary conditions provoked by the influx of US capital in Sonora, Chihuahua, and Coahuila. Then he states: "Only in Monterrey, the capital of neighboring Nuevo León, did a core of ambitious and intelligent Mexican entrepreneurs survive the invasion of American capital."[35]

Perhaps due to its superiority, members of the Monterrey elite did not feel threatened by foreign capital and were willing to work in cooperation with foreigners. North American technical assistance was crucial to the industrial takeoff. Through a US intermediary, J. M. Schnaider was brought in from St. Louis, Missouri, in 1890 to design the plant and set up the machinery for the Cuauhtemoc Brewery. Later, skilled technicians arrived from the United States to begin production. Ten years later US engineers repeated this process when they arrived to build the steel mill and mount the machinery of the Fundidora. This latter enterprise was owned by the most powerful of the local families but also included capital from French, Spanish, and North American investors. Many local enterprises, big and small, included a combination of local and foreign capital. Notarial records of the period show many firms with foreign and Mexican names as the major investors. One such corporation was the Monterrey Building and Improvement Company, which was a diverse group set up to develop the northern part of the city and which included names like Buckner and Robertson, along with those of González, Treviño, and Madero.[36]

Unlike other regions of Mexico, foreigners, and especially North Americans, did not arrive suddenly in Monterrey to disrupt traditional forms of life. Texan exiles from the Civil War formed the beginning of a respectable US community during the 1860s. It grew considerably after the arrival of the railroad in 1882 because of the abundant economic opportunities in the area. By 1895 there were 1,419 foreigners registered in Monterrey, 900 of whom were North Americans. In 1911, the US Consulate reported that about five thousand North Americans lived in the district, which included Monterrey and the rural towns of Nuevo León.[37]

The US colony during the late *porfiriato* was an enclave with its own clubs, schools, and churches. It included businessmen, administrators, professional people, engineers, technicians, farmers, and skilled workers.[38] The largest US enterprise was the American Smelting and Refining Co. (ASARCO), owned by the Guggenheims. It followed the typical pattern of other US firms of funneling huge profits out of the country. However, it paid its workers a higher salary than the Mexican firms and forced them to raise their wages.[39] In addition, ASARCO was not typical of most US firms in Monterrey. Many of these enterprises were modest. North Americans busily produced and sold bricks, nails, hats, furniture, coaches, sewing machines, farm implements, flour, mineral water, tobacco products, and many other items. They and Canadians took charge of providing basic services for the city, like public transportation, water, drainage, and electricity.[40]

It would not be difficult to find cases of exploitation of and injustice toward Mexican workers on the part of US businessmen. The unequal pay given to skilled Mexican workers has been cited, and this provoked anger and resentment. Less known are the instances in which North Americans acted with fairness and social responsibility. Joseph A. Robertson, the most visible and dynamic of the US businessmen and the intermediary who helped in the establishment of the Cuauhtemoc Brewery and ASARCO, founded various companies and published a bilingual newspaper, *The Monterrey News*. Robertson owned the biggest brick factory in town, supplying the local market and sending huge quantities of brick to San Antonio. One year after its founding, the firm had provided housing for its office staff and ninety houses for its workers. With his son, T. Ayers, Robertson obtained a concession to operate a lottery that would provide the state government with funds to establish a vocational school "to educate young people of the working class so that they can compete with the foreign artisans who occupy the most important jobs."[41]

Robertson was very much a part of the Porfirian system. He was a wealthy landowner who bought Mexican farming and mining properties and established, with Gerónimo Treviño, a *compañía deslindadora* in Tamaulipas. These companies, which usually included joint US-Mexican capital, surveyed public lands for the purpose of settlement and kept up to one-third of the land surveyed, with the possibility of buying the other two-thirds. This venture yielded 123,000 acres to the two capitalists.[42] However, Robertson also suffered some business failures, and it seems clear that he and many other North Americans in Monterrey reinvested their profits in Mexico and did not fit the prototypes of the greedy US capitalists that drew the ire of Mexican nationalists.

Another characteristic of Monterrey that bears examination is its degree of national identity. It is true that two foreign invasions—by the United States (1846–1848) and the French (1862–1867)—forged a national consciousness in the Mexican people. However, in the border region a countervailing force also functioned throughout the nineteenth century: the development of a regional identity. The northern states were in constant conflict with the national government because it failed to protect them from Indian attacks and placed prohibitive tariffs and restrictions upon commerce. In 1852 federal deputies from Nuevo León expressed their repudiation of a national government that was incapable of generating prosperity or even the minimal conditions for the security of its citizens, a situation that motivated many *norteños* to emigrate to the United States. They spoke of a lack of respect for the nation: "The lower classes instinctively seek their material improvement and do not heed that which is called honor or patriotism, concepts that are unknown to them."[43] When Santiago Vidaurri took power in Nuevo León in 1855, he challenged the national government to act. Throughout the following decade he established a regional hegemony based on a powerful military force and a public discourse that extolled the virtues of regional values while condemning the failures of the national government.[44]

It is curious that, despite these regionalist inclinations, Monterrey came to be considered as the center of Mexico's "new nationalism" during the *porfiriato*. This was grounded "in the growing fear that foreigners, especially North Americans, were gaining greater control of the Mexican economy. . . . Nationalists regarded Monterrey, a city in which Mexicans owned most of the industrial enterprises, as one of the few centers [that] resisted foreign domination." There was also a sense of nationalism among skilled workers who demanded the same pay as that being paid to foreign workers for the same work. This sentiment was whipped up by newspapers like *El Trueno*, which blasted the inequality and asked: "Why is the good and honest labor of our national workers despised? Because we are not *gueros* [blondes]!"[45] As in the rest of Mexico, most of these expressions emanated from an urban, educated, middle class that often used a nationalist discourse to criticize the government.[46]

The existence of this new nationalism may seem to argue against my thesis that these patriotic sentiments did not become widespread in Monterrey during the revolution. It does not. I will show that, once the revolution began, with its attendant death and destruction, the closing of factories, the disruption of economic life, and the hunger and misery that it caused, most people of all social classes yearned for a return to the peace and prosperity of earlier times, and they looked to the United States for economic support in terms of investments and renewed trade. In this way, the armed phase of the revolution, at least in Monterrey and Nuevo León, may have done more to diminish rather than exacerbate nationalism.

A View of the Revolution from Monterrey

What was the attitude of the population of Monterrey toward the revolution? If it can be shown that there was little inclination toward revolution, it follows that there was probably little propensity for revolutionary nationalism. The available information indicates that the city and most of the state were quite conservative and not inclined to revolution. People were "busy making and selling things," and violence was bad for business, the lifeblood of the city. Businessmen favored order and thus were pro-government. That is why they favored first Díaz, then Madero, and then Huerta. Hanna wrote that these entrepreneurs "seem to care but very little who has charge of the government so long as such peaceful state of affairs is brought about as will allow them to conduct their business in the usual prosperous manner."[47] The working class was also little inclined toward revolution. In contrast to the rest of Mexico, workers received a minimum wage and accident compensation, and mainly belonged to mutualist societies "rather than combative unions."[48]

This does not mean that the inhabitants of the region did not want change. In fact, when the Madero revolution broke out, a majority of the people were in favor of the movement, perhaps because Madero was residing in Monterrey at the time or they were just tired of the political straitjacket imposed by the Porfirian government. However, the empresarial elite and most of the political class continued to support Porfirio Díaz.[49] The authorities in the towns of Nuevo León reported in November 1910 that everything was peaceful in spite of Madero's call for armed revolt. In that same month, Nuevo León joined other states in giving the Díaz government a vote of confidence. In the following months the state government reported that the public peace had not been disrupted.[50]

Throughout 1911 and 1912, when there were many uprisings against the Madero government, Nuevo León remained at peace. During a tour of the northern states, the US ambassador, Henry Lane Wilson, reported that these states and those of Guanajuato, Zacatecas, and Aguascalientes, "with the exception of the State of Nuevo León, are all affected by the revolutionary movement."[51] In March 1912, Philip Hanna wrote that order and tranquility prevailed in Monterrey, not because the people were "especially fond of President Madero, personally, but because they believe that continued revolution is disastrous to the business interests of Mexico." The rising tide of revolts was beginning to affect the economic activity of the city, but "Monterrey would not know that there was any revolution in the country excepting for the information contained in the newspapers and correspondence received by them from other parts of the country."[52]

When Huerta engineered the overthrow of Madero, Nuevo León quickly declared its allegiance to the new government. Only one small town (China) in Nuevo León expressed its disagreement with the designation of Salomé Botello, a Huerta follower, as governor of the state. Less than two months later, with music, parades, and a big ceremony, Monterrey celebrated the anniversary of the battle of April 2, 1867, Porfirio Díaz's famous victory at Puebla, which helped hasten the end of Maximilian's empire. The Porfirian restoration seemed imminent. Enrique Gorostieta, linked by marriage to the most important families of Monterrey, was appointed to Huerta's cabinet. When the *carrancista* revolt began to threaten the city, the government of Botello appealed to the inhabitants to form an armed group called the Defensa Social de Monterrey to defend the city against attack. It was composed of businessmen, middle-class citizens, and workers. One historian has written that "[a]mong the first to respond to the call of the governor were the employees and workers of the Compañía Fundidora de Fierro y Acero de Monterrey." This gives the impression that in Monterrey there was no impulse toward revolution. The revolution came from outside. If anything, a strong counterrevolutionary current was prevalent.[53]

A Consul General of the United States

A discussion of nationalism in Monterrey should include the role played by Philip Hanna, the chief consular representative of the United States. Hanna was a career diplomat who had served in Puerto Rico and Venezuela during periods of armed revolt, so he was no stranger to revolutionary violence. Appointed consul general in 1899, Hanna quickly established rapport and friendly ties with all sectors of the population, from the business and political elite to the lowest classes of society. He was on excellent terms with the military and political leaders of all factions. Several members of the Madero family gave him credit for saving their lives after they were imprisoned by the Huerta government.[54] When the Constitutionalists took control of Monterrey, the military commanders, generals Pablo A. González and Antonio I. Villarreal, immediately paid a visit to the consulate. Hanna confided that these leaders expressed their profound concern for the way he was mistreated by the *huertista* authorities and that they gave "evidence of their love and respect for our country, our people and our flag."[55] Later, when the *villistas* took the city, their military chief, Felipe Ángeles, and Pancho Villa himself called on Hanna and expressed their deep admiration for the United States, its people, and its political leaders.[56]

Hanna's relations with the other foreigners were characterized by respect and solidarity. He supported all foreigners, not just North Americans, in their rejection of forced loans from the different revolutionary factions. He gave support to the Spaniards who suffered confiscations at the hands of the Constitutionalists and gave food to the Chinese, who were a prominent target of Mexican nationalists. Hanna reported that during the Constitutionalist attack on Monterrey in October 1913, "from fifty to one hundred and fifty Americans and foreigners slept in the Consulate General every night for more than a week," and he provided them all with food.[57] It is little wonder, then, that Hanna was held in high regard and that the US Consulate General became a central point for the organization of the foreign colony of Monterrey. That is why most of the consular representatives decided to stay with Hanna during his brief imprisonment. And that is why the consular officials of nine nations met at the US consulate on a daily basis in times of crisis to discuss ways to defend the lives and properties of their citizens.[58]

Unlike many US diplomats, Hanna demonstrated in word and deed that he cared for Mexico and its people. While working closely with the state government to avoid mass starvation in 1915, Hanna wrote to Governor Pablo A. de la Garza: "I shall be very glad to be of all possible assistance to you . . . in keeping hunger away from our dear Monterrey where I have spent more than a fourth of my life."[59] When he learned that Mexicans were not being allowed into the United States at Laredo, he wrote to Washington that this was wrong and that it "would be far better to invite all Mexicans of every political faith and faction to visit our country, be our guests, and make the whole of them feel at home up there for a year or two . . . They would doubtless immediately again fall deeper than ever before in love with their best friend, the United States, and soon lose their bitterness for each other."[60] This recommendation of how to end the fighting in Mexico reveals his faith in teaching by example.

Hanna was always concerned with applying the positive aspects of US culture to Mexico. One of these was love of country. He wanted North Americans to come to Mexico with huge quantities of Mexican flags and "hoist them on all school houses and public buildings," stating that the only hope for Mexico and its people "is to teach them honest respect for their own flag, this applies to the high class as well as the low."[61] This is quite startling. At a time when many North Americans were concerned with a Mexican nationalist backlash against the US presence, here was a US diplomat who called for greater Mexican patriotism.

However, where Hanna made a mark was in the area of humanitarian assistance, much in keeping with his former role as a Methodist minister. Hunger and disease were the twin scourges of the revolution, but Hanna viewed the issue of relief from more than an altruistic position. He knew that "if the food supply gives out and the thousands of men are hungry they will commit desperate acts."[62]

In late 1914 and early 1915, Monterrey, Mexico City, and other parts of the country suffered a severe food shortage that threatened the population with mass starvation. Hanna used the US press, civic organizations in San Antonio, and the American Red Cross to help combat the food crisis in Monterrey. One of his reports reached the *New York Times*:

> There is an alarming shortage of corn, beans, rice, and staple food supplies. I have purchased about 1,500 bushels of shelled corn such as the Mexicans use for making tortillas, which is the principal food of the poor people. The ladies and citizens of San Antonio, Texas, have sent me a carload of food and clothing. I have use of the large Mexican Monterey Hospital as a supply and

distribution station. Several outlying towns are appealing to me for help. If the winter keeps cold there will be great suffering with hunger and cold. I need 2,000 cheap blankets. After four years of war this whole country is short of food. I will make all supplies and money go as far as possible.[63]

Needy families received tickets to go to a relief station on a regular basis for rations of corn, beans, and rice. However, assistance, Hanna noted, was also provided to another group: "There are many refined, once well-to-do families who do not go to the relief station but come to the Consulate General at night and we supply them with such food as their needs demand."[64]

In July 1915, when the crisis was abating, the state government asked the representatives of the foreign community to evaluate the food situation. All of the consuls gave credit to the consulate general, the American Red Cross, and the Chamber of Commerce, made up of the city's principal business leaders, for their humanitarian actions. José P. Laguera, the Spanish consul informed the governor:

> In the solution to the past distressing situation, it is important to take into account the immense aid provided by the American Red Cross under the direction of Consul General Philip C. Hanna, who has distributed more than three thousand aid tickets that represent no less than twenty thousand souls who are provided corn and beans two times a week.[65]

The successful operation of the Red Cross in Monterrey contrasts with its frustrated efforts in other parts of Mexico, where its agents were accused as spies by the government of Venustiano Carranza. According to George E. Paulsen, in some places the "local papers condemned the Red Cross effort and denied that famine existed." People were urged to refuse corn provided by Mexico's "enemies" and maintained that its acceptance would be considered treasonous. Paulsen argues that "[p]atriotism and nationalism, perhaps more than racism, required Mexican leaders to insist that they alone had the responsibility of taking care of the Mexican people."[66]

This sentiment did not have the same impact in Monterrey, where the sensibility of the consul general helped to ameliorate suspicions. It cannot be denied that large impersonal forces like nationalism have a significant impact on human affairs. However, it is also true that the actions of individuals like Hanna and organizations like the Red Cross can make a difference. It is likely that among the people of Monterrey the actions of Philip Hanna and the American Red Cross generated a kinder view of North Americans.

The Economic Imperative

A final factor in debilitating the nationalist backlash in Monterrey during the revolution involves a number of issues that I refer to as the *economic imperative*, a force more powerful than nationalism because it concerns people's most essential needs. On a basic level this refers to a desire among most people for a return to normalcy, which implies peace, renewed economic activity, and employment. On a higher level it included an almost instinctive drive to get back to the usual operation of market forces. And this, of necessity, would require the involvement of the United States. The economic imperative was something that was felt not only in Monterrey but in the rest of the country as well.

Monterrey escaped the first two years of the revolution relatively unscathed, but beginning in 1913 and until about 1917, the city endured the rigors of the conflict: paralysis of industrial production, unemployment, social dislocation, hunger, disease, death, and destruction. The city and its surrounding region felt the same disillusionment that prevailed in much of the country. Hanna wrote that in the countryside of nearby Torreón, the *villista* movement could not make headway because the people were tired of fighting. Alan Knight captures this state of mind in the words of a Sonoran military officer who declared that "he was sick and tired of revolution; he was ready to quit . . . when children had to rob horse troughs to live."[67]

By the end of 1915, after Woodrow Wilson had recognized the Carranza government, Hanna began to see signs of economic improvement in Monterrey. He wrote that there was "a more hopeful feeling relative to the return of peace and a very large majority appear to believe that the revolution in this part has ended." Many North Americans and other foreigners were returning to see whether they could renew their mining and manufacturing activities. They found, however, that much instability still existed in the countryside, which affected the mining operations. Moreover, they discovered that most of the railroad cars had been destroyed by the fighting; without these, they could not "move the products of the mines to the smelting plants or to the ore markets."[68] An additional obstacle arose during the Pershing expedition of 1916, when the US government decreed an embargo on most goods bound for Mexico, a measure that, according to the British vice consul in Monterrey, had caused "a great deal of unnecessary suffering through the closing of industrial plants for lack of supplies."[69] However, by 1917 conditions for business had improved. Hanna reported that "commercial travelers [were] beginning to visit parts of quiet territory. More mines [were] reopening giving employment to many Mexicans at good wages."[70]

Even in the thick of the revolution, the laws of the market never ceased to work. Farmers, ranchers, manufacturers, and industrialists continued trying to produce and sell their products under severe restrictions and adverse conditions.[71] Although they were often thwarted, they did not cease to try. Two stock raisers from Nuevo León, Victoriano Garza of Sabinas Hidalgo and Juan Serrano of Cadereyta, tried desperately to get their cattle to Texas markets in 1914. Garza managed to evade military authorities and smuggle 166 head across the Rio Grande at San Ignacio, Tamaulipas.[72] On the southern side of the river, US and Mexican stock raisers sought to protect their interests by moving their herds to the United States. Between 1913 and 1915, according to Manuel Plana, "229,054 head of cattle, 189,411 goats, and 267,552 sheep crossed the border at Piedras Negras," a flow "so significant as to constitute a veritable decapitalization."[73]

Monterrey's major industries did not suffer major damage and were affected not so much by the revolutionary violence as by the disruption of the railroads, exorbitant taxes, forced loans, and serious currency fluctuations.[74] Yet even during the conflict, Monterrey's capitalists continued to look for ways to continue operating. The steel production at Fundidora, the most important plant, did not exceed the level of its 1910 output (67,944 tons) until 1925. However, it hit its lowest point in 1915, when it produced 6,656 tons, and began a steady climb in 1916, with 19,247 tons, and continued to rise thereafter. Its sales also reached their nadir in 1915, with a value of 98,676 pesos. In 1916 its sales totaled $1,588,930, and by 1920 it superseded all previous years with sales of $8,096,402.[75]

A more favorable climate for economic recovery was promoted by Carranza, who was a master at manipulating Mexican nationalism against the United States but also knew that his northern neighbor would play an essential role in Mexico's economic recovery. Even if Carranza's nationalism was genuine, as Katz affirms, the official rhetoric was superseded by practical considerations. That "intangible, cerebral sentiment," in the words of Alan Knight, "could not stand against pressing economic needs."[76] Thus the Carranza government took a series of measures designed to jump-start the economy. It began to return lands and factories to their owners in order to stimulate production. To combat inflation, it "returned to a metal currency by January 1917," and "Mexico enjoyed financial stability for the next four years." It also began courting foreign businessmen by offering guarantees so they would invest.[77] Not all of Carranza's reforms were welcomed by foreign companies. His tax policies were roundly condemned. However, Doug Richmond argues that they were successful: "[E]xports nearly doubled from 1916 to 1920. The economy recovered unexpectedly soon."[78]

Various departments of the national government worked to strengthen ties to the United States. Manuel Carpio, of the ministry of foreign relations, urged the governor of Nuevo León to exhort local authorities to promote the creation of friendship societies with the people of the United States.[79] Several newspapers abandoned their nationalist rhetoric and adopted a friendlier tone. Monterrey's principal newspaper, *El Porvenir*, editorialized about the reasons that Mexicans disliked their northern neighbor, but it recognized that the United States was a rich and powerful nation because of its level of organization and national discipline, as well as its emphasis on education. Mexico could achieve the same greatness "through education, with hard work, with prudence and the ability to follow her example."[80]

The Mexican ambassador in Washington, D.C., Ignacio Bonillas, worked to change Mexico's image in the United States. In 1917 he requested complete information on Nuevo León's industries, commerce, and infrastructure, as well as other data that would show the positive aspects of the revolution and the work of reconstruction under way in order to rectify "the campaign of falsehoods disseminated by our enemies."[81] Mexican financial and commercial agents in the major cities of the United States addressed the Nuevo León government in a similar vein. From New York, M. Rollano wrote that it was essential to "promote the work of reconstruction . . . above all in this country that weighs heavily on our future." Samuel Vázquez suggested from Los Angeles that he wanted to mount a permanent exposition of Mexican products to promote trade because "it is logical to suppose that our future well-being depends on the intensity of our commercial exchange."[82] These sentiments were echoed by a former governor of Nuevo León, Antonio I. Villarreal, considered one of the fire-breathing radicals of the revolution. At a luncheon with prominent businessmen in 1920, Villarreal stated that "Mexico must cultivate the goodwill of the United States to assure [*sic*] future prosperity."[83]

The state government received a steady flow of correspondence from Mexican consular representatives in the United States asking for information on Nuevo León's products and investment opportunities. Queries came from San Antonio, Chicago, New York, New Orleans, and other cities. One of these letters is particularly revealing. Nicéforo Zambrano, the Mexican consul in San Francisco, informed Governor José E. Santos that he had been invited by the local chamber of commerce to participate in an international trade conference. This was the moment, he wrote, "to put on display the immense opportunities for foreign capital to invest in agriculture, industry, mining, and other sectors." He asked Governor Santos to send all available information and an English-speaking person because the conference was "extremely important."[84]

This occurred in March 1920. A few months earlier, when Zambrano was still governor of Nuevo León, he railed against North Americans who came to Mexico to despoil her treasures like the Spanish conquerors centuries before. Many of these North Americans, he declared, insulted the Mexicans by saying that "our country is in the most complete state of anarchy, that no one can live here because it is infested with bandits, that there is no government to offer guarantees, that the army cannot extinguish the Revolution [and] that we are all thieves." Zambrano's anger was aroused by an incursion of US troops into Chihuahua, which some perceived as the prelude to an invasion of Mexico. He declared that Nuevo León, along with the rest of the states, was prepared to drive back the invasion and "join together as if a single man."[85] Nothing reveals with greater clarity the rhetoric and reality of nationalism than the words and actions of this Nuevo León governor. For Mexican politicians Uncle Sam–baiting became an almost existential necessity. However, it was even more imperative to get the country back on its feet, and for this the United States was necessary.

Commerce was a crucial component of the economic imperative. Nuevo León required products that it could obtain only from the United States or from US companies in Mexico. Similarly, it had to sell its own products, and, given the battered condition of the domestic market, the best option was outside the country, mainly the United States. The two leading corporations in Monterrey, ASARCO and Fundidora, began laying the groundwork for a rapid expansion based on exports to the United States. By 1921 ASARCO had begun its "most important period of expansion and profit," and by 1925 it "had regained its envied position as the leading and largest metallurgical organization in Mexico."[86] Fundidora had depended almost exclusively on the domestic market (and particularly on government contracts) during the *porfiriato*, but its collapse during the revolution obligated the firm to look outward. Oscar Flores affirms that the entry of the United States into World War I was "like a shot of fresh energy to the Mexican economy." By 1918, Fundidora was selling 80 percent of its production in the United States and Cuba.[87]

However, while the Mexican government and private firms were reaching out to the US economy, a similar process was occurring in reverse. In spite of the national provisions of the Constitution of 1917 and continuing violence in the countryside, political and business leaders from Texas and throughout the southern United States sought to renew their economic exchanges with Mexico. As early as November 1918, Texas governor William P. Hobby was seeking a meeting with the governments of the three border states, Tamaulipas, Coahuila, and Nuevo León, "in order to discuss issues of great importance for these states and the two countries."[88] It is not known whether this meeting ever took place, but if it did, there is little doubt that renewed commerce was on the agenda.

The interest on the part of North American firms to invest in Mexico grew in strength as the revolution came to a close with one last spasm in early 1920, when Álvaro Obregón overthrew the government of Venustiano Carranza. In October of that year, the Houston Chamber of Commerce organized a trip to Mexico to get a "firsthand" look at the situation and to "further in every possible way the re-establishment of commercial relations." The visitors were pleased at what they saw in Monterrey: "We began there to revise our opinion that the Mexican people fostered a dislike for Americans," an idea promoted by the press of both nations. The visitors also found "on every hand evidences of work and industry. There were practically no signs of revolution or warfare. The streetcars were running, factories, foundries and mines in full operation and their stores all open and apparently doing a brisk business."[89] This was followed by many such trips. In 1923, the Mexico Tours Association of Spartanburg, South Carolina, organized an excursion to Mexico City and Monterrey. A pamphlet with the complete itinerary informed readers that they would find the Mexicans "a kindly, patient, friendly people, whose courtesy and hospitality to you will give the lie to that overly worked bit of propaganda known as 'anti-Americanism in Mexico,' for no such antipathy exists, among the people as a whole." Although it would take years to restore the confidence of most investors, it is clear that after a decade of revolution, the reconstruction of Mexico's image was under way, promoted by interested people of both countries.[90] This image allowed little room for nationalist sentiments that would put the country's economic recovery at risk.

Conclusion

Various factors attenuated the development of intense anti-US nationalism in Monterrey and its surrounding region during the revolution.[91] The capital of Nuevo León did not share the revolutionary conditions of other cities and regions. Throughout the *porfiriato* it developed a powerful industrial base in a country that was overwhelmingly agrarian. Industrial growth was spearheaded by a local capitalist elite that owned most of Monterrey's factories, was seldom in competition with foreign capital, and was usually willing to enter into alliances and cooperative ventures with foreigners. The US community in Monterrey, which was dominant among the foreigners, was essentially an enclave, but its presence was not considered malignant and did not generate broad nationalist rejection as in other parts of the country. Among a sector of the population that was proud of the achievements of local capital, there was a spirit of nationalism directed against the United States, but it does not appear to have been profound. These characteristics and what followed after

1910 do not fit the pattern of the revolutionary upheaval that characterized other parts of the country, that of a peasant uprising spurred by a nationalist drive to recover the lands and resources usurped by foreigners.

The very characteristics of the city and the region lent themselves to an ambivalent attitude toward the revolution. There was a desire for political change but not for violence, which would put at risk the peace that was essential to business. Monterrey was a conservative city and, though the years of conflict deeply affected it, the revolution was not generated internally; it came from outside.

The role played by Philip Hanna, the US consul general, also contributed to the reduction of hostility toward North Americans. For his sensibility and his untiring support of humanitarian causes, Hanna was held in high regard by all sectors of the population and by the other members of the foreign community. Unlike most US diplomats, he did not express a negative view of the Mexicans and always concerned himself with improving relations between the people of the two countries.[92]

A final factor is harder to pin down, but it cannot be ignored because it involves powerful economic forces that affect people's daily lives in a way that patriotism and nationalism cannot. After years of conflict there was a generalized desire for peace and a return to normal life. For all of Mexico, but especially for Monterrey, this meant a return to economic activity, and this necessarily involved the United States. Mexico needed its northern neighbor for its products, markets, opportunities, capital, and commerce. Without denying the importance of nationalism, this economic reality was imperative then, no less than it is now. The imagined community would have to coexist with the very real struggle for survival.

The study of nationalism in Monterrey during the Mexican Revolution brings us face to face with a crucial issue: how to reconcile national identity with acceptance of that which is foreign. In this case study, objective, structural, and historical conditions combined with human agency to create a situation in which a greater degree of tolerance and acceptance of foreigners were able to develop.

Notes

1. The eyewitness was Juan Luis Cantú, reporter for the newspaper *El Noticiero* and author of *Memorias de un modesto e ignorado revolucionario*, vol. 2 (Monterrey: author, 1949), 123.
2. Cantú, *Memorias*, 124. Hanna's imprisonment made front-page headlines in the *New York Times*, Apr. 27, 1914, 1. Other sources for this incident are Samuel Guy Inman, *Interven-*

tion in Mexico (New York: Doran, 1919), 147–48; telegram, Hanna to Secretary of State (hereafter cited as SS), Apr. 24, 1914, 812.00/11719, US Department of State, Papers relating to the Foreign Relations of the United States (hereafter cited as FRUS), 659–60, http://digital.library.wisc.edu/1711.dl/FRUS.FRUS1914; Hanna to SS, May 2, 1914, 812.00/11975, National Archives and Records Administration, Washington, D.C., Record Group 59, Records of the Department of State, Decimal Files, Internal Affairs of Mexico (hereafter cited as IA), 1910–1929. This last source includes a detailed report by the vice consul, T. Ayers Robertson, of the siege of Monterrey, including the imprisonment of the consul general.

3. Cantú, *Memorias*, 124.
4. Quoted in Inman, *Intervention in Mexico*, 147–48. It is reported that consular representatives from ten nations went to the government palace and asked Governor Botello for Hanna's release. When he refused, they spent the night there in solidarity with the American diplomat. Cantú, *Memorias*, 125.
5. Moisés González Navarro argues that the nationalist creed that developed during the *porfiriato* stressed "Mexico for the Mexicans" and was used by the most varied groups. Thus, Huerta used it in his struggle against the United States, and the Constitutionalists used it to "justify the limits on privileges to foreigners." Moisés González Navarro, *Los extranjeros en México y los mexicanos en el extranjero, 1821–1970*, vol. 3 (México: El Colegio de México, 1994), 73.
6. Benedict Anderson, *Imagined Communities: Reflections on the Origin and Spread of Nationalism* (London: Verso, 1983), 15–16. Nationalism can refer to a movement for autonomy by a particular group or "a psychological bond that joins a people and differentiates it, in the subconscious conviction of its members, from all other people in a most vital way," according to Walker Connor, "A Nation Is a Nation, Is a State, Is an Ethnic Group, Is a . . . ," in *Nationalism*, ed. John Hutchinson and Anthony D. Smith, Oxford Reader (Oxford: Oxford University Press, 1994), 36. Anthony Smith points out the principal components of nationalism, including "citizen self-government, a territorial home and a distinctive ethnic history," as well as "other elements such as language, will or religion." He also refers to the "pictorial abstraction" of nationalism, which, among ideologies, makes it "one of the most remote from immediate social and economic concerns, and so can embrace many groups with conflicting goals within its fold." See Anthony D. Smith, "Introduction: The Formation of Nationalist Movements," in *Nationalist Movements*, ed. Anthony D. Smith (New York: St. Martin's, 1976), 2, 26, An excellent source, which brings together the best scholarship on the subject, is Hutchinson and Smith, *Nationalism*.
7. Frederick C. Turner argues that "the anti-Americanism which gripped Mexico during the Revolution significantly shaped the growth of Mexican nationalism." See Frederick C. Turner, "Anti-Americanism in Mexico, 1910–1913," *Hispanic American Historical Review* 47(4) (1967): 518. The effects are visible even today in the distrust by the Left and by a large sector of the population of foreign domination of strategic sectors, such as the state-

run oil company, PEMEX, which has prevented its modernization at a time when both production and government revenues have fallen significantly.

8. John Mason Hart, *Revolutionary Mexico: The Coming and Process of the Mexican Revolution* (Berkeley: University of California Press, 1987), 348. In a more recent work, Hart has moderated this position somewhat: "By mid-1912 a growing wave of rural violence against the Porfirian latifundia system, often nationalistic and sometimes anti-American, swept the country." See John Mason Hart, "Social Unrest, Nationalism, and American Capital in the Mexican Countryside, 1876–1920," in *Rural Revolt in Mexico: US Intervention and the Domain of Subaltern Politics*, ed. Daniel Nugent, expanded ed. (Durham: Duke University Press, 1998), 82. Carlos Trejo Lerdo de Tejada, a federal deputy during the Madero presidency and a voice for many fervent nationalists in Mexico during the revolution, wrote that the conflict was the "bloody preamble of a cleansing and liberating upheaval" against North American capitalism. Carlos Trejo Lerdo de Tejada, *La revolución y el nacionalismo: Todo para todos* (La Habana: Imprenta La Estrella, 1916), 250.
9. Ramón Eduardo Ruíz, *The Great Rebellion: Mexico, 1905–1924* (New York: Norton, 1980), 107, 119. The author includes many expressions of anti-US nationalism (see pp. 107–109). Lorenzo Meyer and Josefina Zoraida Vázquez have also commented on the impact of nationalism: "There is no doubt that the Mexican Revolution, as a reaction to the great economic and cultural penetration of foreign interests and values during the *porfiriato* aroused enormous nationalist energy." Josefina Zoraida Vázquez and Lorenzo Meyer, *México frente a Estados Unidos* (*Un ensayo histórico, 1776–1993*), 3rd ed. (México: Fondo de Cultura Económica, 1994), 147.
10. Alan Knight, "The United States and the Mexican Peasantry, circa 1880–1940," in Nugent, *Rural Revolt in Mexico*, 27; Alan Knight, *US-Mexican Relations, 1910–1940, An Interpretation*, Monograph Series 28 (San Diego: Center for US-Mexican Studies, University of California, 1987), 87. A discussion of the major arguments of Hart and Knight can be found in John Foran, "Review: Reinventing the Mexican Revolution: The Competing Paradigms of Alan Knight and John Mason Hart," *Latin American Perspectives* 23(4) (1996): 115–31.
11. Ruíz, *Great Rebellion*, 103; Hart, *Revolutionary Mexico*, 177; Hart, "Social Unrest, Nationalism and American Capital," 72; Knight, *US-Mexican Relations*, 21; Moisés González Navarro, "Xenofobia y xenofilia en la Revolución mexicana," *Historia Mexicana* 18(4) (1969): 571.
12. González Navarro, "Xenofobia y xenofilia," 572.
13. Knight, *Mexican Revolution*, vol. 1, reprint from 1986 version published by Cambridge University Press (Lincoln: University of Nebraska Press, 1990), 67. The complexity of this topic is illustrated by Friedrich Katz, who argues that a principal by-product of the revolution, the Constitution of 1917, was a very nationalistic document that "drastically restricted the rights of foreigners in Mexico and under certain circumstances made their holdings subject to confiscation." Yet, at least until 1920, foreign property had been largely

untouched and US investments "were more important than they had been at the beginning of the revolution in 1910." In fact, capital from the United States had displaced European interests and "had assumed an economic supremacy in Mexico it had never enjoyed before." See Friedrich Katz, *The Secret War in Mexico: Europe, the United States, and the Mexican Revolution* (Chicago: University of Chicago Press, 1981), 569.

14. Knight, *Mexican Revolution*, vol. 1, 340; González Navarro, "Xenofobia y xenofilia," 577. In one letter to Washington, D.C., Hanna wrote the following: "Without doubt there is some jealousy problem brought about on account of a few Americans who appear to take pride in impressing upon the Mexicans the greatness and importance of the United States Government, etc. etc. That class of Americans in Mexico are [*sic*] largely responsible for the misunderstanding that exists between the Americans and Mexicans in this country." Hanna to SS, Mar. 20, 1911, 812.00/1111, IA.
15. T. Ayers Robertson to SS, Aug. 12, 1915, 812.00/15829, IA; Knight, *Mexican Revolution*, vol. 1, 428. In the Senate investigation of Mexican affairs after the revolution, the testimony of Wallace Thompson, former news editor of the *Mexican Herald*, includes an account of how skilled German workers at the *fundidora* used tequila to induce a crowd to break up a pro-Allied celebration of the signing of the armistice in November 1918. The crowd chanted "Death to America" and "Long live Germany," according to Thompson. This witness also stated that "German propagandists were working all over Mexico . . . to convince the Mexicans that the United States had planned definitely to annex all of northern Mexico." See "Investigation of Mexican Affairs, Preliminary Report and Hearings of the Committee on Foreign Relations," US Senate, vol. 2, 1920, pp. 1918–1919.
16. Knight, *Mexican Revolution*, vol. 1, 171; Turner, "Anti-Americanism," 504–505; *El Monterrey News*, Nov. 12 and 13, 1910, 1. A US mining engineer in Durango commented on the role that newspapers played in arousing hostility against North Americans: "[T]he majority of the Mexican business men and the majority of Mexican laboring men, who work for Americans, are when let alone, friends to our country and people. If the newspapers of Mexico would not fool and mislead the Mexicans, they would, as a rule, be more friendly toward and more appreciative of Americans." Quoted in Hanna to SS, Apr. 17, 1918, 812.00/21909, IA.
17. González Navarro, "Xenofobia y xenofilia," 578; T. Ayers Robertson to SS, Aug. 12, 1915, 812.00/15829, IA; Knight, *Mexican Revolution*, vol. 1, 321; Knight, *Mexican Revolution*, vol. 2, reprint from 1986 version published by Cambridge University Press (Lincoln: University of Nebraska Press, 1990), 71, 344–45.
18. Hanna to SS, Mar. 20, 1911, 812.00/1111, IA. Two years later Hanna wrote the following: "True it is that some of the Mexicans claim to hate the Americans and the US—but the fact is, it is all Mexican hatred, Mexicans hating Mexicans, and Mexicans fighting Mexicans—and it is their own family quarrel." Hanna to William Jennings Bryan, Nov. 28, 1913, 812.00/10306; see also Knight, *Mexican Revolution*, vol. 2, 71.

19. Turner, "Anti-Americanism," 503; Gene Z. Hanrahan, ed., *¡Abajo el Gringo! Anti-American Sentiment during the Mexican Revolution* (Salisbury, N.C.: Documentary Publications, 1982), 97–98; González Navarro, "Xenofobia y xenofilia," 576.
20. González Navarro, "Xenofobia y xenofilia," 580.
21. Knight, *Mexican Revolution*, vol. 1, 321.
22. This applies to all aspects of the revolution and not just nationalism. A vast body of literature that is supported by regional studies and, to a lesser degree, by the new "cultural history" and subaltern studies has enriched the study of the revolution and reinforced the concept, earlier advanced by Katz, that the conflict between 1910 and 1920 "did not constitute one revolution, but a series of very different revolutions and revolts that were centered in the states of Morelos, Chihuahua, Coahuila, and Sonora." Katz, *Secret War*, 569. A splendid analysis of the contributions of regional and cultural history to the study of the revolution is provided by Luis Barrón, *Historias de la Revolución mexicana* (México: Centro de Investigación y Docencia Económicas and Fondo de Cultura Económica, 2004); see also Elisa Servín, Leticia Reina, and John Tutino, *Cycles of Conflict, Centuries of Change: Crisis, Reform, and Revolution in Mexico* (Durham: Duke University Press, 2007).
23. Avishai Margalit, "The Moral Psychology of Nationalism," in *The Morality of Nationalism*, ed. Robert McKim and Jeff McMahan (Oxford: Oxford University Press, 1997), 75.
24. Quoted in Inman, *Intervention in Mexico*, 146.
25. Knight, *US–Mexican Relations*, 23–24.
26. Hanna to SS, May 18, 1912, 812.00/3994, and Apr. 25, 1913, 812.00/7326, IA. An incident that reflects the inclination of the rebel factions to protect US property occurred during the first battle of Monterrey, in October 1913. In a lengthy report on the battle, Vice Consul T. Ayers Robertson wrote the following:

    > As evidence of the care exercised by the [Constitutionalist] Rebels with respect to American property, the case of the lumber yards of Fernando Martínez, a Mexican, and the Derby Lumber Company, an American concern, may be cited. These two properties are separated only by a party wall of *sillar*. This wall extended about five feet above the roof of the lumber yards. The Rebels completely burned the Martínez Yard. While it was burning there were ten Rebels stationed on the roof of the Derby Yard to prevent the flames spreading to it. The Derby Yard was undamaged.

    See Hanna to SS, Oct. 31, 1913, 812.00/9690, IA.
27. Telegram, Hanna to SS, Apr. 1, 1916, 812.00/17715, IA. The argument that North Americans were generally well treated must remain tentative, for there is still much that we do not know. For example, Hanna abandoned Monterrey and set up headquarters at the Menger Hotel in San Antonio in June 1916 and remained there until February 1919. The *San Antonio Express* reported that Hanna and his staff were ordered out of Mexico (along

with other diplomatic representatives) because of the growing hostility between the United States and Mexico over the Pershing expedition. *San Antonio Express*, May 10, 1918.

28. Descriptions of Monterrey on the eve of the revolution can be found in Alex M. Zaragoza, *La élite de Monterrey y el estado mexicano, 1880–1940* (Monterrey: Fondo Editorial de Nuevo León, 2008); Oscar Flores, *Monterrey, 1890–2000: Industry, Commerce, Banking and Finance in Monterrey, Mexico* (Monterrey: Universidad de Monterrey, 2009); Oscar Flores, *Monterrey en la Revolución* (Monterrey: Universidad de Monterrey and R. Ayuntamiento de Monterrey, 2006); H. Hamilton Fyfe, *The Real Mexico: A Study on the Spot* (New York: McBride, Nast, 1914); Jaime Eloy Rodríguez, "A Divided City: Social and Urban Patterns in Mty, Mexico, 1876–1911" (PhD diss., Columbia University, 2004); Horace D. Marucci, "The American Smelting and Refining Company in Mexico, 1900–1925" (PhD diss., Rutgers University, 1995); Ruíz, *Great Rebellion*, 18.
29. Flores, *Monterrey en la Revolución*, 23; Rodríguez, "Divided City," 58.
30. Juan Mora-Torres, *The Making of the Mexican Border: The State, Capitalism, and Society in Nuevo León, 1848–1910* (Austin: University of Texas Press, 2001), 106. One scholar estimates that in 1911 the *comunidades* occupied 70 percent of the state's lands. See Flores, *Monterrey en la Revolución*, 47.
31. Mora-Torres, *Making of the Mexican Border*, 106, 116.
32. Two important sources for the study of the Monterrey elite are Mario Cerutti, *Burguesía, capitales e industria en el noreste de México: Monterrey y su ámbito regional (1850–1910)* (Monterrey: Facultad de Filosofía y Letras, Universidad Autónoma de Nuevo León, 1989); and Zaragoza, *La élite de Monterrey*.
33. Isidro Vizcaya Canales, *Los orígenes de la industrialización de Monterrey*, reprint from 1969 edition (Monterrey: Fondo Editorial de Nuevo León: 2006), 82. According to Zaragoza, in 1903, Europeans had invested 400,000 pesos in industrial enterprises, whereas the United States had 3.36 million, 2.5 million of which were concentrated in the Guggenheim firm, ASARCO. Local capital dominated with 17 million. Zaragoza, *La elite de Monterrey*, 97.
34. Zaragoza, *La elite de Monterrey*, 97.
35. Ruíz, *Great Rebellion*, 118.
36. Anexo 826, 533–34, Memoria de Gobierno, B. Reyes, 1903–1907, Archivo General del Estado de Nuevo León (hereafter cited as AGENL), Monterrey, Nuevo León; Mora-Torres, *Making of the Mexican Border*, 258; Flores, *Monterrey*, 1890–2000, 91, 92.
37. Telegram, Hanna to SS, Mar. 19, 1911, 812.00/995, IA; Rodríguez, "Divided City," 71, 80.
38. One traveler described the North American community in 1913 as follows: "Life is lived in a leisurely fashion, with plenty of quiet diversion in the shape of lawn-tennis, bridge, picnics into the mountains, tea-parties on verandas looking on to gardens filled with roses all the year round." After 1914 this community, like the Southern oligarchy after the Civil War, would be gone with the wind. See Fyfe, *Real Mexico*, 44.
39. According to Mora-Torres, in 1890 the Guggenheim smelter "set the wage for unskilled

workers at one peso, forcing the other enterprises to do the same." Mora-Torres, *Making of the Mexican Border*, 214.

40. Vizcaya, *Los orígenes*, 88–91. A broad range of products and services was advertised in *El Monterrey News*. See, for example, July 27, 1909, 2.
41. Anexo 779, 500, Memoria de B. Reyes, AGENL; Vizcaya, *Los orígenes*, 91. A study of Robertson's economic and social activities can be found in J. A. Vázquez, *Robertson, impulsor de la industria regiomontana (1890–1910)* (Monterrey: Congreso del Estado de Nuevo León, 1999).
42. John Mason Hart, *Empire and Revolution: The Americans in Mexico since the Civil War* (Berkeley: University of California Press, 2002), 514. Robertson used his newspaper, *El Monterrey News*, to offer thousands of rich pasture and agricultural lands in a region southwest of Tampico in Tamaulipas. See various issues, 1909–1910.
43. Quoted in Alberto Barrera Enderle, "Plaza pública y discurso regionalista en Nuevo León, 1848–1856," in *Sociedad, milicia y política en Nuevo León, Siglos XVIII y XIX*, coord. Artemio Benavides Hinojosa, Colección Cuadernos del Noreste, no. 2 (Monterrey: Archivo General del Estado de Nuevo León, 2005), 58.
44. Barrera Enderle, "Plaza pública," 55, 64. An excellent source for Vidaurri's regional power is Mario Cerutti, *Economía de guerra y poder regional en el siglo XIX* (Monterrey: Archivo General del Estado, 1983). To this propensity for regionalism must be added an ingredient that Eric Van Young refers to as *localocentrism*, "the tendency of villagers to see the social and political horizon as extending only as far as the view from their pueblo church tower." Eric Van Young, "Revolution and Imagined Communities in Mexico, 1810–1821," in *Nationalism in the New World*, ed. Don H. Doyle and Marco Antonio Pamplona (Athens: University of Georgia Press, 2006), 196.
45. Quoted in Mora-Torres, *Making of the Mexican Border*, 197, 214, 215, Attacks upon North Americans were not uncommon in Monterrey's newspapers. In 1910 Philip Hanna protested to the state government about the scurrilous anti-American articles that appeared in the newspaper *El Espectador*: "In the eleven years that I have lived in Monterrey I have learned to love Mexico and her people . . . it pains me to have anything done that mars the good understanding between the people of our countries . . . and give out the impression that law-abiding foreigners are not welcome in this great free land of liberty." Hanna to Governor José María Mier, July 7, 1910, folio 79/48, Relaciones Exteriores, Cónsules (hereafter REC), caja 5 (1907–1913), AGENL.
46. There was an active opposition to Governor Bernardo Reyes of Nuevo León by middle-class groups tired of his long authoritarian rule. See Mora-Torres, *Making of the Mexican Border*, 216–25; and Knight, *Mexican Revolution*, vol. 1, 49.
47. Hanna to SS, May 18, 1912, 812.00/3994,IA; Flores, *Monterrey en la Revolución*, 45; Knight, *Mexican Revolution*, vol. 1, 401.
48. Knight, *Mexican Revolution*, vol. 1, 138, 431. Mario Cerutti has found that the wages of the workers of Monterrey were greater than in other regions of northern and central Mexico.

See Mario Cerutti, "Industrialización y salarios obreros en Monterrey (1890–1910)," *Humanitas, Anuario de la Universidad Autónoma de Nuevo León* 21 (1980), 473.

49. As late as May 10, 1911, when the Díaz government was in its death throes, dozens of Monterrey's leading citizens sent the old dictator a telegram expressing their unconditional support "in the event that the nation requires our humble services." See *El Monterrey News*, May 10, 1911, 1.
50. Correspondence from the towns of Nuevo León can be found in caja 122 (1910), Correspondencia de Alcaldes Primeros, Monterrey, AGENL; see also Memorias de Gobierno, Leobardo Chapa, 1907–1911, 5, AGENL; Hanna to SS, Mar. 16, 1911, 812.00/1043, IA; Michael Snodgrass, *Deference and Defiance in Monterrey: Workers, Paternalism, and Revolution in Mexico, 1890–1950* (Cambridge: Cambridge University Press, 2003), 32.
51. Henry Lane Wilson to SS, Mar. 20, 1912, 812.00/3365, 753–54, FRUS. In September 1912, the governor of Nuevo León, Viviano Villarreal, reported that public order in the state had not been affected by the revolts, including that of Bernardo Reyes, former governor of the state: "Nuevo León preserves her love of order and at the same time sends volunteers to fight in favor of the government [of Madero]." See Memorias de Gobierno, Viviano L. Villarreal, 1912. Informe de Septiembre, 1912, 10–11, AGENL.
52. Hanna to SS, May 18, 1912, 812.00/3994, and Mar. 22, 1912, 812.00/3381, IA.
53. Flores, *Monterrey en la Revolución*, 58; Rocío González Maíz, "Mitos nacionales y realidades regionales: La revolución en Nuevo León," *Identidad, Revista del Instituto de Investigaciones Históricas de Nuevo León* 2(3) (July 2007–June 2008): 72; Zaragoza, *La elite de Monterrey*, 140; Programa para celebrar el XLXI aniversario de la batalla del 2 de abril 1867, Colección Juntas Patrióticas, caja 8 (1910–1919), AGENL; Cantú, *Memorias*, 50. Thomas Bowman, the consul who replaced Hanna, wrote as follows in 1920: "Monterrey is an industrial center, well advanced as compared with other parts of Mexico, and there has never been shown the marked enthusiasm for revolutions here as in certain other communities of the Republic." Bowman to SS, May 18, 1920, 812.00/24079, IA.
54. Evaristo Madero to William Jennings Bryan, Dec. 26, 1913, 812.00/10385, IA.
55. Telegram, Hanna to SS, May 1, 1914, 812.00/11797, IA.
56. Telegram, Hanna to SS, Mar. 14, 1915, 812.00/14593, IA.
57. Telegram, Hanna to SS, Nov. 5, 1913, 812.00/9581, IA.
58. Telegram, Hanna to SS, Mar. 21, 1913, 812.00/6814, IA; Cantú, *Memorias*, 125.
59. Hanna to Gov. Pablo A. de la Garza, July 6, 1915, Relaciones Exteriores, Cónsules, caja 6, AGENL.
60. Telegram, Hanna to SS, Nov. 29, 1913, 812.00/9979, IA.
61. Telegram, Hanna to SS, June 13, 1916, 812.00/18414, IA. The position of some Mexican nationalists coincides with Hanna. Carlos Trejo Lerdo de Tejada wrote in 1916 that it was vital to inculcate pride of country and to use science and reason to construct a national soul that would be based on "true patriotism, a supreme collective force that makes a nation strong." Trejo Lerdo de Tejada, *La revolución y el nacionalismo*, 254.

62. Hanna to SS, Mar. 3, 1912, 812.00/3085, IA.

63. *New York Times*, Dec. 27, 1914, 6. Social conditions during the revolution have not been studied extensively. Heather Fowler-Salamini has stated that not enough has been written about the way people coped with hunger, disease, violence, and other rigors imposed by the revolution. Heather Fowler-Salamini, "Review: The Boom in Regional Studies of the Mexican Revolution: Where Is It Leading?" *Latin American Research Review* 28(2) (1993): 175–90.

64. Hanna to SS, January 1915, 812.00/14361, IA. Hanna also supplied medicine to those who required it, regardless of their social status. In early 1915, he reported that he had acquired large quantities of vaccine from the United States to combat the black smallpox, which was ravaging parts of Mexico. Telegram, Hanna to SS, Feb. 20, 1915, 812.00/14428, IA.

65. José P. Laguera to Gov. Pablo A. de la Garza, July 6, 1915, REC, caja 6, AGENL. In this same file there are many similar statements from the consular representatives of the other nations.

66. George E. Paulsen, "Helping Hand or Intervention? Red Cross Relief in Mexico, 1915," *Pacific Historical Review* 57(3) (1988): 317, 324–25.

67. Quoted in Knight, *Mexican Revolution*, vol. 2, 415; Zaragoza, *La elite de Monterrey*, 133; Snodgrass, *Deferance and Defiance*, 37; telegram, Hanna to SS, Aug. 4, 1916, 812.00/18853, IA.

68. Hanna to SS, Dec. 4, 1915, 812.00/16945, IA.

69. Quoted in Hanna to SS, July 23, 1916, 812.00/18811, IA.

70. Telegram, Hanna to SS, Mar. 21, 1917, 812.00/20697, IA.

71. Stephen Haber expresses this sentiment: "Even with these adverse conditions, however, many enterprises continued to operate . . . many firms, especially in the consumer goods sector, continued to function even during the worst phases of the fighting." Stephen H. Haber, *Industry and Underdevelopment: The Industrialization of Mexico, 1890–1940* (Stanford: Stanford University Press, 1989), 137.

72. Mayor Tomás Lozano to Gobierno Militar de Nuevo León, June 1, 1914, Sección Militares, caja 420, AGENL; Juan M. Serrano to A. de la Paz Guerra, June 24, 1914, Secretaría de Gobierno, caja 9, AGENL.

73. Manuel Plana, "The Mexican Revolution and the US Border: Research Perspectives," *Journal of the Southwest* 49(4) (2007): 607.

74. This pattern was not confined to Monterrey. According to Stephen H. Haber, "[m]ost of Mexico's manufacturing plants emerged intact from the fighting." Haber, *Industry and Underdevelopment*, 124.

75. Mora-Torres, *Making of the Mexican Border*, 258, 262. The author uses the company report for 1927. Other Monterrey firms demonstrate the same pattern of growth. In 1917 the Cuauhtemoc Brewery began a rapid recovery, and by 1920 it "had its second-best year ever, shipping close to 15 million liters of beer." See Haber, *Industry and Underdevelopment*, 138.

76. Knight, *US-Mexican Relations*, 60; Katz, *Secret War*, 325. Knight further argues that "[f]oreigners might not be loved but, now more than ever, foreign companies constituted islands of higher employment, wages and consumption in a sea of destitution." Knight, *Mexican Revolution*, vol. 2, 412.
77. Douglas W. Richmond, "Carranza: The Authoritarian Populist as Nationalist President," in *Essays on the Mexican Revolution: Revisionist Views of the Leaders*, ed. George Wolfskill and Douglas W. Richmond (Austin: University of Texas Press, 1979), 59–60; Zaragoza, *La elite de Monterrey*, 148; Flores, *Monterrey en la Revolución*, 226.
78. Douglas W. Richmond, *The Mexican Nation: Historical Continuity and Modern Change* (Upper Saddle River, N.J.: Prentice Hall, 2002), 233.
79. Manuel Carpio to Gobierno de Nuevo León, Jan. 19, 1920, file 70/02, caja 70, Ministerio de Relaciones Exteriores, AGENL.
80. *El Porvenir*, "Como debemos proceder los mexicanos de hoy con respecto a los E. Unidos," Feb. 6, 1919, 1, 4.
81. Ignacio Bonillas to Gobierno de Nuevo León, May 17, 1917, Correspondencia Gobernadores (hereafter CG), Pablo A. de la Garza/Raul Madero/Alfredo Ricaut, caja 1, AGENL.
82. Samuel Vázquez to Governor José E. Santos, Nov. 10, 1919, CG, José E. Santos, caja 1, AGENL; M. Rollano to Governor of Nuevo León, July 18, 1918, CG, Pablo A. de la Garza/Raul Madero/Alfredo Ricaut, caja 1, AGENL.
83. Quoted in Thomas Bowman to SS, May 25, 1920, 812.00/24155, IA.
84. Nicéforo Zambrano to Governor José E. Santos, Mar. 9, 1920, REC, caja 7, AGENL.
85. Anexos 1 and 2, Memorias de Gobierno, Nicéforo Zambrano, 1917–1919, AGENL. Three years earlier, as treasurer of the Carranza government, Zambrano had dined with Hanna in San Antonio, where he expressed his friendship toward North Americans and his desire to obtain an interview with President Woodrow Wilson. Telegram, Hanna to SS, Dec. 19, 1916, 812.00/20098, IA.
86. In order to defend its operations against the antiforeign precepts of the Constitution of 1917, ASARCO created a number of holding companies under Mexican registry and transferred its properties to those firms. Marucci, "American Smelting and Refining Company," 488–89, 491.
87. Flores, *Monterrey 1890–2000*, 99–100. The rapid recovery after 1917 allowed the Monterrey elite to weather the revolution and maintain its strength and cohesion. Zaragoza, *La elite de Monterrey*, 25. This parallels the experiences of other empresarial groups in Puebla, Chihuahua, and Sonora and reflects the importance of regional studies in interpreting the revolution. See Fowler-Salamini, "Boom in Regional Studies," 182; and Barrón, *Historias de la Revolución Mexicana*, 40. Stephen Haber addresses this issue in the most emphatic terms: "[N]ot only did the nation's industrialists stay put during the Revolution, but they were already trying to influence government policy even before the fighting had stopped." Haber, *Industry and Underdevelopment*, 140.
88. J. L. Garza to Governor Nicéforo Zambrano, Nov. 13, 1918, REC, caja 6, AGENL.

89. William H. Moseley, *Mexico Today as seen by our Representative on a Hurried trip completed October 30, 1920* (New York: American Exchange National Bank, 1920), 3. http://www.archive.org/details/mexicotodayassee00moserich. In February 1919, a group of North American businessmen in Monterrey organized the American Chamber of Commerce and named as its president T. Ayers Robertson, the vice consul and son of Joseph Andrew Robertson, who had left Monterrey to establish a business in San Antonio. Feb. 11, 1919, *El Porvenir*. A less optimistic view of the economic prospects in Monterrey and the rest of Mexico can be found in Wallace Thompson, *Trading with Mexico* (New York: Dodd, Mead, 1921).

90. Arturo M. Elías to Gobierno de Nuevo León, July 18, 1923, REC, caja 7, AGENL. According to Haber, the zeal of North American investors was tempered by uncertainty generated by the revolution because there had been a change in "the rules of the game" and "the fear of a renewed round of violence lurked in the minds of the investment community." It was not until after 1940, when social peace was achieved, that the confidence of old and new investors was restored. Haber, *Industry and Underdevelopment*, 196–97.

91. Some readers may object that my study concentrates heavily on Monterrey and that I have paid little attention to the Nuevo León countryside, where rural workers may have appealed to nationalism to rise in revolt against oppressive conditions. I must first say that, because of the limited space available in a work of this nature, one cannot cover all of the ground. Second, the archival records of Nuevo León are replete with acts of violence in the rural areas, but they were largely generated by three sources: by those who came from outside the state; by dissidents who had previous grievances with the local political establishment; and by those of a criminal bent. These two latter groups took advantage of the national uprising, the first to fight for local power by force of arms, and the second to appropriate property from its rightful owners. Examples can be found in Correspondencia Gobernadores, 1913–1920, and a special collection called "Persecución de Bandoleros" (1918), AGENL.

92. Upon retiring from the consulate general at the end of 1919, Hanna wrote the following to Governor José E. Santos: "I shall always continue to hold the warmest affection for Mexico and its people, who are very dear to me." Hanna to Santos, Oct. 31, 1919, REC, caja 6, AGENL.

CHAPTER 4

Creating a Schizophrenic Border

Migration and Perception, 1920–1925

Linda B. Hall

When Álvaro Obregón came to the presidency of Mexico on December 1, 1920, Mexico was just emerging from the devastation of a ten-year civil war, and disorders continued in the countryside. As a Sonoran from northern Mexico, he was intensely aware of the significance of the United States, and he wanted its respect for his citizens there, as well as respect and respectability for his country and administration. His highest internal priorities as chief executive were a complete pacification of his war-torn country and its economic recovery.

Three months later, on March 4, 1921, Warren Harding was inaugurated as president of the United States. Also emerging from a war, World War I, and facing economic problems, circumstances in the United States differed greatly. The economic difficulties would be short lived, the country had attained the status of a world power, and its long-term prospects were strong. Unlike Mexico, its fight had not occurred on its own soil. Yet the world war itself and the Russian Revolution, though at more of a distance, had been profoundly disturbing, and the very nature of the United States seemed to be changing.

One of the most important factors in this transformation had been huge numbers of persons arriving from other countries, some to return but many to remain. In the decade before World War I, immigration, though only a fraction of it from Mexico, had been averaging about one million annually. These figures had begun to seem overwhelming, and the economic devastation in Europe, as well as the political changes and economic problems there, promised to keep people coming, leading to a racist debate about just who would be most appropriate as residents and as citizens of the polity. Just to the south, Mexico, with its devastating decade of violence, had had an impact on the Southwest and beyond as more than 1.5 million Mexican workers and refugees poured in. The late 1910s had witnessed the xenophobia of the "Red scare" and its heavy crackdown against labor; Senator Albert Fall's 1919–1920 investigation of Mexican affairs, which emphasized Mexico's violence on the one hand and its indigenous racial character on the other; and prohibition of alcoholic beverages—which continued to come in illegally from Mexico (and elsewhere). All of these factors worked against Obregón's objectives and made friendly relations and mutual understanding difficult.

The border between the two countries had been porous and flexible during the previous decade. Workers and refugees went north, while businesspeople and their workers, particularly in mining and the suddenly booming oil industry, journeyed south. By the early 1920s, many in the United States had come to view this openness with alarm. World War I, as Mae M. Ngai points out, "marked the consolidation of the international nation-state system, based on Westphalian sovereignty, hardened borders, state citizenship, and passport controls."[1]

The world war itself had strengthened attitudes in the United States against foreign lands and foreign peoples, leading to nostalgia for a homogeneous past that was largely a fantasy, but a comforting one. Furthermore, the Russian Revolution, much more than the Mexican Revolution, had shaken any previous faith that had existed in the United States that monarchies or dictatorships would yield inevitably to democracies, and signs of social change in Mexico made citizens jittery about "Reds" and "Bolsheviks." Simultaneously, Obregón, although dealing with his own economic problems, was eager to diminish Mexico's reputation for disorder so as to facilitate trade with and investment from the nations of the world, particularly from his neighbor to the north. Though the United States finally recognized his administration, in 1923, this acknowledgment did little to help his citizens abroad or diminish the United States' fears of the border. Instead, Mexicans, who were *not* targeted in the new immigration laws that were passed in 1921 and 1924, had emerged by the time he left office as what Ngai terms the "iconic illegal aliens."[2] Mexicans, for the many reasons described later, faced increasingly negative attitudes and more severe restrictions and enforcement in crossing the border and working in the United States. While Mexicans remained essential to certain kinds of employers north of the border, attitudes toward Mexicans themselves became more overtly racist. Continual reports about Mexico in the mainstream press portrayed it as unstable, radical politically, and still violent, as well as a refuge for criminals and draft dodgers from the United States, increasing the country's worries about Mexico and Mexicans as dangers close at hand. By the time Obregón left office, the border had taken on a new character, one more policed, unfriendly, and even violent than it had been in the previous decade, when it had provided a refuge for Mexicans fleeing the violence of the revolution.

While growers in the Southwest argued in April of 1920 for the continued availability of unrestricted migration by Mexican workers, other voices insisted inaccurately—around the time of Obregón's inauguration, just nine months later—that Canadian and Mexican immigration in the previous fiscal year (ending June 30) had broken all records. On the very day that Obregón came to power, the *New York Times* reported that Democratic senator William H. King of Utah was preparing a bill for the new Congress calling for a six-month suspension of all immigration while administrative details were worked out to control the flow and particularly to ensure that "all persons who were inoculated with 'red' tendencies," that is, all potential agitators, would be stopped at the border.[3] Though this initiative came to naught, at that particular moment immigration issues in the United States became profoundly divisive.

The almost completely unregulated migration across its southern border into the United States during the previous decade had reached high levels; registered legal migration of Mexicans and other nationals amounted to 890,371, including both those who expressed their intention to stay permanently (261,699) and temporary workers, who stayed for a lengthy period of time (628,672). Many others crossed without going through official checkpoints and procedures; probably as many as 1.5 million Mexicans spent substantial parts of the revolutionary decade (1910–1920) in the United States, in addition to the many who went back and forth across the border almost daily to work jobs close to the border. Mexicans came across the border virtually unimpeded despite the passage in 1917 of legislation that imposed a literacy test and a head tax; those regulations were largely suspended, either officially or unofficially, until the end of World War I and the beginning of the new decade. The major initial attempts to enforce the laws restricting Mexicans came after Obregón's inauguration.[4] Migration north, for Obregón, raised issues of economic strength versus weakness, of humanitarian treatment for the migrants, and of national pride. Working against him were the notions of subversion and disorder discussed earlier. The struggle was one not just of realities but also of perceptions, and it was one that Obregón largely lost.

At the same time, the United States had been coping with another enormous migration, chiefly from Europe, and problems with Asiatic immigration. The Chinese had been excluded since the 1880s, although some movement continued illegally; the Japanese had been limited by a gentlemen's agreement that Theodore Roosevelt had arranged with Japan in the wake of anti-Japanese hysteria after that nation had begun to emerge as a world power with its victory over Russia in 1905. Japan agreed to provide no more passports to its workers bound for the United States, ending the possibility of any large migration, but a few Japanese and even Chinese continued to arrive. Pressure from the

Western states continued to push presidential administrations in the 1910s and 1920s for Japanese exclusion, and anti-Japanese sentiment remained strong.[5] Yet after World War I, even European immigration became suspect, particularly that from the southern and eastern Mediterranean, whose peoples were believed to be less racially desirable than the blue-eyed blondes of the imagined homogeneous past. Soon new immigration laws pushed these suspect groups to Mexico, where they became associated with illegal immigration coming in along the land border between the two countries.

Mexican immigrants who intended to stay and declared so on crossing do not seem to have been excessive during these years, as revolutionary violence waned and the economy very slowly improved. This is difficult to determine, however, because the statistical categories differed from those of the previous decade and because much migration was irregular and uncounted. The reports from the commissioner general of immigration during the years 1921–1925 provided two categories: "immigrant aliens" (permanent arrivals) and "nonimmigrant aliens" (temporary arrivals). In the case of Mexico, the former group now dwarfed the latter. It seems certain, therefore, that the statistics did not include most of the temporary workers, who came for several months at a time. During the 1910s, they had fallen under the category of "nonstatistical aliens," although they were counted, but that useful category dropped from sight in the next decade.

Furthermore, the annual reports ran through the fiscal year ending on June 30, so that precise calendar-year figures are unavailable.[6] Still, the statistics that we have are instructive because they show that legal immigration through Mexican land entries and seaports was far smaller than that at Ellis Island in New York; between July 1, 1920, and June 30, 1921, for example, only 29,790 persons had come in legally through Mexico's land entries and 117 through seaports, whereas 560,971 entered through New York.[7] The hysteria over the supposed hordes flowing across the Mexican border seems to have been out of proportion to any real threat, though in fact border inspectors were clearly understaffed and underpowered.

The figures for the five fiscal years from June 30, 1921 through June 30, 1925, indicate a waxing and waning of legal Mexican immigration, with particularly large figures for 1922–1923 and 1923–1924. Net increases in the number of Mexicans entering the United States for the former year (62,224) and the latter (89,190) were significantly higher than the two previous years or the following year, when the numbers began to drop again. The early period, 1920 to 1922, was a time of recession in the United States, with widespread though spotty unemployment that left many Mexican workers already there without jobs and resources.[8] The increased movement during the next three years seems to have been fueled by an increasing demand in the United States for Mexican labor, given some drop-off in European immigration caused by the quota system installed in 1921 and the improving economic situation in the United States (see table 4.1).

Mexico in 1920 still suffered considerable political flux; when Obregón was inaugurated in December, he presided over a very fragile state, not a rapidly developing leviathan as some authorities have claimed.[9] Furthermore, the United States withheld recognition, severely limiting his options in dealing with the problems of expatriate Mexican workers. Yet the situation was reasonably promising. During his campaign and the early part of his presidency, Obregón had established useful ties with border politicians and businessmen who in general supported his recognition. These groups were eager for comfortable trade relationships, investment opportunities, and access to Mexican labor, particularly for agriculture, mining, and railway work. Governor Thomas Campbell of Arizona had described Obregón during a meeting in July of 1920 as a man with a "head on his shoulders . . . a heart in his body . . . and the backbone to back him up."[10] Governor William Hobby of Texas had similarly entertained Obregón in October 1920, when he stated publicly, though perhaps not eloquently, his desire for the United States and Mexico to be "pals" and, in fact, to be the "Mutt and Jeff of the Western Hemisphere."[11] The *New York Times* noted at the same time that the now president-elect, visiting El Paso, Texas, had won "border recognition" and that he had told "applauding Texans he welcomes friendship more than government action." The meeting had included both Hobby and Campbell, along with New Mexico governor Octaviano Larrazola and the governors of the Mexican border states of Chihuahua and Sonora.[12]

The American Chamber of Commerce in Mexico a month later declared that business conditions had recently become "more stable and settled" and that more than one hundred businesses had begun operating in Mexico in the previous two years.[13] At the time of Obregón's inauguration, the Los Angeles Chamber of Commerce cheerfully announced that its planned excursion to attend had resulted in 151 reservations, including "business men [sic], bankers and industrial heads in the city [who] are taking advantage of the chamber's invitation to visit Mexico and stop off at various American and Mexican cities en route." Hoping that the visit would become an annual event, the chamber announced its plan to publish a newsletter, *The Hot Tamale*, during the trip. It intended, it declared, to assure the Mexicans that "the glad hand really extends across the border at all times."[14]

Although slightly ominous notes were not lacking—Senator Albert Fall of New Mexico was denied a visa at the border to attend the inauguration, and

Table 4.1. Legal Mexican Migrants Entering and Departing from the United States

Fiscal Year Ending June 30		*Immigrant*	*Nonimmigrant*	*Total*
1921	Entering	30,758	3,904	34,662
	Departing	5,705	4,959	10,664
Net Increase				23,998
1922	Entering	19,551	3,477	23,028
	Departing	6,285	2,390	8,675
Net Increase				14,353
1923	Entering	63,768	3,519	67,287
	Departing	2,660	2,403	5,063
Net Increase				62,224
1924	Entering	89,336	4,553	93,889
	Departing	1,926	2,773	4,669
Net Increase				89,190
1925	Entering	32,964	4,727	37,691
	Departing	2,954	2,652	5,606
Net Increase				32,085

Source: CGI 1922–1925.

the Department of State ordered George D. Summerlin to turn down his invitation—the climate seemed reasonably favorable.[15] Texas governor Hobby attended with a large party, though the International and Great Northern Railroad initially stopped his train at Laredo. Railway officials were afraid to permit the valuable dining and baggage cars to cross the border given the potential "danger of the cars falling into the hands of bandits." After negotiations, a local Laredo banker provided a $60,000 cashier's check as bond so that the party could continue on to Mexico City.[16]

The Los Angeles visitors enjoyed the Mexican capital and socialized with Obregón and his wife. They then returned home safely and uneventfully, stopping off in San Antonio, Texas, where their chamber of commerce counterparts took them on a city tour that predictably included the Alamo. Yet even this visit was not completely free of bad publicity for Mexico. A sensational report datelined San Antonio claimed several days later that the "Los Angeles Special Is Nearly Bandits' Prey." Though the businessmen reportedly had no problems from start to finish and were delighted with their reception in Mexico, the press claimed that bandits in northern Mexico had been ordered to waylay and rob them on the trip back. Moreover, the bandits themselves were said to have been "executed by their chieftains when they refused to carry out the plot," yet another example of arbitrary violence, according to a Mexican rancher who had spoken to a Texas reporter.[17]

These ceremonial visits from border businessmen and politicians, though friendly, did little to diminish the major problems between the two countries. Among the most serious issues were the Mexican citizens in the United States and those that continued to cross the border. Many had made their way into the United States during the revolutionary decade and were still spread throughout the country. Though most resided in the Southwest, they were by no means confined to that region. Worker shortages in the United States during World War I had pulled them on to employment opportunities far from the border. The new president quickly received reports from New York to Arizona to Kansas City that Mexican workers were suffering unemployment and other vicissitudes as a result of the economic downturn. In Arizona, between 2,500 and 3,000 migrant workers had been abandoned by cotton growers miles from any transportation and without funds. In Kansas City, slumps in the meat-packing industry and in railway employment gravely impacted the city's Mexican population. The Mexican consul reported in New York that factories there were closing, Mexicans were out of work, and the prisons were full of his compatriots, who had been forced to commit crimes both petty and serious by "hunger and desperation." The consul's solution was to ask his government to ban further migration into the northern republic, a remedy that the Obregón administration could not afford to take given unemployment and economic devastation in Mexico itself. He also advised publicizing the difficult conditions in the United States within Mexico to discourage migration, which the government endeavored to do.[18] Despite the misery, employers were reluctant to have any quotas placed on Mexican workers coming into the United States.

While policymakers wanted no responsibility for Mexican workers who might suffer from the country's economic conditions, businesses wanted them close at hand should they need them.

Obregón linked his concerns about his country's economy with the plight of unemployed workers north of the border and hoped to make more jobs available in Mexico itself. The failure of the Harding administration to recognize his government, along with its increasingly rigid prohibitions and attitudes toward foreign workers and its acquiescence in their mistreatment, led him to retaliate by ordering his own foreign relations ministry (Secretaría de Relaciones Exteriores) to prohibit the entrance of non-Mexican workers into the country. During the revolution of the previous decade, one of the major issues, particularly in northern Mexico, where many expatriate citizens worked in mining and other jobs, had been the high salaries that such workers enjoyed relative to their Mexican counterparts and the frequent use of non-Mexicans in supervisory positions. Obregón suggested that Relaciones Exteriores restrict immigration into Mexico, "using all legal means that it has available to ensure that, in the republic, Mexicans would be preferred over all other workers." The mechanism would be its consuls, "especially in the United States," who could refuse visas to non-Mexican workers, with the restriction to remain in force "as long as the present conditions of unemployment continue to exist [in Mexico]." Exceptions would be those who came to settle permanently and brought with them the tools and capital for colonization. The same day, he and his secretary of government, close collaborator, and fellow Sonoran Plutarco Elías Calles, signed a memorandum of understanding on the matter.[19]

By the third week in March, the president had issued an executive decree thus limiting foreign laborers; the *Christian Science Monitor* on March 21, 1921, noted that Obregón had reacted to Mexico's "present scarcity of employment, notably in the oil regions." The report further pointed out that approximately one thousand workers had visited various Mexican consulates in the border states in recent days; only about 25 percent of them had obtained visas.[20] The next day, the *Chicago Daily Tribune*, no friend to Mexico, printed the following editorial comment:

> It may go hard with the United States government to take a tip on a matter of national policy from the so frequently erring government of Mexico, but pride should not blind us to our own best interest. On the contrary, the spectacle of our neighbor, ragged and battered, under-nourished [*sic*], ignorant, needy, and neglected, but still capable of one definite act for the protection and benefit of its citizenry, should emphasize our own slackness on the same point.[21]

These sentiments were widespread throughout the United States and would soon culminate in new, restrictive immigration legislation, though not yet directed specifically against Mexicans.

Ten days later, President Obregón sent Relaciones Exteriores a memo ordering the ministry to instruct Mexican consuls in the United States to provide funds for the repatriation of all Mexicans suffering from unemployment and economic want; for that purpose he transferred a quarter-million pesos to the Relaciones Exteriores. Three months later, on May 3, 1921, he declared publicly that his government, regardless of cost, would repatriate all Mexicans in the United States to protect them from the authorities, and on May 4 he asked the Mexican congress for a law to restrict immigration into Mexico. All of these actions received strong editorial support from the local newspapers. By September 1921, 23,354 workers had been repatriated at a cost of approximately three million pesos, but in October, unfortunately, the program had to be suspended for lack of funds.[22] Although the number of returnees was substantial, it does not seem to have been reflected in the figures for Mexicans returned noted earlier (table 4.1). Regrettably, the program of repatriation was largely futile, as the economic situation in Mexico offered these workers even worse conditions than they had endured in the United States and frequently led to their rapid return back across the border.[23] The following year, the intransigence of the problem was underlined by the failures of the migration offices that the Obregón administration had set up along the border and in the interior of Mexico to help control the flow of workers; some of these officials had developed a cooperative relationship with labor contractors from the United States and were profiting illegally by charging contractors and migrants for their services.[24]

Obregón remained concerned about this issue, and among his papers is an unsigned proposal dated June 1922, which emphasized the continuing significance of workers north of the border in providing sizable remittances to their financially struggling families in Mexico. The proposal noted that Italians and Poles in the United States were well treated and attributed this situation to the solidarity of these two national groups and the attention given to them by the Italian and Polish governments.[25] Yet economic constraints made it extremely difficult for the Mexican government to shore up consular offices or to engage in other cultural programs abroad, though subsequent administrations would begin to do so. Obregón was unable to establish an economic climate that would attract Mexicans back to their homeland, but he developed a bill that would at least provide some protection for Mexicans in the United States. The proposal he sent to the Mexican congress in October 1923 called for all Mexicans in foreign countries to be registered and afforded them "contractual protection of rights," as described in the Mexican Constitution of 1917. The law was not passed until 1926, during the presidency of his successor, and changed little even then. Still, it stood as a statement of his goals on the matter.[26]

In the United States, by early 1921, continuing fear about overwhelming numbers of immigrants from all points of origin led to a reevaluation of immigration policy extending beyond the rather limited changes brought about by the 1917 law. In part a reaction to the average immigration of about one million persons annually before World War I, it created quotas, largely directed toward Europe, that were designed to reduce immigration from that continent to about 350,000 a year.[27] Signed into law on May 19, 1921, it was always envisioned as just a first step, a temporary measure passed despite its late date as "war emergency legislation" and then extended to June 30, 1924, still legally provisional. The first resulting law was put together quickly to deal with the situation while Congress and the Harding administration sought a more permanent solution.[28] It established the principle of a quota system that permitted a yearly entry of 3 percent from each European nation based on the number already in the country as of the census of 1910. Migrations from the Western Hemisphere, including, importantly for our purposes, Canada and Mexico, remained unrestricted in numerical terms, though this exemption from the quota would not prevent Mexicans, within a few short years, from becoming the quintessential illegal aliens.[29]

Part of the problem was that, according to the law, otherwise excluded aliens could legally enter without quota restrictions after a waiting period (initially one year) in Western Hemisphere countries. Canada and Mexico, along with Cuba, immediately developed as locations where these migrants could wait in reasonable comfort and proximity until the year expired and then enter without concern about quota limitations. This loophole led to an immediate perception of the land borders with two contiguous countries as soft and penetrable—an accurate impression, as it happens—along with the Florida Gulf and Atlantic coasts, where boats from Mexico and particularly Cuba could drop off otherwise inadmissible migrants.[30] Although more than twice as many legal aliens entered via Canada as came through Mexico throughout this period, the Mexican border began to be perceived as the major problem (table 4.2).

The *Christian Science Monitor* in July 1921 particularly targeted Mexico for criticism in this regard. It noted that "Aliens [Are] Evading Immigration Law," lurking in Mexico, and "watching for their opportunity to get across the border."[31] In January 1922, the *Washington Post* trumpeted similarly that "Aliens [Are] Evading Laws: Officials Say Thousands Come through Mexico and Canada." According to the story, the problem was so grave that the sec-

Table 4.2. Legal Immigration over the Canadian and Mexican Borders, Land and Sea Ports, July 1, 1920–June 30, 1925

Year	Canada	Mexico	Total
7/1/1920–6/30/1921	93,043	29,907	122,950
7/1/1921–6/30/1922	53,163	19,247	72,410
7/1/1922–6/30/1923	127,034	63,635	190,669
7/1/1923–6/30/1924	219,736	89,042	308,778
7/1/1924–6/30/1925	108,212	32,532	140,744
Total	601,188	234,363	835,551

Sources: CGI 1922, 40; CGI 1923, 40; and CGI 1925

retary of labor, James J. Davis, was spending more time on immigration than on any of the other functions of his department. It further insisted that "if the bars were let down millions of foreigners would flock in and further add to the problem of unemployment, which threatens, some administration officials believe, to again become acute." It was "almost *impossible*," according to officials, "to prevent the illegal entrance of foreigners into the United States through Mexico and Canada." The article asserted without evidence that the illegal border traffic surpassed the legal immigration at Ellis Island, viewing with alarm the "high-powered automobiles driven by daring chauffeurs" that easily evaded immigration agents in "smaller government-owned machines." A perhaps more realistic report from the *New York Times* in February 1922 indicated the authorities' belief that no more than two thousand illegal aliens had made their way across the southern border in the previous nine months, but the notion of Mexico as the vulnerable underbelly of the United States appeared more often in the news.[32]

The Congress, while not immediately able to spend a great deal of money to reinforce the border against illegal entry, nevertheless moved quickly to close the one-year residence loophole. When Congress extended the 1921 law through 1924, it changed the waiting period to five years. This provision, passed on May 11, 1922, gave an immediate push in the direction of illegal entry, putting the issue of enforcement directly on the table.[33]

A discouraging report three weeks later, published in the *Los Angeles Times* but datelined Laredo, Texas, pointed out that only fifty-six inspectors served that immigration district, which extended from the mouth of the Rio Grande four hundred miles west. The director in charge of the district, E. W. Smith, noted that the new law would drive to Mexico many Europeans who were seeking access to the United States but were unable to enter because of the quota or other restrictions. Smith commented:

> It's no easy task to patrol the sluggish old river, with its banks lined with trees and shrubbery, forming perfect hiding places in daytime and good blinds at night, when most of the crossing will be done. Unless the inspectors actually see a boat or someone in the river, or happen to be on hand as the aliens reach the American bank, there is little to hinder them entering this way.

The reporter, not Smith, went on to mention the following:

> Scarcely a day passes that from one to a dozen Turks, the Italians, Greeks, or men, women, and children of other nationalities are captured or held up on the border as they attempt to enter this country surreptitiously. There is no means of knowing how many escape the vigilance of the immigration inspectors. Every Spanish steamship that enters the port of Vera Cruz unloads several hundred aliens from the countries of Europe and it is well known that most of these head for points near the Rio Grande as fast as trains can carry them and their limited luggage.[34]

It is noteworthy here that the reporter emphasized migrants from southern Europe and the eastern Mediterranean, who were considered less desirable than the fairer, blonder northern Europeans.

This dual vision of vulnerability and menace had a powerful effect in linking unregulated migration across the Mexican border to criminality, lawlessness, and racial taint. In addition to these migrants, of course, there were large numbers of Mexican workers who were entering the United States, many legally but many by irregular means, and there were racial, class, and, most noxiously, hygienic concerns about them. As Mexicans became linked to Europeans and, even "worse," Asians entering legally or illegally through their country, this stigma against working-class Mexicans deepened.

A border incident around this time indicated the officials' fears of radical labor activists slipping into the United States. When Mexican union officials went to the border in January 1921 to greet a delegation of the American Federation of Labor, headed by Samuel Gompers, traveling to Mexico to attend a meeting of the Pan American Federation of Labor in Mexico City, they were prevented from crossing to the side even temporarily. Meanwhile, the labor demonstration that had been arranged to welcome Gompers was called off, apparently by those who had come to welcome him.

At the same time, Obregón left Mexico City, perhaps to avoid a connection with the meetings.[35] He may have been worried about being associated with a gathering that could be construed as radical in the United States or might cause disorder in Mexico City. During the meetings in the Mexican capital, even Gompers expressed apprehension about rising immigration into his own country. He asserted, hyperbolically, that 1.5 million immigrants were entering the United States each year, that 15 million Europeans were poised to set sail for America, and that unemployment had reached 2 million in the United States. Meanwhile, the meetings were considered insufficiently radical by other militant Mexican laborers, who paraded through the streets of Mexico City protesting "all labor unions [inasmuch] as they considered themselves the true Bolsheviks."[36]

Moreover, the media portrayed Mexico as harboring not only dangerous Reds but also "draft dodgers," men who had fled the draft in the United States during World War I to take refuge south of the border. Frequently, the two categories became conflated, and these men were stigmatized as political radicals who belonged in neither country. On balance, however, the critics preferred that those who had avoided military service in Europe in this way be returned to the United States to face charges. During Obregón's campaign for the presidency in 1920, he was asked whether he would send back "these slackers" who, according to popular belief, numbered several thousand. The press claimed that one of them, Linn E. Gale, was publishing *Gale's Magazine* in Mexico City as an organ of the International Workers of the World and the Mexican Communist Party. "General Obregón" apparently received the idea of the repatriation of such radicals "in the most friendly spirit" but declined to commit himself, given that he was not yet president. According to the *New York Times*, Gale was urging Obregón "to do for Mexico a work comparable to what Lenin is doing for the Russian workers" and to recognize Bolshevik Russia."[37]

The idea that Mexico was full of deserters had been promoted for several months before Obregón's election by Senator Fall, who claimed that thirty thousand men had thus escaped the dangers of war in Europe.[38] Among the headlines emerging from his committee hearings, one declared, "Mexico Is Sewn with the Seeds of Bolshevism," a story based on the testimony of an anonymous traveling salesman who claimed to have heard a speaker in Sonora singing "the hymn of the Bolsheviki."[39] A more optimistic article appeared in the *Christian Science Monitor* two days after Obregón's election; the magazine's understanding was that "General Obregón is . . . determined to crush Bolshevism in Mexico after he assumes the presidency, if it has not been accomplished before that time. He recently declared that Mexico did not wish to be classed with Soviet Russia among the nations of the world," a danger given the coincidence in time between the Russian Revolution and Mexico's own.[40] Around the same time, notices appeared in the press that Robert Haberman, characterized as a "Bolshevik leader and agitator," had been chased out of Mexico City by Secretary of Education José Vasconcelos during the interim government preceding Obregón's inauguration. Haberman, who had been serving as head of the Bureau of Foreign Languages, the article claimed, had "filled the schools with a horde of foreign agitators." Worse, he had set up a "clever spy system in all government departments." Warned of his impending arrest, Haberman had fled to northern Mexico.[41]

Obregón, tired of war and trying to pull his country together, had probably already been angered by Mexican and foreign anarchists when a labor demonstration on September 28, 1920, two months before his inauguration, turned into an invasion of the National Palace. The demonstrators took over a balcony, where they waved the red and black anarchist flag, cheered for Russia and for other European workers, denounced the Mexican congress and the Supreme Court, and declared that they had bombs ready for all Mexico City newspapers, which, they declared, were all " 'organs of capitalism.' " As the rhetoric began to get further out of hand, suggestions were publicly made for attacks on the archbishop's palace, the erection of a guillotine in the central plaza meant for the journalists on hand, the construction of street barricades, and the ransacking of stores.[42] None of these fit well with the president-elect's hopes of presenting Mexico as a newly peaceful and responsible nation, one that was worthy of recognition by the United States.

Very soon after his inauguration as president five weeks later, Obregón brought those he perceived as foreign radicals to heel. In an interview with a *New York Times* reporter on April 3, 1921, he declared his determination "to stamp out so-called Bolshevism in the Republic. I will not permit foreigners to preach doctrines contrary to our laws." When queried about his timeframe for the "cleanup," he announced that he had begun the night before with the arrest of Linn Gale. Gale, in fact, was a bona fide draft dodger who had escaped twice and been reapprehended, the first time the day that he was to appear before the local draft board in Albany, New York, his home, and then again after he had made it to Pontiac, Michigan, probably hoping to abscond into Canada. This third time, he and his wife had fled across the Rio Grande.[43]

Unfortunately for Obregón, who was continually working to achieve his own objectives while satisfying his more radical supporters and opponents in Mexico and the United States, the Mexican Left protested Gale's deportation to the United States on the grounds that he would immediately be thrown into prison. Obregón then decided to send him to Guatemala, where Gale believed he would be received as a political refugee; when leaving Mexico, Gale declared that he was in fact German, as was his wife (Wilhelmina) and that his real name was Wertenberfeld. German or not, Guatemalan officials quickly said that they would not grant him asylum and that they would pass the pair on to Honduras or El Salvador. The Gales instead returned to Veracruz but were eventually deported overland through Laredo, Texas, where Gale was handed over to military authorities at Fort McIntosh. He faded gradually from the Mexican scene, but by September 1921, six months after his deportation, he had offered to tell the government everything he knew about "radicals in the United States and Mexico, in return for a promise of freedom." At this point, even the American Civil Liberties Union, according to director Roger N. Baldwin, refused to defend him. Baldwin's letter to Gale's lawyer referenced Gale's "complete disregard for principle, friendship and obligations, offering to do practically anything which promises to bring his freedom" and to escape from the consequences of having evaded the draft. His lawyer replied that indeed the former radical "has authorized me to make public the information that he has renounced his former political beliefs and convictions, that he has legally severed his connection with the radical movement, and consequently would not be justified in receiving any further aid or support from them."[44]

Other unfortunate incidents continued to reinforce the idea of Mexico and the border—and, by extension, Mexicans—as inherently dangerous. Obregón must have been dismayed by a series of reports that individuals responsible for notorious crimes were taking refuge in his country. In a case that vied in notoriety with O. J. Simpson's alleged attempted escape to Mexico many decades later, headlines shortly after Obregón's inauguration trumpeted that Clara Barton Smith, who, according to her own account, had been the mistress of Oklahoma oilman and Republican national committeeman Jake Hamon since she was seven years old, had escaped south of the border after shooting her lover. Hamon had tried to keep her from harm, first by walking to the hospital from an Ardmore hotel and then claiming that he himself had inflicted the wound when he was cleaning his pistol prior to a hunting trip. Nevertheless, after visiting her lover in the hospital, Smith prudently fled south through Texas, and murder charges were filed against her after Hamon's demise. A Dallas taxicab driver chronicled her story after transporting Clara to El Paso, where she crossed the line into Mexico. Lurid details included her questioning the cabbie about what he thought Hamon's chances for survival might be. After he learned that the gun had been old and possibly rusty, he assured her that even if Hamon did not die from the wound, he would probably expire from blood poisoning. Meanwhile, the official Mrs. Jake Hamon claimed that Clara Smith did not exist at all and that her husband was a devoted family man.

After retaining lawyers from a Fort Worth firm, Smith returned voluntarily to the United States. Still, the case remained front-page national news for months, kept there by bizarre details such as Clara's intention to claim one-quarter of her deceased lover's $20 million fortune, based on a will that had mysteriously disappeared, and the shocking details of the violent fight that had led her to discharge her weapon "accidentally."[45] Clara, now generally using the surname of Hamon (acquired some years earlier through a marriage of convenience to Jake Hamon's nephew Frank), was quickly acquitted after a single jury vote; as the *Washington Post* reported, "She used a private passage from the courtroom to escape crowds which threatened to overwhelm her with congratulations."[46] After settling with the other Mrs. Hamon for $10,000 and a number of oil leases, marrying a film producer, and making an unsuccessful film about her experiences, Clara faded from the news, but her dramatic escape to Mexico had made an unfortunate impact.[47]

Worse, in a case similar to the kidnapping of the consul in Puebla, W. O. Jenkins, in 1919, "bandits" captured and held for ransom A. Bruce Bielaski, former chief of the Federal Bureau of Investigation, during an excursion to Cuernavaca. Reinforcing the notion of Mexico as a refuge for dangerous individuals, a story in the *New York Times* mentioned that "Prominent American radicals," a number of whom were known to be in the vicinity, might have been responsible for the crime.[48] Less than five days later, Bielaski managed to escape, Indiana Jones–style, by dropping off a cliff and swimming a river. He described his captors as peasants—not radicals—and "extremely careless," but he mentioned that Bolshevik signs filled the country.[49]

Throughout Obregón's term, further sensational stories about criminals fleeing to Mexico and the disorder there continued to plague his government and damage his country's reputation. Cop killer "Little Phil" Alguín and another murderer named Clara, this time surnamed Phillips, who had beaten her husband's girlfriend to death with a hammer and whom the newspapers nicknamed "the tiger girl," both fled to Mexico in February 1923. They arrived there from Los Angeles—though not together. Alguín was captured and returned to California after a long manhunt, the only continuing controversy having to do with who received the substantial reward money. Phillips moved on to Honduras, where Los Angeles authorities pursued her. She eventually wound up serving a life sentence in San Quentin prison, where the prison optometrist observed several years later that she was as beautiful as ever.[50] In each case, lawmen entered Mexico in search of the fugitives and returned to the United States without difficulty.

Meanwhile, a rash of safecracking and second-story break-ins in Mexico City and Tampico underlined the notion of Mexico as a refuge for undesirables.

Figure 4.1. Woman behind bars. Courtesy of Archivo Casasola, Fototeca del INAH.

The press attributed these crimes to a group of criminals from the United States, as the locals were not believed to have the necessary skills. A ring of "oil promotion swindlers" wanted in the United States peddled fake stocks by mail; Denver forger W. Ellis, alias Emerson, was reportedly located in Mexico City, and to top it all, even after Mexico's recognition by the United States, law-enforcement officers complained that the "extradition of fugitives [is] prevented by red tape." In fact, one story noted that "hundreds of offenders are said to be living in apparent security against molestation" as "The authorities of that country are too busy trying to round up a horde of domestic criminals to pay much attention to foreign refugees." These Mexican malefactors, who were presumed to be roaming the countryside, were reported to have been "released from prison by rebel forces" during the revolutionary decade.[51] Precisely these offenders might be planning a move into the United States, or, of course, they might already be there. None of the extensive publicity on any of these cases was at all helpful to the United States' perceptions of Mexico, and all increased public and congressional desire for more restrictive legislation and for additional controls and enforcement along the border (figure 4.2).

At the same time, as Obregón's administration continued, immigration officials in the United States began focusing with specific alarm on Mexico. Reports to the secretary of labor from the commissioner general of immigration between 1922 and 1925 (all published in December of the year in the title and summarizing the previous fiscal year [July 1 through June 30 of the year in question]) reflect the growing concern. Thus, in December 1922, the report looked back at one full year of operation of the first emergency measure, the Immigration Law of 1921. Noting that various kinds of barriers had existed before the quota—racial, largely in relation to Asian immigration, and other more individual criteria ("physical, mental, moral, and, in a limited way, educational," this latter in regard to literacy)—it went on to review the effect of the new law. In particular, it noted that the new "stringency" had "accentuated" alien smuggling over land borders, both Canadian and Mexican. The commissioner of immigration at Montreal noted that "dope, liquor, Chinese, and alien smuggling has become a lucrative business" that was being carried on by "international gangs in which there have been found the hardest, most daring, and cleverest criminals, backed by no limit of funds and possessed of the highest powered vehicles, boats, etc., the automobile predominating as a means of traveling." Thus the illegal traffic in living human beings became linked to other major problems, particularly the growing concern about psychoactive drugs and prohibited alcohol; in later reports the word "contraband" was extended to include the movement of human beings. The report of the supervising inspector of the Mexican border district further noted that the first few months of 1922 had seen a significant increase in the number of aliens trying to enter the country illegally. Fortunately, in spite of weakened enforcement capabilities as a result of declining appropriations, "the movement was apparently checked for the time being."[52]

Figure 4.2. A murderer holding a bloody knife. Courtesy of Archivo Casasola, Fototeca del INAH.

The next year, the inspector in charge of the San Antonio district emphasized that "the experience of the past two years in dealing with Europeans unable to secure entry through our seaports who looked at the back door of this country as a favorable means of ingress has demonstrated the ever-existing and increasing need for a strong border patrol." In 1923, the concern with the Canadian and Mexican land borders had increased, along with the figures for legal migration. While the latter had totaled 309,556 in 1921–1922, the number had soared to 522,919 the following year and were coupled with significant drops in departures—one departure for every three entries the earlier year and only one for approximately 6.5 entries the second year. The report pointed out inaccurately but dramatically that almost all of that increase was due to movement over the land borders despite the fact that by now a five-year waiting period in a Western Hemisphere country was required for aliens to enter without quota restrictions. Given that much of the border migration was believed to involve southern and eastern Europeans, the report noted a significant and increasing congressional concern over the "fundamental racial character" of the country along with a "steadily growing demand for restriction." In this vein, the report noted that the immigration reports had begun keeping track of the "races of peoples" and their "country of origin."[53] Interesting for our purposes here is that categories for Mexicans were included in both groups, reflecting the confusion that has persisted for decades.

An ominous event in late 1922 with regard to immigration policy took place when Dr. Harry H. Laughlin, "expert eugenics agent" of the Committee on Immigration and Naturalization of the House of Representatives and staff member of the Eugenics Record Office of the Carnegie Institution of Washington, D.C., appeared at congressional hearings. He reported on his study of the "individual physical, mental and moral quality, and more particularly the potentiality of the immigrant as a parent of desirable Americans of the future." The specific issue that he was investigating was "the occurrence of the degree of specific degeneracy within the several nativity and racial groups of the United States." Taking as his database the "inmates of the custodial institutions of the several states and of the Federal Government," he examined ten "social inadequacies" among various immigrant groups, ranging from insanity to disease (including syphilis, leprosy, and tuberculosis) to "inebriety (including drug habitués)" to crime. He further insisted that "these degeneracies and hereditary handicaps are *inherent in the blood*." His study concluded that only three national groups were lower on these scales than Mexicans: those of Bulgaria, Spain, and, lowest of all, Serbia. In particular, Mexicans were very high on the scale of "crime," in which category they scored even lower than the Bulgarians, though the Spanish and the Serbians were worse yet. Laughlin made it quite clear at the hearing that his intention was to describe the "socially inadequate person," that is, "one who by his or her own effort, chronically, and regardless of etiology or prognosis, fails in comparison with normal persons to maintain himself or herself as a useful member of the organized social life of the state."[54] Clearly policy oriented, Laughlin designed his account to persuade legislators that some national and racial groups were desirable as immigrants and others not. Although at least one scholar attacked Laughlin's statistics and methodology as misleading and described his argument that these inadequacies revealed an "inborn racial quality" as totally specious, the report nevertheless helped shift the quota basis from the 1910 census to that of 1890 in order to favor northern Europeans (see table 4.2).[55]

Equally ominous was the 1923 commissioner general's report, in its section on "Smuggling and Surreptitious Entry," which singled out the Mexican rather than the Canadian border. This emphasis appeared despite the fact that, in terms of registered movement, the Canadian figures for land and seaport arrivals were twice as large as the Mexican figures, 127,034 versus 63,635 (see table 4.2). There was no specific comment about the Canadian side with regard to the migrants' negative characteristics, but those coming across the Mexican border were implied to be inferior, both racially and physically, compared to those arriving from across the northern border. The reports also indicated that "diseased" Near Eastern and Japanese immigrants who had been excluded by passport regulations were coming up from Mexico; further, a typical smuggling route ran from southern Europe to the Mexican coast and then up to the Texas border, thus ostensibly attracting more undesirable southern Europeans than did Canada. At the same time, many Mexicans themselves, given the increasing collection of head taxes and the enforcement of literacy requirements, simply avoided official border crossings and in this way earned the status of "illegal." These surreptitious entries had led to a situation in which it was "not possible even to estimate the number of Mexicans who enter the country without inspection." Meanwhile, Mexicans continued to move into areas in the United States beyond the Southwest, particularly into the "Middle Western States," but also increasingly to the north and east, including industrial areas in Pennsylvania, where "European laborers . . . had been checked by the quota law."

All of these developments seemed alarming to the immigration officers, though perhaps not to employers. The El Paso District supervisor again pointed out the need for more money for border enforcement; the Immigration Service's "mounted guards" were overwhelmed and imperiled, and the "smugglers on this border travel [are] armed with deadly weapons, and shoot to kill rather than be apprehended and imprisoned." One mounted guard had died in the violence during the previous fiscal year, another had been shot but survived, and the third had been beaten severely. The supervisor urgently pointed out that more officers were badly needed and that "the expenditure of vast energy and huge sums of money in guarding the portals at Ellis Island against the entry of the proscribed seems a vain and futile thing so long as the back-yard [*sic*] gate swings loosely on its hinges."[56]

The 1924 report indicated with alarm yet another huge increase in registered migration for all ports of entry over the previous year: 706,896, an increase of 183,977. These figures reflected several major issues: The quotas did not apply to Canada, Mexico, and the "New World"; those for "Southern and Eastern Europe" were restrictive, but those for northern Europe were rarely filled. In addition, there were many exceptions to the law, which had been extended by liberal court decisions and only recently reversed by the Supreme Court. Again, the numbers from the two contiguous countries had surged: They were now up to 219,736 from British North America and 89,042 from Mexico. In May 1924, just before the end of the fiscal year being examined, a new immigration law restricted quotas to 2 percent of those persons of the same "national origin" who had been present in the United States as determined by the census not in 1910, when there were more southern Europeans, but in 1890, when the population of the United States had been, as many who thought of the United States as white and blonde believed, more homogeneous.

Again, the workforce of the immigration service patrols was viewed as inadequate. The statement of the San Antonio headquarters reflected the sense of threat, indicating that it was very difficult "to apprehend aliens as they cross the river." The report noted that controlling the border would be a type of war, requiring an army to carry out that mission successfully. The only possibility for catching "these contraband aliens" was at the point where "trails from the river began to merge," by implication extending the jurisdiction of officers well back from the international line. Finally, the author of the report noted with relief that Congress had increased by a significant amount its appropriations for border protection. The assumption was that "if the number of men asked for is given and they are men who have a thorough knowledge of the Spanish language and Mexican border conditions and are temperamentally fitted for this particular type of work," it might be possible to control the "smuggling situation."[57] Unfortunately, most of the men who were eventually hired to control the border did not speak Spanish; this lack of language skills, along with the nature of the men hired, made border crossing a much more difficult ordeal for migrants.

At about the same time, the constant preoccupation of the Congress with other immigrants of undesirable racial characteristics (e.g., the Japanese) became increasingly focused on Mexico. In a March 1924 report that accompanied a new immigration bill being sent to the House from its Committee on Immigration and Naturalization, sponsoring Representative Albert Johnson of Washington State noted that "the surreptitious entries of Japanese, partly through Canada, but perhaps more extensively through Mexico, must be very great." He offered no evidence for this supposition, nor could he suggest even an approximate figure. He did, however, offer a probable route: Beginning at some unidentified location in South America, the aliens, he assumed, worked their way north through Mexico, up into the Imperial Valley and then farther into California, thus connecting Mexico to what Johnson called "unassimilable aliens."[58]

The Johnson-Reed Immigration Act of 1924 changed the situation substantially. It established temporary annual quotas of 2 percent of the foreign-born population by national origin according to the census of 1890; the secretaries of state, commerce, and labor were to come up with definitive quotas by 1927. Aliens entering the United States needed passports and visas, which were to be obtained in their own countries, moving most examinations offshore. Yet there were still no quotas for Western Hemisphere citizens despite the interest of Secretary of Labor James J. Davis in establishing limits. The Senate voted down such quotas sixty to twelve. It seems the public, racial doubts or not, preferred to maintain Mexicans as a convenient reserve labor force. Though for some time Secretary of Labor Davis continued to advocate for Western

Hemisphere quotas, he eventually changed his mind or at least his belief that any such limits would be enforceable. His confusion was palpable in a 1929 letter on the subject:

> The Mexican people are of such a mixed stock and individuals have such a limited knowledge of their racial composition that it would be impossible for the most learned and experienced ethnologist or anthropologist to classify or determine their racial origin. Thus, making an effort to exclude them for admission or citizenship because of their racial status is practically impossible.[59]

In this statement he reflected the ambivalence about Mexican "race" that pervaded attitudes in the United States and at the same time made clear that, for him at least, race should be the basis of immigration policy. "National origin" was rather unclearly associated with some notion of race; it would be years before just what it meant began to be unraveled. Though Mexicans were stigmatized in the discussion, it proved ultimately impossible to exclude them on this basis.[60] Nevertheless, in 1939 Harry H. Laughlin was still reporting to civic groups that Mexican immigration into the Southwest might constitute a "Conquest by Immigration."[61]

The 1924 laws contributed to a more cheerful tone in the 1925 report of the commissioner general of immigration. This statement looked back on a year in which quota immigration had been significantly reduced, the 2 percent limit having gone into effect and visas now being required from consulates in immigrants' countries of origin. These measures had cut down substantially on arrivals, at least legal ones. Further, the border patrol, as it was now referred to, though usually still not capitalized, had received $1 million for salaries and $38,000 for vehicles. Four hundred and fifty men, including officers, had now come aboard; some recruits had come from the railway postal-clerk register and the immigration inspectors' list. However, immigration inspectors already enjoyed a higher grade and therefore greater pay than patrol inspectors, so few applied. Postal clerks were not well qualified for the work, leading to a turnover of approximately 25 percent in the first three months. Therefore, temporary appointments that did not fall under civil-service regulations had been adopted until a "patrol-inspector register" could be set up, obviously removing a layer of scrutiny in hiring that might have avoided problems later. Yet the report did not reflect any concern about the success of the rapid hirings. Instead, "the immigration patrol force" was claimed to have attracted "men of the highest type, many of whom served as officers in our Army and Navy in the late World War."[62] This assessment of their caliber has been questioned in the years since the hiring.

Violence and racism along the border became significantly worse; it may be that the recent participation by many in World War I led them to interpret the border with Mexico as a front line of battle. Certainly, as historians have pointed out, the haste to enlist officers led to major problems. Many were "former cowboys, skilled workers, and small ranchers," almost all young, almost all veterans of the war or with other military experience, and a number associated with the Ku Klux Klan. Only one in the El Paso district was Hispanic, Pete Torres, a New Mexican with a reputation for being "a little quick on the trigger."[63] However, despite a probable lack of Spanish skills, the force on both the Mexican and Canadian land borders made impressive though perhaps somewhat inflated achievements: They investigated 1,252,379 persons (2,783 per border patrol employee), stopped and searched 418,128 cars and buses, and apprehended 14,711 illegal migrants. Not all of the problems had been completely resolved, however; the commissioner general noted that agents were already questioning the rules of engagement. The El Paso headquarters, for example, protested restrictions against firing until fired upon and averred that conditions were even worse than "those generally obtaining in actual warfare." On the Canadian border, in contrast, inspectors reported that the smuggling of aliens had been brought under control.[64]

Exempt from the quota, Mexicans traveling across the border became subject to onerous regulations and increased enforcement. New visa requirements added not only bureaucratic harassment but actual cost for those who came to work; both those who crossed the border daily to work on the side and those who ranged farther and came for months at a time had to pay not only the $8.00 head tax but also a one-time visa charge of $10.00. Odious medical line inspections, in which immigrants walked one by one in front of a medical officer, were eliminated at Ellis Island in 1924 and for Europeans and Mexicans who came to the border on first-class rail lines but still applied to all other Mexicans. Even worse were the practices of bathing and delousing, which, for workers who came across the border daily, had to be repeated each week, stimulating yet another kind of crime—the creation of false documents, in this case showing that the bathing requirement had been fulfilled.[65] More and more Mexicans came across without going through this expensive and degrading process; they were increasingly associated with illegalities, while border enforcement became associated with criminal pursuit. Although in 1925, the commissioner general's report *did* acknowledge the cooperation of both the Canadian and the Mexican governments in controlling the international boundaries, word and deed reinforced the criminalization of the Mexican border. The "clandestine entry of aliens" had given rise to what, in the enforcers' minds, had clearly become a border war.[66] Employers in the United

States continued to need Mexican labor, yet Mexican laborers were pursued as criminals, as border-patrol jurisdiction was moved ever deeper into the interior of the country and border-patrol officers made arrests on the basis of race. Ngai points out that by 1930 the Border Patrol was not simply policing the border but also operating well into the interior. As Henry Hull, the commissioner general of immigration at that time, explained it, the organization was "a scouting organization and a pursuit organization . . . [Officers] operate on roads without warrants and wherever they find an alien they stop him. If he is illegally in the country, they take him to headquarters."[67] Unfortunately, many legal residents and citizens who were or appeared to be of Mexican descent became fair game, unprotected by the norms of law.

Notes

1. See Mae M. Ngai, "The Strange Career of the Illegal Alien: Immigration Restriction and Deportation Policy in the United States, 1921–1925," *Law and History Review*, 21(1) (Spring 2003): 74–75. According to Ngai, *Impossible Subjects: Illegal Aliens and the Making of Modern America* (Princeton, N.J.: Princeton University Press, 2004), 10, "Westphalian sovereignty . . . sanctified the integrity of the territorial nation-state and the principle that no nation can interfere in the affairs of another."
2. Ngai, "Strange Career," 72.
3. *Los Angeles Times*, Apr. 11, 1920, 9; hereafter cited as *LAT*. *Atlanta Constitution*, Dec. 16, 1920, 9; hereafter cited as *AC*. *New York Times*, Dec. 2, 1920, 12; hereafter cited as *NYT*. See also the table for earlier migration in Linda B. Hall and Don M. Coerver, *Revolution on the Border: The United States and Mexico, 1910–1920* (Albuquerque: University of New Mexico Press, 1988),127.
4. Hall and Coerver, *Revolution*, 126–28; John Higham, "American Immigration Policy in Historical Perspective," *Law and Contemporary Problems* 21(2) (1956): 228; Lawrence A. Cardoso, *Mexican Emigration to the United States, 1897–1931* (Tucson: University of Arizona Press, 1980), 38, 51–54.
5. Higham, "American Immigration Policy," 227.
6. Commissioner General of Immigration, "Annual Report of the Commissioner General of Immigration to the Secretary of Labor" (Washington, D.C.: USGPO, 1921–1925). Cited hereafter as CGI, followed by date and page number. See description of categories in CGI 1922, 3.
7. CGI 1922, 24.
8. Mark Reisler, *By the Sweat of Their Brow: Mexican Immigrant Labor in the United States, 1900–1940* (Westport, Conn.: Greenwood, 1976), 24–49; Thomas C. Cochran, *American Business in the Twentieth Century* (Cambridge, Mass.: Harvard University Press, 1972), 105.

9. See, for example, Adolfo Gilly, *La revolución interrumpida*, first repr. (Mexico: Ediciones Era, 1994), 348–67, and John Hart, *Revolutionary Mexico: The Coming and Process of the Mexican Revolution*, 10th anniversary ed. (Berkeley: University of California Press, 1997), 370–74.
10. Thomas Campbell, speech at a barbecue given by the combined chambers of commerce of Nogales, Arizona, and Nogales, Sonora, July 11, 1920, Fidecomiso Archivos Plutarco Elías Calles y Fernando Torreblanca, Papers of the Secretario Particular de la Presidencia, 13–010201, 29/8. Cited hereafter as FAPEC-SP, followed by document location.
11. *San Antonio Express*, Oct. 7 and 8, 1920. For a longer discussion, see Linda B. Hall, *Oil, Banks, and Politics: The United States and Postrevolutionary Mexico, 1917–1924* (Austin: University of Texas Press, 1995), 131–33.
12. *NYT*, Oct. 8, 1920, 15.
13. *LAT*, Nov. 14, 1920, I6.
14. *LAT*, Nov. 21, 1920, I11; Nov. 26, 1920, II9; Dec. 1, 1920, II1.
15. *LAT*, Nov. 21, 1920, I1; Nov. 28, 1920, I1.
16. *NYT*, Nov. 29, 1920, 15.
17. *LAT*, Dec. 9, 1920, II1.
18. Mexican consul, New York, to Secretario de Gobernación, Dec. 22, 1920, Departamento de Trabajo, Archivo General de la Nación, vol. 334, Expediente 23. Hereafter cited as AGN-DT, followed by volume and folder number. *LAT*, Apr. 11, 1920, XI9. Informe, Eduardo Ruiz to Obregón, Feb. 18, 1921, Archivo General de la Nación, Ramo Obregón-Calles, 407-A-2. Cited hereafter as AGN-OC, followed by folder number. See also Hall, "Alvaro Obregón and Mexican Migrant Labor," 763. Thomas Campbell to Obregón, Feb. 9, 1921, AGN-OC 407-C-2. Paul S. Taylor, *Mexican Labor in the United States* (New York: Arno, 1970), vol. 1, 17–18. Cardoso, *Mexican Emigration*, 101. Mexican consul, Kansas City, Missouri, to Jefe del Depto. de Trabajo, Apr. 5, 1921, AGN-DT 333/25.
19. Obregón to Secretaría de Relaciones, Feb. 16, 1921, AGN-OC 605-T-2. See also Cardoso, *Mexican Emigration*, 99.
20. *Christian Science Monitor*, Mar. 21, 1921, 2. Cited hereafter as *CSM*.
21. *Chicago Daily Tribune*, Mar. 22, 1921, 8. Cited hereafter as *CDT*.
22. "Crisis obrera en los Estados Unidos," Legajo 3, 1921, 205–206, in Archivo Fernando Torreblanca and Plutarco Elías Calles, section Alvaro Obregón IV.2. Archive hereafter cited as FAPEC-AO. Report, Mexican Consul, Los Angeles, in Subsecretary to Secretary of Industria, Comercio y Trabajo, May 19, 1921, AGN-DT 333/23/1. For newspaper support, see *Excelsior*, May 9, 1921.
23. "Informe Presidencial," Sept. 1, 1921, in "Material para un libro," Legajo 7, 337, FAPEC-AO IV.2. *El Universal*, Oct. 24, 1921. Cardoso, *Mexican Emigration*, 103.
24. J. Garza Zertuche to Depto. Consular, Mar. 4, 1922, 36–16–94; Garza Zertuche to Sec. Relaciones Exteriores, Feb. 17, 1922, 36–16–98; L. Montes de Oca to Sec. del Estado y del Despacho de Relaciones Exteriores, Apr. 21, 1922, and Oficial Mayor, Depto.

Consular, Relaciones Exteriores, Mar. 15, 1922, 36–16–363; Garza Zertuche to Sec. de Relaciones Exteriores, June 19, 1922, and June 24, 1922, 36–16–106; Garza Zertuche to Depto. Consular, Oct. 25, 1922, and Subsecretary, Relaciones Exteriores, Nov. 14, 1922, 36–16–122, all in Archivo Histórico de la Secretaría de Relaciones Exteriores. Hereafter cited as ASRE. Cardoso, *Mexican Emigration*, 112.

25. See Francisco E. Balderrama, *In Defense of la Raza: The Los Angeles Mexican Consulate and the Mexican Community, 1929 to 1936* (Tucson: University of Arizona Press, 1982), 31–32, 67–69.
26. Cardoso, *Mexican Emigration*, 106–109. Fernando Saúl Alanis Enciso, "No cuenten conmigo: La política de repatriación del gobierno mexicano y sus nacionales en Estados Unidos, 1910–1928," *Mexican Studies/Estudios Mexicanos* 19(2) (Summer 2003): 421.
27. Ngai, "Strange Career," 75.
28. Robert DeC. Ward, "Our New Immigration Policy," *Foreign Affairs*, 3(1) (Sept. 15, 1924), 99.
29. Higham, "American Immigration Policy," 227.
30. CGI, 1922, 4, 15–29.
31. *CSM*, 7/9/1921, 2.
32. *Washington Post* (hereafter WP), Jan. 16, 1922, 1; emphasis mine; *NYT*, Feb. 5, 1922, 26.
33. CGI, 1922, 4.
34. *LAT*, June 4, 1922, III 13.
35. *LAT*, Jan. 5, 1921, I1.
36. *LAT*, Jan. 17, 1921, 2.
37. See, for example, *NYT*, June 7, 1920, 9. For Gale's relationship to other Communist groups and to the government of Obregón's predecessor, Venustiano Carranza, see Douglas W. Richmond, "Nationalism and Class Conflict in Mexico, 1910–1920," Americas 43(3) (January 1987): 302.
38. *CDT*, Jan. 12, 1920, 2. On Senator Fall, see also Hall, Oil, Banks, and Politics, 36–59.
39. *AC*, Dec. 16, 1920, 1.
40. *CSM*, Sept. 7, 1920, 2.
41. *WP*, Oct. 7, 1920, 2. Vasconcelos continued as secretary of education when Obregón took office.
42. *WP*, Sept. 28, 1920, 14.
43. *NYT*, Apr. 3, 1921, 7.
44. *NYT*, Apr. 23, 1921, 4; Sept. 18, 1921, 25. See also Pablo Yankelovich, "Explotadores, truhanes, agitadores y negros: Deportaciones y restricciones a estadounidenses en el México revolucionario," Historia Mexicana 57(4) (April–June 2008): 1175–76.
45. *LAT*, Nov. 27, 1920, 8; AC, Dec. 8, 1920, 1; WP, Dec. 8, 1920, 2 and Dec. 23, 1920, 1; *LAT*, Dec. 24, 1920, I1; NYT, Dec. 23, 1920, 1, and Mar. 16, 1921, 3.
46. *WP*, Mar. 18, 1921, 1.
47. *LAT*, May 12, 1921, II 1; NYT, May 13, 1921, 5; AC, May 15, 1921, D6.

48. *NYT*, June 26, 1922, 1.

49. *NYT*, June 29, 1922, 1; June 30, 1922, 3.

50. *LAT*, July 16, 1922, I1; Feb. 10, 1923, I1; Apr. 19, 1923, II21; May 28, 1923, II1; Dec. 18, 1925, 10.

51. *NYT*, June 5, 1921, 25; July 11, 1924; LAT, July 6, 1924, E7.

52. CGI 1922, 9–10, 13–14; 1923, 19, 23–24; 1924, 18; 1925, 18.

53. CGI 1923, 1, 3, 6–7, 10–12, 19.

54. Congress, House Committee on Immigration and Naturalization, *Analysis of America's Modern Melting Pot: Hearings before the Committee on Immigration and Naturalization*, House of Representatives, 67th Congress, Third Session, Nov. 21, 1922, Serial 7-C. (Washington, D.C.: USGPO, 1923), 730. Emphasis mine.

55. Congress, *Analysis*, 733, charts between 740–41 and 750–51. See the critique in Joseph M. Gillman, "Statistics and the Immigration Problem," *American Journal of Sociology* 30(1) (July 1924): 29–30, 46.

56. CGI 1923, 1, 3, 5, 7, 12, 15–19, 40–41.

57. CGI 1924, 1, 16–17. For an outstanding discussion of "national origins," see Mae M. Ngai, "The Architecture of Race in American Immigration Law: A Reexamination of the Immigration Act of 1924," *Journal of American History* 86(1) (June 1999): 67–92. The issue of Mexican immigration is specifically addressed on pp. 88–92.

58. Congress, House Committee on Immigration and Naturalization, "Restriction of Immigration," House of Representatives, 68th Congress, First Session, Report 350 (Washington, D.C.: USGPO, 1924), 8–9.

59. Ngai, *Impossible Subjects*, 50–55.

60. For an outstanding discussion of "national origins," see Ngai, "Architecture of Race," 67–92.

61. Harry H. Laughlin, *Immigration and Conquest: A Report of the Special Committee on Immigration and Naturalization of the Chamber of Commerce of the State of New York* (New York: Chamber of Commerce of the State of New York, 1939), 37–38.

62. CGI 1925, 14–15.

63. See, for example, Ngai, *Impossible Subjects*, 74, and George J. Sánchez, *Becoming Mexican American: Ethnicity, Culture, and Identity in Chicano Los Angeles, 1900–1945* (New York: Oxford University Press, 1993), 59.

64. CGI 1925, 16–19.

65. Ngai, "Strange Career," 85–86, 88.

66. CGI 1925, 19.

67. Ngai, "Strange Career," 69–70.

CHAPTER 5

Revolutionary Mexican Nationalism and the Mexican Immigrant Community in Los Angeles during the Great Depression

Memory, Identity, and Survival

Francisco E. Balderrama

My study of the Mexican Revolution began very early in my career as a historian. It was at the age of six during the first grade, but this was not part of the first-grade curriculum of Sister Anne Marie at Saint Michael's Elementary School in Los Angeles, California, during the 1950s. Rather, my grandfather Francisco Balderrama Terrazas presented the Mexican Revolution as a history lesson at home. Coming from the small town of Satevó, Chihuahua, my grandfather masterfully told tales of the valor of the Division of the North and especially the enigmatic Francisco Villa. The exciting stories extended beyond the northern state of Chihuahua to include the entire Mexican nation and even reached across the border to Columbus, New Mexico, the site of Villa's famous raid. Grandfather also discussed a pantheon of revolutionary leaders from the inspiring brothers Ricardo and Enrique Flores Magón to the martyred Francisco I. Madero and Emiliano Zapata, as well as the politically astute Venustiano Carranza and Álvaro Obregón. Accounts also included the villains of the revolution, such as the usurper Victoriano Huerta and the meddling US president Woodrow Wilson.

Grandfather did not confine his storytelling to home but continued the conversation at our family's small grocery store in East Los Angeles, where customers enthusiastically shared their own tales or passionately debated revolutionary issues. My family's teaching of history also included field trips on family outings to see the natural wonders of the Golden Gate of San Francisco and the Grand Canyon of the Southwest. All of these sites were introduced by my family with the lesson that "all of this once belonged to Mexico before the Mexican-American War." Learning the legacy of the Mexican-American War was valuable; however, the Revolution of 1910 always ranked as the most enthralling lesson.

Years later, I discovered in the course of my studies that my experience was far from unique. The distinguished historian of Mexico Ramón Eduardo Ruiz recounted that during his childhood in Southern California "he would listen to his father . . . discuss what had taken place in the country he had recently fled. A magnificent storyteller, my father eagerly shared his wealth of anecdotes and opinions with all his children."[1] Elena Herrada of Detroit, Michigan, shared a similar experience. Her grandfather José Santos Herrada told her countless episodes of the Mexican Revolution, including its leaders, battles, and especially the ideals of the revolutionaries.[2] Often these talks about the revolution took place on Sunday morning visits to the "Detroit Industry Frescoes" painted by the great Mexican muralist and revolutionary Diego Rivera. These frequent visits to the Rivera masterpiece also celebrated the heritage of revolutionary art because "it belongs to us, the people."[3] Clearly, many Mexican immigrants valued the legacy of the Mexican Revolution and employed storytelling to pass on this treasured heritage to posterity as they struggled to adapt to US culture and society.

The presence of the Herrada, Ruiz, and Balderrama families in the United States was a result of the first massive movement of Mexicans north to the United States during the early twentieth century. The movement northward became truly enormous. According to official statistics compiled by both the Mexican and US governments, scholars conservatively estimate that more than half a million Mexicans entered the United States legally between 1899 and 1928. In 1930, the United States census reported some 1,422,533 Mexican nationals and Mexican Americans residing in the United States. This exodus meant that some 10 percent of the Mexican population lived on North American soil and thereby created *México de afuera*, or Mexicans and Mexican Americans outside Mexico.[4]

By 1930, massive immigration had created a formidable Mexican presence in Los Angeles and Southern California: at least 170,000 Mexicans and Mexican Americans, a larger Mexican population than El Paso or San Antonio, ranking as second and third, respectively, in concentration. The Mexican community also had the distinction of being the largest ethnic community in Los Angeles. The city also became the final destination for many Mexican immigrants who had resided elsewhere in the United States. An analysis of consular *matrícula*, or matriculation records, as well as oral-history testimony confirms that most Mexican immigrants had lived and worked in other parts of the United States before becoming residents in Southern California. Obviously, this fact underscores the opportunities that Los Angeles and Southern California provided over other US cities and regions.[5]

The massive movement north from Mexico to Los Angeles coincided with the Revolution of 1910. Historians often regard the epic crusade to oust dictator Porfirio Díaz and the subsequent civil war from 1910 to 1920 as the key forces that drove Mexicans across the border to the United States. Surprisingly, the immigration figures during the violent years of 1910 to 1920 were lower than both before or after Mexico became engulfed in a civil war. Numerous immigrants testify that they left Mexico as a result of the revolution. Among them are community leader Lucas Lucio, merchant Eduardo Negrete, and farmworker Celso Medina, who all fled the fighting and chaos for the peace and security of the United States.[6] Other immigrants fled the violence especially because they were fighting on the losing side. Long Beach resident Genaro Torres served as a colonel in Francisco Villa's army until captured after the battle of Agua Prieta in 1915 and faced death; however, he escaped by crossing the nearby border at Douglas, Arizona.[7] On the winning side of the battle of Agua Prieta was Los Angeles inhabitant Francisco R. Ramírez, who wrote in detail of his service and bravery in battle to his former commander, President Plutarco Elías Calles, who was now the *jefe máximo*, who ruled behind the scenes. The occasion for the letter to the *jefe máximo* was the slashing of Ramírez's work days and salary by Southern Pacific Railroad, as the Great Depression hit Los Angeles in 1931. Without his usual pay, Ramírez could not make his mortgage payment and feared that his wife and two children (the oldest seven and the youngest four), would be homeless. Ramírez therefore asked his former commander to "recognize his service" and provide him a loan so that he could make his house payment and keep his home (figure 5.1).[8]

Famous generals and key political figures joined the ordinary revolutionary soldiers immigrating to Southern California. At various times Los Angeles became the destination of many renowned insurgents: President Adolfo de la Huerta taught voice lessons in East Los Angeles, Education Minister José Vasconcelos borrowed books at the downtown Central Public Library, and President Plutarco Elías Calles purchased *pan dulce*, or pastries, at the Esperanza Bakery, Ricardo and Enrique Flores Magón gave speeches at the Los Angeles Plaza, and José David Alfaro Siqueiros painted *América Tropical* at Olvera Street.[9]

Among the working-class Mexican immigrants and rebels were counterrevolutionaries. Los Angeles had significant numbers of *cristeros*, or exiled Mexican clergy and Catholic families who had fled after their unsuccessful uprising against the Mexican government from 1926 to 1929. During the 1930s they dedicated themselves to battling both religious persecution and the strict

Figure 5.1. Family of Mexican refugees. Courtesy of The University of Texas at Arlington Special Collections.

enforcement of the anticlerical Mexican Constitution of 1917. The Mexican government's program of socialistic education during the 1930s, especially sexual education, horrified the *cristeros*. San Antonio, however, was a magnet for counterrevolutionaries, including *porfiristas*, *reyistas*, and *huertistas*. The wealthy, or ricos, along with some middle-class expatriates, were obsessed with news from Mexico because they yearned to return to the Mexico of Porfirio Díaz, or the *porfiriato*, but not the Mexico of the revolution.[10] The counterrevolutionaries failed to realize that the 1910 revolution had revitalized the ideals of nationalism, which embodied social justice, land reform, *mexicanismo*, and anti-imperialism as cardinal principles. These concerns were manifested with the revolutionary cry of "*México para los Mexicanos*" (Mexico for the Mexicans). The Revolution of 1910 vibrantly symbolized that "*los de abajo*," or the underdogs, had fought and won the battle against not only foreign economic domination and exploitation but also political tyranny and social injustice at home. Mexico's revolution truly inspired oppressed people around the world, and especially for *México de afuera*. Furthermore, the revolutionary heritage of Mexicans north of the border had mellowed since the civil war and the overthrow of Díaz. "Pancho Villa, Emiliano Zapata, and [Venustiano] Carranza were all good men with the right ideas," as José Santos Herrada observes.[11] By the 1930s, the passionate sentiments dividing the *villistas*, *carrancistas*, *zapatistas*, or other fractions had subsided, and a common revolutionary identity had emerged.

For the Mexican people, only their proximity to the United States, viewed as both a blessing and a curse, rivaled the impact of the 1910 revolution. A lament commonly heard in Mexico intones: "Poor, Mexico, so far from God and so close to the United States!" Both realities have had a decisive influence on the lives and attitudes of Mexicans who immigrated to the United States during the early twentieth century. Even prior to the advent of large-scale immigration, there had always been a strong sense of identification with the *madre patria*, or motherland. Cinco de Mayo, for instance, was celebrated in Los Angeles in 1863, only a year after the spectacular victory of General Ignacio Zaragoza over the French. During the French invasion, *Mexicanos* in the United States did more than merely engage in ceremonial observances. Under the leadership of Placido Vega, a special agent of the Mexican government, loyal Mexicans throughout the Southwest formed *juntas patrióticas*. They raised funds and troops in support of Benito Juárez's beleaguered government. Their efforts helped Juárez resist the French attempt to conquer Mexico and reestablish a French empire in the Americas.[12]

Bonds linking *México de afuera* and *la madre patria* became even stronger during the early twentieth century. An excellent example of the close ties was the 1929 campaign tour in the United States made by Mexican presidential candidate José Vasconcelos. When President-elect general Álvaro Obregón was assassinated in August 1928, Vasconcelos, former education minister and famous philosopher, viewed Obregón's death as an opportunity to return the presidency to civilian control. This could best be ensured, he reasoned, if the presidency passed into his hands. To enhance his ambition, his scheduled itinerary changed dramatically after the announcement of Obregón's death. Rather than giving lectures on university campuses or to international groups, he addressed his speeches almost exclusively to the burgeoning Mexican colony, or *colonia mexicana*, in a bid for its political support. Vasconcelos visited a number of important *colonias mexicanas*, including Calexico, San Antonio, McAllen, Brownsville, San Diego, and Chicago, but probably the most significant stop was Los Angeles, where the most Mexicans in the United States might be enlisted to join his campaign.[13]

In Los Angeles, Vasconcelos compared the Mexicans in the United States to the Zionist Jews for retaining their faith and desire of eventually returning to their native land. However, the former Mexican minister of education was not hailed as Moses leading *la raza* or Mexicans and Mexican Americans to the promised land of Mexico. Vasconcelos did receive an enthusiastic reception in the *colonias*, but his platform of higher wages, better working conditions, and improved educational opportunities for Mexicans in the United States largely explain his success. On the other hand, the government party's candidate for the presidency, Pascual Ortiz Rubio, also had numerous supporters who were just as active as the Vasconcelos followers in trying to win the endorsement of *México de afuera*. Nonetheless, Vasconcelos's trip generated a great deal of political excitement. Mexican nationals and Mexican Americans fiercely debated the political situation occasioned by the sudden murder of Obregón and the resulting presidential election of 1929.[14]

The Exhilaration and Expectations of the Vasconcelos vs. Ortiz

The Rubio campaign of 1929 for the *colonia mexicana* in Los Angeles quickly diminished with the stock market crash that year and the outbreak of the Great Depression. Widespread unemployment and underemployment paralyzed the economy and disrupted countless lives throughout the United States. However, Mexicans and Mexican Americans faced an even greater threat than being jobless—expulsion or unconstitutional deportation from the United States. During the presidential administration of Herbert Hoover and under the direction of Attorney General William N. Doak, the Immigration and Naturalization Service orchestrated deportation campaigns targeting ethnic communities to save jobs for "real" Americans, including the Mexican community. These *razias*, or raids, terrorized Mexicans and Mexican Americans throughout the United States. An especially tragic example was the Los Angeles raid at La Placita on February 26, 1931, when federal immigration agents detained four hundred persons near the historic area that commemorated the founding of Los Angeles. More important, these raids also encouraged deportation campaigns by major corporations, local businesses, and charitable organizations to ship Mexican families to Mexico. County relief agencies emerged as the leading force driving the removal of Mexicans because many people mistakenly regarded the removal of Mexicans from the relief rolls as an effective way of controlling public expenditures.

Whether these agencies and organizations were public or private, local or state, they lacked the legal authority to deport individuals. In accordance with the US Constitution, the right and responsibility to deport is reserved for the federal government and under the Immigration and Naturalization Service and the Border Patrol. The administration of Republican Herbert Hoover and Democrat Franklin D. Roosevelt, however, allowed local authorities to expel Mexican nationals and Americans of Mexican descent. By the outbreak of World War II and the ending of the Great Depression, more than one million Mexicans and Mexican Americans had been expelled from the United States. The Los Angeles campaign of expulsion was especially effective because it ousted one-third of its Mexican population. Moreover, Los Angeles became the model for other cities to deal with unwanted Mexicans and Mexican Americans especially because of its success in reducing the largest Mexican community in the United States. The Los Angeles campaign for removal of its Mexican population also popularized the use of the word "repatriation" after the Los Angeles legal counsel warned the "deportation desk" of Los Angeles Charities not to use the word "deportation" because only the federal government had the right to deport. Whether called deportation or repatriation, the removal remained especially brutal and heartless. Most Mexican nationals that were "repatriated" had lived and worked in the United States for a considerable time ranging from fifteen to thirty years. Furthermore, the overwhelming majority of the children of Mexican immigrants were born in the United States and therefore US citizens by birth.[15]

During the difficult years of unconstitutional deportation during the Great Depression, the Mexican community of Los Angeles found comfort and inspiration in revolutionary nationalism. Desperate times in *México de afuera*, particularly in Southern California, also provided Mexican politicians with a clearly defined issue upon which to vent the emotional ideals of revolutionary nationalism, especially concerns for social justice, sentiments for *mexicanismo*, and anti-American feelings. Instead of addressing the problems of the Mexican nation, politicians diverted public attention to the various transgressions of the colossus of the north. As an example, when Mexican strawberry pickers went on strike in Southern California in 1933, the *jefe máximo*, Plutarco Elías Calles, contributed $4,500 to the strike fund and instructed his government ministers and labor leaders to support the strikers. He also wrote to President Franklin D. Roosevelt, seeking his help in bringing about a quick settlement. In Mexico and *México de afuera*, Calles was hailed for his humane intervention, but his supposed concern masked his diminishing support for Mexico's own labor unions and their pleas for assistance.[16]

The Mexican Consular Service received special respect and affection in *México de afuera* probably because it was a local institution of the Mexican government with the singular responsibility to protect and defend the interests of Mexicans abroad. Since the dictatorship of Porfirio Díaz, the Mexican government and its consuls had been concerned about the growing Mexican presence in the United States. The early revolutionary regimes, particularly of Venustiano Carranza, had appointed a number of highly visible and active consuls, but it was during the 1920s' administration of President Álvaro Obregón that the Mexican government had to deal for the first time with many Mexicans losing their jobs and becoming stranded in the United States. Obregón therefore expanded the consular service from fifty-one to more than sixty offices in order to respond the crisis. The Mexican government also ordered all consuls to pursue their duties in a more aggressive manner but also cautioned them never to antagonize the host nation. Diplomatic courtesy and tact were to be observed at all times in order to avoid becoming *personae non gratae*. Consuls who forgot or overlooked this admonishment found themselves in diplomatic hot water and were transferred or relieved of their duties. Even though historians differ on the effectiveness of the Mexican Consular Service, especially with regard to the labor movement, the consuls were largely considered not merely the official representatives but also personifications of the Mexican government.[17] The Mexican community therefore frequently treated the consuls with awe and great respect. Consuls were charged with protecting not only the interests of Mexican nationals residing abroad but also their children, who were Mexican citizens by blood. Their presence was a reassuring sign to *México de afuera* residents, especially newly arrived immigrants, that they had not been forgotten by their government. The availability of a consul meant there was someone they could turn to when everything else failed. Many consuls, especially during the Great Depression, worked hard to earn and maintain the confidence and allegiance of the Mexican communities. Unfortunately, consular activities often had to be curtailed due to a lack of government funding. More significantly, Mexican consuls were frequently intervening on behalf of Mexican workers against powerful US agriculturalists and industrialists, who often had the full support of local, state, and federal authorities.

Underscoring the weakness of the Mexican Consular Service and the Mexican governments during the Great Depression, especially the administration of President Pascual Ortiz Rubio, was the tragic incident on June 8, 1931, in Ardmore, Oklahoma. Emilio Cortés Rubio, the president's nephew, and his companion, Manuel García Gómez, were shot to death by deputy sheriffs William Guess and Cecil Crosby. The young men were on their way home after attending college in Atchison, Kansas. Mexicans everywhere were shocked and dismayed. As far away as Southern California, Alfonso Jiménez of El Monte, Lucas Lucio of Santa Ana, and Catarino Cruz of the city of Orange vividly recalled the episode decades later.[18] Initially, many individuals responded to the news of the killings with stunned disbelief. How could such an outrageous act have taken place? Certainly, no one could condone such a terrible deed. Justice was bound to be sure and swift. In San Antonio, some four thousand persons greeted the train carrying the young men's bodies back to Mexico. A formidable delegation of municipal authorities, state representatives, and both US and Mexican consuls met the train at the border. Thousands of people attended the interment services in Morelia, Michoacán, where the state governor and future president Lázaro Cárdenas pledged to erect a monument to the students. Mourners also turned out not only to pay their respects but also to demonstrate their grief and protest the untimely deaths.[19]

The deaths of the two students, which many viewed as murder, became a cause célèbre in Mexico and *México de afuera*. Mexican newspapers on both sides of the border covered the subsequent inquest and trial in minute detail. Banner headlines greeted each new development and revelation. Ignacio Lozano's newspapers, *La Prensa* and *La Opinión*, assigned special reporters to follow the proceedings, for this was not merely another Mexican victimized by local police. The death of the president's nephew elicited diplomatic concern from both Mexican and US officials. However, in spite of Oklahoma governor William "Alfalfa" H. Murray's intercession and promise of justice and the considerable national and international media attention, the trial did not result in a guilty verdict. Officers Guess and Crosby were acquitted of all charges. The jury declared that the deaths were a case of mistaken identity and that the officers' actions were deemed appropriate because the students had guns in their car. The stunning verdict was a blow to the weak administration of Ortiz Rubio. More important, it was a kick in the teeth to the Mexican community in the United States because it underscored the Mexicans' place as second-class residents. It also highlighted the weakness of the Calles-era governments of Mexico. Two years later, the Roosevelt administration, upon the recommendation of the State Department and with the consent of the US Senate, paid $15,000 each to the families of the deceased students. The awards were made "without reference to the liability of the killings."[20] Months earlier, Ortiz Rubio had resigned from the presidency and departed for New York City due to a lack of political support, which affected his ability to govern effectively.

Spanish-language newspapers were another key institution that maintained strong ties with *la madre patria*. On the other hand, the English-language press usually viewed Mexicans and their problems or activities as not newsworthy. This editorial policy reflected the views of Anglo community leaders and established institutions. They considered the Mexican *colonia* as mainly an assortment of unskilled workers outside of the US socioeconomic mainstream. Any responsibility or obligation to them was dismissed as inconsequential. Differences in language, culture, and ethnicity, along with the Mexican community's largely working-class status, produced a distant and an indifferent relationship with the larger American society. In sharp contrast, the Spanish-language newspapers, particularly San Antonio's *La Prensa* and Los Angeles's *La Opinión*, were the leading dailies in terms of circulation, financial success, longevity, and reputation. Ignacio Lozano founded *La Prensa* in 1917 and *La Opinión* in 1926. The Lozano newspapers had the unique distinction of being located in the cities with the largest concentrations of Mexicans in the United States. These newspapers focused their attention primarily on reporting newsworthy events occurring in Mexico rather than local news. In the stories and editorials they printed, Mexican issues and themes were given extensive and continuous coverage. Both newspapers reflected Lozano's conservatism and were extremely critical of Mexico's revolutionary government. Due to the newspapers' opposition, the Mexican government officially banned *La Prensa* and *La Opinión* from Mexico until the 1930s.[21]

The Lozano newspapers reflected not only their publisher's concerns but also the foremost interests of an immigrant community of *recién llegados*, or recent arrivals. Many residents of *México de afuera* dreamed of returning to the Mexican motherland, and the Lozano dailies provided them with detailed information about Mexico, from politics to celebrities. Stories about local activities also appeared, but the Mexican community in the United States was a secondary focus for the tabloids. Spectacular local events, however, such as scandalous mistreatment of Mexicans and sensational court trials involving Mexicans, received extensive coverage.

Among the unforgettable cases was one that involved Juan Reyna, who was remembered over the years in the Mexican community of Los Angeles as a classic example of prejudice and discrimination, especially of law enforcement and the Los Angeles criminal-justice system. *La Opinión* and other *colonia mexicana* newspapers responded with details of his arrest, sensational trials, and mysterious death in prison, as well as the elaborate funeral procession and burial. According to various newspapers accounts, on June 10, 1930, foundry worker Juan Reyna was driving in downtown Los Angeles when his car went out of control and struck a parked car, which, unluckily, was a police vehicle. Reyna was arrested amid shouts of "you dirty Mexican" and "you filthy Mexican." While being escorted to the police station by three detectives, Reyna managed to disarm one of them. He then shot and killed one sleuth while wounding another before being subdued. During his trial, Reyna expressed no regret or remorse for his actions. Rather, he declared that he wished he had killed all three officers for having called him "a dirty and filthy Mexican." Immediately, the Mexican Consulate and the *Sociedad de Madres Mexicanas* responded on his behalf. Since 1926, the *Madres Mexicanas* had assisted Mexican and Mexican American prisoners facing criminal and civil charges by informing family members, raising defense funds, and securing legal counsel.[22] After an initial mistrial, a second trial found Reyna guilty of manslaughter instead of murder. Recognizing the mitigating circumstances, the judge gave Reyna a minimal sentence of one to ten years in San Quentin. He also recommended that Reyna be considered for parole after completing a single year of his sentence. Many Southern Californians regarded the sentence as compassionate, but his supporters remained hopeful that the decision would be overturned and that Reyna would soon be released.[23]

While a host of Mexican union and civic organizations joined the Mexican Consulate and the Sociedad de Madres Mexicanas in organizing for a new trial, Reyna suddenly died in his jail cell on May 4, 1931. *Corridos*, or popular narrative ballads, immortalized Juan Reyna for knowing "how to defend your dignity, and even expose your life, to honor your nationality." Local Los Angeles residents Alejandro Castro, Lucas Lucio, and Eduardo Negrete vividly recall the crusade to save Reyna and the numerous monetary contributions of Southern California residents. They also remember that the poorest individuals contributed pennies to Reyna's defense, as reported daily in *La Opinión*. Even though Reyna's support extended throughout the Southern California Mexican community, it was especially strong among his fellow members of the Partido Liberal Mexicano (PLM). The PLM, originally founded by the *magonistas* (Enrique and Ricardo Flores Magón in 1906), had by the 1930s become less concerned with anarchism, the Mexican political scene, and particularly the fulfillment of revolutionary principles. Instead, the Partido Liberal Mexicano of the Great Depression was far less radical than it had been during the early twentieth century. In addition, it maintained ties with the Mexican labor movement and the Mexican government. At this time, the PLM claimed a membership of some eleven thousand in Southern California.[24]

Juan Reyna's funeral in Watts, California, on May 7 and 8 was a perfect setting in which to display the ideals of revolutionary Mexican nationalism. While calling for an investigation of Reyna's outrageous death, the Partido Liberal Mexicano conducted a wake at its meeting hall in Watts, which included an honor guard recruited from a variety of political, social, and recreational organizations such as the Confederación de Uniones Obreras Mexicanas (CUOM), an important confederation of local labor unions. With *La Opinión* publicizing the event, the response was monumental. A cortege of workers arrived at the Southern Pacific station in Watts to deliver Juan Reyna's body to the PLM hall for an all-night viewing, which was attended by hundreds. By morning, the crowd had increased to around four thousand mourners, who attended services at the Watts Methodist Church and drove to the cemetery in a funeral procession more than four miles long. Upon the conclusion of the religious services, CUOM president Armando Flores convened a community meeting, where numerous speakers called for justice and a full investigation. Among them was Elena de la Llata, president of the Cruz Azul Mexicana, an organization composed exclusively of women dedicated to helping Mexican families in need of clothing, shelter, and food. The Cruz Azul Mexicana assistance became critically important to thousands of Mexicans in Los Angeles, and its efforts extended even to Mexico City for fund-raising activities on behalf of the Los Angeles *colonia mexicana* during the Great Depression.[25] De la Llata praised

Reyna for being not only a "good Mexican" but also a "martyr."[26] All of the speakers also joined the president of the Cruz Azul Mexicana in repeating the accusation that the police had attacked Reyna because he was Mexican. Armando Flores probably best conveyed the magnitude and seriousness of the offense when he declared that the police had "insulted him as a Mexican."[27]

In recounting his own life, long-time labor activist Bert Corona provides an insight into the gravity of this insult to Juan Reyna and other Mexicans of the 1930s by observing that "the immigrant workers—learned what the Revolution had been all about . . . they learned tales of valor, of weakness, of cowardice, and of sacrifice."[28] Moreover, the Mexican immigrant workers carried these stories with them as they laid railroad track, harvested fields, and labored in factories. While they endured low wages and deplorable working conditions, Mexican workers and their families also encountered discrimination and segregation throughout US society. As they struggled to find a place for themselves in California society, sentiments of revolutionary Mexican nationalism provided comfort and support to Mexican immigrants and their children.

Many Mexicans, however, often left their town and region without a sense of their nationality as Mexicans. Yet once in the United States, "they . . . learn immediately what their mother country means, and they always think of it and speak of it with love," the distinguished Mexican anthropologist Manuel Gamio observed.[29] Speaking of this same generation of Mexican immigrants, scholar Ramón Eduardo Ruiz notes that "they never lost sight of who they were: Mexicanos."[30] This was the experience of Juan Reyna and others in Los Angeles when Mexican revolutionary nationalism inspired them to fight for their rights. A number of Los Angeles and Southern California *colonia* residents confirm this view. They remember Juan Reyna as a "fighter" and a "defender of his nationality," especially because he became a member and a leader of both the Partido Liberal Mexicano and the Confederación de Uniones Obreras, where he emerged a "true revolutionary."[31]

Among Juan Reyna's most powerful advocates was KMPC radio announcer Pedro J. González. González and his radio show provide another insight into the Mexican revolutionary nationalism. Since its establishment in 1929, González's morning radio program in Los Angeles from 4 to 6 A.M. attracted a following in the Mexican immigrant community, and its "los madrugadores" (early risers) musical group had become a regional sensation. As far away as San Diego, Mexican families would tune in to hear "los madrugadores" and González perform. Among the listeners was the Ruiz family, who joked that "if you listen carefully, you can hear the rooster crow."[32] "Los madrugadores" were so successful that the group achieved very respectable record sales even during the difficult years of the Depression. González, however, did more than play music. With the onset of the deportation raids and repatriation pressures, he protested and defended the rights of Mexicans. His protests reflected his youth, when González had served in the revolution as a telegraph operator for the *villista* forces, an experience that shaped his view of life: "I have very patriotic feelings and very revolutionary feelings when I see the bad treatment given to the Mexicans."[33]

González's powerful influence stunned the political establishment of Los Angeles when he announced to his Depression audience of unemployed Mexicans and Mexican Americans where work was available. With shovels and axes in hand, hundreds of Mexican workers appeared at the site within hours of the announcement, ready to work. This event also shocked Los Angeles district attorney Buron Fitts, who worried about the power of González and his activist ideas: "What if this madman, troublesome as he is, and on top of that a Villista, what if he tells all Mexicans—here, in Arizona, New Mexico, and other states, or wherever they can hear his program—every Mexican would rise up with a bottle of gasoline and start burning all the American houses!"[34] Soon after this incident, the district attorney's office filed charges and secured a conviction of Pedro González for rape in 1934, with a sentence of one to fifty years. Even though the young woman later recanted her testimony and reported that the district attorney's office and the Los Angeles Police Department had pressured her to file the charges, the judge refused to admit the woman's affidavit, and González remained in San Quentin prison. Two Mexican presidents supported the defense committees in California in lobbying for González's release and return to the airwaves, but it was not until 1940 that the governor of California finally released González, who, however, was released only on condition of accepting deportation to Mexico. On his trip to Mexico, his train stopped in Los Angeles, where a sizeable crowd from the Mexican community gathered at the train station to wish González a final farewell. The tearful crowd also pleaded with the former radio star to sing and play his guitar one last time before his train departed to Mexico.[35]

As noted earlier, Pedro J. González's expulsion and sad farewell were far from being a singular event. Moreover, the massive movement of Mexicans and Mexican Americans from the United States to Mexico during the Great Depression reveals the impact of revolutionary ideals on the Mexican immigrant population. Mexicans who were forced to go to Mexico often dreamed of a new life there and were inspired by nationalistic rhetoric. It is therefore not surprising that references were frequently made to the promises of the revolution and the willingness to contribute to Mexico's development. Southern California community leader and Orange County representative for the Mexican Consulate, Lucas Lucio, for example, recalled the revolutionary sentiments of the Mexican families residing in the Bastanchury *colonia mexicana* of Orange County. "They wanted to contribute to Mexico and fulfill the goals of the revolution," Lucio observed, even though they were "very poor" and "went on the half fare of the Southern Pacific to Mexico without any money."[36]

Among the repatriation colonization efforts in the Los Angeles area was a group from San Fernando and San Pedro, who settled the Ejido Erienda in San Ysidro, Baja California. The San Pedro colonists included the Ríos family, whose daughter Ramona was a bright and confident young girl who enjoyed her life in the United States, especially going to school and playing softball. Soon Ramona would find that her intelligence, confidence, and maturity would be severely tested. Conditions at the Ejido Erienda were so desperate that she and her family were surviving by "eating beans by the spoon without tortillas."[37] Starvation appeared imminent. Ramona, however, wrote to the governor for food, supplies, and seeds for the agricultural colony. Her letters to Mexican government officials were patriotic declarations that expressed the sentiments of revolutionary Mexican nationalism. Specifically, she spoke of the promise of Mexico for Mexicans and land for the people—the ideals of the revolution.[38]

Facing expulsion from elsewhere in the United States, other Depression-era Mexican nationals and people of Mexican descent resorted to Mexican revolutionary nationalism in order to survive. More than one hundred families from Wyoming and Nebraska wanted to develop an agricultural colony and petitioned President Pascual Ortiz Rubio in highly patriotic terms. Under the banner of the Mexican Constitution of 1917, the "Union, Progress, and Country," another group from the agricultural colony of Goodyear, Arizona, petitioned President Ortiz Rubio as follows: "We are hungry, shoeless, and unclothed . . . without a miserable piece of bread for our children." Nonetheless, they proclaimed unity and country as their revolutionary motto.[39]

The presence of the Mexicans and Mexican Americans in Los Angeles and Southern California has changed dramatically since the dark days of the Great Depression. Not only has the Mexican-origin population continued to grow, but Los Angeles County has also become the home of the largest Latino population of any county in the nation.[40] Los Angeles is now unquestionably a leading Latino city and the long-time home of numerous Mexicans and Mexican Americans. More important, Mexican Americans occupy highly visible and very powerful positions. Among them are the mayor of the city, a county board supervisor, and an archbishop of the Roman Catholic Church. Furthermore, there are Mexican/Latino caucuses in the Los Angeles City Council, California state legislature, and the state's congressional delegation. In the face of massive budget cuts and layoffs of city workers for the fiscal years of 2010–2011, Los Angeles remains steadfast in funding the restoration of the *América Tropical* mural by José David Alfaro Siqueiros, which the Anglo establishment whitewashed during the repressive 1930s.

It is also commonplace to see not just in Mexican neighborhoods but throughout the southland murals depicting Mexican revolutionary themes and issues, including portraits of heroes such as Francisco Villa or Emiliano Zapata, as well as references to the Mexican Constitution of 1917 or the oil expropriation of 1938. Visiting Southern California college and high-school campuses, Mexican and Mexican American youth often wear T-shirts with images of revolutionary heroes or slogans. The epic revolution of 1910, now more than a hundred years later, appears to be highly visible and a fundamental part of life in the Los Angeles Latino community of the twentieth-first century.

The legacy of the Mexican Revolution is apparent not only in art and fashion but, more important, in the minds and souls of the Mexican community. In 2010 a newspaper article discussed a student protest against recent budget cuts at California State University and the University of California. In the article *Los Angeles Times* columnist Hector Tobar interviewed a student who was sharing his frustration at struggling to pay fee increases of 32 percent while financial aid was becoming less available. Moreover, he was unable to complete his program of study because fewer key classes were being offered. "Being pushed against the wall, but I am still here" was how the student summarized his difficult situation.[41] Asked for his name, "Ricardo Flores Magón," the student responded. "It is my protest . . . name," Adan García explained.[42] Obviously, García was inspired by the example of Flores Magón, who confronted ruthless pressure to back down but was never willing to compromise his revolutionary principles. When invoking the name of Ricardo Flores Magón, student Adan García joined the ranks of Los Angeles Mexicans of the Great Depression, such as foundry worker Juan Reyna, radio announcer Pedro J. González, and repatriate Ramona Ríos, who drew inspiration and courage from the Mexican Revolution of 1910.

Notes

1. Ramón Eduardo Ruiz, *The Great Rebellion: Mexico, 1905–1924* (New York: Norton, 1980), ix.
2. Interview with Elena Herrada, Detroit, Mich., May 8, 2004.
3. Ibid.
4. México, Secretaría de Relaciones Exteriores, *Memoria de la Secretaría de Relaciones Exteriores de agosto de 1928 presentada al H. congreso de la Unión por Genaro Estrada* (México, D.F.: Imprenta de la Secretaría de Relaciones Exteriores, 1929), 1549–50; US Department of Commerce, Bureau of the Census, *Fifteenth Census of the United States, 1930: Population,*

Special Report of the Foreign-Born White Families by Country of Birth of Head (Washington, D.C.: USGPO, 1933), 199.

5. Los Angeles Consular Matrícula Register for 1930 in Archivo de la Secretaría de Relaciones Exteriores, México, D.F., ASRE IV-103–26. Among the numerous interviews are those with the following people: Flavio Valenciana, Riverside, Calif., Dec. 26, 1989; Lucas Lucio, Santa Ana, Calif., Mar. 16, 1976; and Eduardo Negrete, Fullerton, Calif., Mar. 26, 1976.
6. Los Angeles Consular Matrícula Register for 1930 in Archivo de la Secretaría de Relaciones Exteriores, México, D.F., ASRE IV-103–26; interview with Celso Medina, El Modena, Calif., Apr. 12, 1976.
7. Interview with Daniel Torres, Long Beach, Calif., June 17, 1994; Safe Conduct Pass, Agua Prieta, México, Jan. 31, 1916, courtesy of Daniel Torres.
8. Francisco R. Ramírez to President Plutarco Elías Calles, May 23, 1931, ASRE IV-374–22.
9. John W. F. Dulles, *Yesterday in Mexico: A Chronicle of the Revolution, 1919–1936* (Austin: University of Texas Press, 1967), 263; William David Estrada, *The Los Angeles Plaza: Sacred and Contested Space* (Austin: University of Texas Press, 2008), 131, 133–67.
10. For Los Angeles *cristeros*, see Francisco E. Balderrama, *In Defense of La Raza: The Los Angeles Mexican Consulate and Community, 1929–1936* (Tucson: University of Arizona Press, 1982), 73–90, and for San Antonio *ricos*, see Richard A. García, *Rise of the Mexican American Middle Class: San Antonio, 1929–1931* (College Station: Texas A&M University Press, 1991), 221–52.
11. Herrada interview.
12. Placido Vega's activities with the *juntas patrióticas* are documented in "Colección de Documentos de la Comisión Confidencial," in the Bancroft Library, University of California–Berkeley.
13. John Skirkus, "Vasconcelos and México de Afuera (1928)," *Aztlán: International Journal of Chicano Studies Research* 7(3) (Fall 1976): 479–97.
14. Ibid.; Douglas Monroy, *Rebirth: Mexican Los Angeles from the Great Migration to the Great Depression* (Berkeley: University of California Press, 1999), 232–33; Juan Gómez-Quiñones, *Roots of Chicano Politics, 1600–1940* (Albuquerque: University of New Mexico Press, 1994), 370–73. The Vasconcelos campaign also strained the relationship between some Mexican community organizations and local Mexican consulates. See ASRE 4–7-9 for the debate over the activities of Los Angeles consular employee Adolfo Moncada Villarreal, who publicly sided against the Vasconcelos supporters. Another important source is *La Opinión*; see, for example, Nov. 25, 1928, and Dec. 9 and 14, 1928.
15. Among the leading repatriation studies are Francisco E Balderrama and Raymond Rodríguez, *Decade of Betrayal; Mexican Repatriation in the 1930s*, rev. ed. (Albuquerque: University of New Mexico Press, 2006), and Abraham Hoffman, *Unwanted Mexican Americans in the Great Depression: Repatriation Pressures, 1929–1939* (Tucson: University of Arizona Press, 1974).
16. The 1933 berry strike of Southern California has received extensive attention. For the Mexi-

can government's activities in support of the striking workers, see Balderrama, In Defense of La Raza, 93–97, and Abraham Hoffman, "The El Monte Berry Strike: International Involvement in a Local Labor Dispute," *Journal of the West* 12 (January 1973): 71–84.

17. See Balderrama, *In Defense of La Raza*, for the only study exploring a specific community and consulate; Gilbert G. González, *Mexican Consuls and Labor Organizing: Imperial Politics in the American Southwest* (Austin: University of Texas Press, 1999), for a thoughtful discussion of the consuls.
18. Lucio interview; interview with Catarino Cruz, Orange, Calif., Mar. 23, 1976; interview with Alfonso Jiménez, El Monte, Calif., Dec. 21, 1976.
19. *La Opinión*, June 11–16, 1931; diplomatic correspondence regarding the incident appears in US Department of State, *Papers relating to the Foreign Relations of the United States, 1931* (Washington, D.C.: USGPO, 1931), 708–29; also see secondary treatments Abraham Hoffman, *An Oklahoma Tragedy: The Shooting of the Mexican Students, 1931* (El Paso: Texas Western Press, 1987), and Luis G. Zorrilla, *Historia de las relaciones entre México y los Estados Unidos, 1800–1958* (México, D.F.: Editoral Porrúa, S.A., 1965), 438.
20. US Department of State, *Papers*, 726.
21. Francine Medeiros, "La Opinión, A Mexican Exile Newspaper: A Content Analysis of Its First Years, 1926–1929," *Aztlán: International Journal of Chicano Studies Research* 11 (Spring 1980): 65–87.
22. Balderrama and Rodríguez, *Decade of Betrayal*, 54–55.
23. Francisco E. Balderrama and Raymond Rodríguez, "Juan Reyna: Victim of Anti-Mexican Hysteria," Western History Association Conference, Los Angeles, Calif., 1987; also see San Francisco Consul General to Secretaría de Relaciones Exteriores, May 7, 1931; Secretario General Comité General de Confederación de Obreros Mexicanos, Cervantes Torres to Secretaría de Relaciones Exteriores, May 28, 1931; Petra Reyna to Los Angeles Consul Rafael de la Colina and de la Colina to Consul General Alejandro Lubbert, May 11, 1931, in ASRE IV-320–17.
24. Nellie Foster, "The Corrido: A Mexican Culture Trait Persisting in Southern California" (master's thesis, University of Southern California, 1929), 121. Interview with Alejandro Castro, El Monte, Calif., Dec. 21, 1976; Lucio and Negrete interviews; Partido Liberal Mexicano Secretary Armando Flores to Secretary of Foreign Relations, Apr. 28, 1930, in ASRE IV-98–38.
25. Balderrama and Rodríguez, *Decade of Betrayal*, 55–56.
26. *La Opinión*, May 9, 1931.
27. Ibid. Also see Los Angeles Consul Rafael de la Colina to Mexican Ambassador, Sept. 24, 1930; Colina to Departmento Consular, Dec. 16, 1931; Secretaría de Relaciones to de la Colina, Dec. 17, 1930; Consul General Alejandro to Secretaría de Relaciones Exteriores, May 7, 1931, in ASRE IV-320–17; Castro, Lucio, and Negrete interviews. Also see Edward J. Escobar, *Race, Police, and the Making of a Political Identity: Mexican Americans and the Los Angeles Police Department, 1900–1945* (Berkeley: University of California Press,

1999), 139–47, and Arturo Rosales, *Pobre Raza! Violence, Justice, and Mobilization among México Lindo Immigrants, 1900–1936* (Austin: University of Texas Press, 1999), 95–96, 134, 175–76.

28. Mario T. García, *Memories of Chicano History: The Life and Narrative of Bert Corona* (Berkeley: University of California Press, 1994), 40.
29. Manuel Gamio, *Mexican Immigration to the United States: A Study of Human Migration and Adjustment* (New York: Dover, 1971), 128.
30. Ramón Eduardo Ruiz Urueta, *Memories of a Hyphenated Man* (Tucson: University of Arizona Press, 2003), 49–50.
31. Castro, Lucio, and Negrete interviews.
32. Ruiz Urueta, *Hyphenated Man*, 30.
33. Pedro J. González interview transcript, Charles C. Young University Research Library, University of California–Los Angeles; Escobar, *Race, Police, and Political Identity*, 147–50. Also see the following films: *Ballad of an Unsung Hero* (30 min.), WNET, 1985; *Break of Dawn* (100 min.), San Diego, Cinewest, KPBS, 1989; and these articles: *New York Times*, Jan. 7, 1985, and Mar. 23, 1995.
34. *San Diego Union*, Oct. 6, 1983.
35. Pedro J. González interview transcript, Pedro J. González Papers (1895–1991), Chicano Studies Research Library, University of California–Los Angeles.
36. Lucio interview.
37. Christine Valenciana de Balderrama, with Francisco E. Balderrama, interview with Ramona Ríos de Castro, Ejido Erienda, San Isidro, Baja California, July 17, 2004.
38. Ibid.; also see extensive correspondence on colonization projects for repatriates in Los Angeles Colonization Desk in ASRE IV-185–32.
39. Luis N. Vera to President Pascual Ortiz Rubio, May 15, 1931, in ASRE IV-353–38, and Santiago L. Gómez to President Pascual Ortiz Rubio, Jan. 21, 1931; El Paso Consul General Luis Medina Barron to Secretaría de Relaciones Exteriores, ca. 1931, in ASRE IV-355–20.
40. US Census Bureau, "Census Bureau Releases State and County Data Depicting Nation's Population ahead of 2010 Census," http://www.census.gov/newsroom/releases/archives/population/cb09–76.html (accessed May 22, 2012).
41. *Los Angeles Times*, Feb. 9, 2010.
42. Ibid. Among the first to recognize and examine Ricardo Flores Magón's contribution to the Mexican community and its political history is Juan Gómez-Quiñones, *Sembradores, Ricardo Flores Magón y el Partido Liberal Mexicano: A Eulogy and Critique* (Los Angeles: Aztlán Publications, Chicano Studies Center, University of California, 1976).

CHAPTER 6

From the *Caudillo* to Tata Lázaro

The Maximato *in Perspective, 1928–1934*

Jürgen Buchenau

On September 1, 1928, President Plutarco Elías Calles delivered to Mexico's assembled congress his final *informe*, the annual state-of-the-nation address. The speech came with much anticipation. Only six weeks before, a Catholic assassin had killed Calles's predecessor, General Álvaro Obregón, who had just been elected to a second term in office. As the Constitution of 1917 had abolished the office of vice president, the nation faced an acute succession crisis. Obregón had not been just any ordinary president-elect. Rather, Mexicans knew him as the "undefeated *caudillo* of the Mexican Revolution" and unquestionably the primary political leader of a nation that had only recently emerged from a destructive civil war. To top it off, Calles could not simply extend his own time in office, the likely solution in most other political contexts of early twentieth-century Latin America. Obregón's supporters blamed the president, as well as labor leader and presidential hopeful Luis N. Morones, for the murder of the *caudillo*, and they knew that the constitution, forged in the memory of General Porfirio Díaz's long dictatorship, forbade Calles from serving a single additional day. As Calles scanned the assembled legislators, he knew that the *caudillo*'s death had created not only a political vacuum but also a menace to the fragile state that the winners of the revolution had built since Venustiano Carranza and Obregón led them to victory over Pancho Villa's and Emiliano Zapata's armies in 1915.

However, a speech that could have thrust Mexico into renewed violence instead became the foundation of a new political order. Calles's oration assuaged Obregón's numerous supporters by delivering praise for the man who had served as his political mentor for much of the preceding fifteen years. But then, in a thinly veiled attack on Obregón, who was known far and wide as a *caudillo*, Calles referred to *caudillismo* as the source of his country's ills.[1] The reference to *caudillismo* placed Obregón's career in the context of other *caudillos* such as Díaz and nineteenth-century strongman Antonio López de Santa Anna.[2]

Having thus linked Obregón's leadership style to Díaz's authoritarian tradition, Calles laid out his plans for the future. Addressing his opponents' worst fears, he announced that he would not serve as president again under any circumstances and asked congress to appoint an interim president pending new elections. In his words, Mexico had entered the transition from a "country of one man" to a "nation of institutions and laws." Calles also called for the creation of a national party in order to combine the hundreds of parties that claimed loyalty to the cause of the revolution, yet operated as the political machines of strongmen. Finally, he welcomed the formation of a Catholic opposition party, a gesture designed to direct his conflict with the church into legislative channels.[3] This conflict had resulted from Calles's anticlerical policies, as well as the Vatican's opposition to the constitutional provisions that enshrined the complete separation of church and state. In July 1926, the clergy had suspended all religious ceremonies, and a few months later, the conflict had played a decisive role in setting off the devastating Civil Code. Calles's speech disarmed his political opposition and assured for the president a continuing role behind the scenes.

Indeed, Calles emerged as the symbolic pater familias of the revolution, or *jefe máximo de la Revolución Mexicana* (supreme chief of the Mexican Revolution). The moniker *jefe máximo* was the creation of one of Calles's opponents, Antonio Díaz Soto y Gama, a former *zapatista* who had become one of Obregón's most ardent allies following Zapata's assassination. Suspecting the government's involvement in Obregón's slaying, Soto y Gama coined the term in order to criticize Calles's repressive practices. The term *jefe máximo* thus imputed to Calles the very role he had publicly rejected: a leader just as authoritarian and dominant as Obregón. Calles never used this term to refer to himself in order to avoid its authoritarian connotations. Nonetheless, the label stuck, identifying Calles for better or for worse with the political system he had helped forge. As a result, one of Calles's most prominent allies, *El Nacional* editor Luis L. León, began to refer to Calles as *jefe máximo*, reinventing the term as one of respect for the only man whom he considered capable of holding the nation together in those difficult times.[4]

This chapter analyzes the politics of the *maximato*, the period dominated by the *jefe máximo*, as a crucial phase of transition from Obregón's overweening shadow toward Lázaro Cárdenas's populist leadership (1934–1940). It particularly focuses on the role of Calles and other significant players in the forging of a new political landscape that featured the rise of the party that claimed to represent no less than the Mexican Revolution itself: the Partido Nacional Revolucionario (PNR, or National Revolutionary Party). Under three different names, that party held on to power until the year 2000 and remains a significant force. Most historians have depicted the *maximato* as a period in which Calles was the dominant political power behind the scenes. Three leaders who served relatively brief terms as president—Emilio Portes Gil, General Pascual Ortiz Rubio, and General Abelardo L. Rodríguez—deferred to Calles in important decisions. Popular lore dubbed these three presidents the *peleles*, or puppets. Calles also played a significant role in creating the PNR and remained thoroughly involved in its affairs. Government officials, foreign diplomats, and entrepreneurs trekked to Calles's whereabouts for consultation.[5] Yet, as the following pages show, this characterization greatly exaggerates Calles's influence and underestimates the role of the so-called *peleles*, and especially Portes Gil and Rodríguez, as well as that of other significant actors in shaping the political and social life of the nation.[6]

The Emilio Portes Gil Years, 1928–1930

Despite having presided over a government that had accomplished a number of important reforms, including a major overhaul of the nation's financial system, the promulgation of a civil code, as well as numerous infrastructure improvements, Calles bequeathed to his successor a multifaceted crisis. The conflict with the church was in its third year. Religious services remained suspended, and the *cristeros* continued to dominate much of the states of Jalisco and Michoacán. Since 1926, Mexicans had found themselves in the throes of a severe recession set off by declining prices for silver and other exports, as well as the economic consequences of the Cristero Rebellion. As a result, a government that had pledged to deliver both social justice and national economic development could no longer promote either of those two objectives. Most citizens doubted that "the revolution," as represented by Calles's government, had delivered on its promises. The campesino and workers' organizations allied with that government did not inspire much hope. Soto y Gama's *agraristas* had proven ineffective, and Morones, the powerful boss of the Confederación Regional Obrera Mexicana (CROM, or Mexican Regional Workers' Federation), symbolized corruption and violence more so than anyone else in the governing elite. To top it off, regional warlords continued to defy the central government. On their own turf, *caciques* such as San Luis Potosí's Saturnino Cedillo and Tabasco's Tomás Garrido Canabal reigned supreme, selectively applying or ignoring federal mandates as suited their needs. In this atmosphere, the continuing rivalry between the president's own adherents and the leaders who had been loyal to Obregón constituted the primary political dynamic at the national level. While the *callistas* interpreted Calles's speech as license to eliminate the *obregonistas* as a political factor, the obregonistas remained powerful in congress, the military, and most state governments.[7]

Given these problems, it was not surprising that an *obregonista* received the nod for the interim presidency. On September 25, 1928—most likely upon Calles's recommendation—the Chamber of Deputies chose Gobernación Secretary Emilio Portes Gil for a term beginning on December 1, 1928, and ending on March 1, 1930. Portes Gil was a civilian *obregonista*, the leader of a regional agrarian party and former governor of Tamaulipas.[8] The nominee drew strength from his regional base, and his candidacy received support from Calles opponents such as Soto y Gama. Thus, the president's decision to support Portes Gil constituted an opportunistic reaction to the political lay of the land. In other words, Calles did not so much impose Portes Gil as he made a pragmatic choice that reflected the strength of *obregonistas* in congress.[9] As a result, Portes Gil approached his term with a great deal of independence from Calles. For example, Calles accepted the nominee's demand for restoration of an agrarian reform fund that had been deleted from the 1929 budget.[10]

With the question of the interim presidency settled, Calles and his allies moved toward the founding of the PNR as a national ruling party. In the late 1910s and early 1920s, the Partido Liberal Constitucionalista had aspired to such a role, as did the Partido Nacional Cooperatista in subsequent years. Both the PLC and the PNC, however, had ended up as vehicles of individual presidential ambitions rather than broad-based parties, and both had therefore disappeared under the Obregón-Calles political machine. Forging a durable national ruling party required uniting the diverse political elements beyond individual ambitions. In particular, such a party would need to unite the foremost groups in the revolutionary political elite. While the disappearance of Calles, Morones, and Obregón as presidential contenders finally made such an ambitious endeavor possible, the evolution of the PNR to a mass-based party was a long-term process. It was not until the late 1930s that the party effectively incorporated the major agrarian and labor movements, as well as the multitude of regional parties.[11]

Most immediately, the PNR needed an organizing committee and a candidate for the 1929 presidential elections. The planning for the new party began at the Mexico City residence of Luis L. León on November 21, 1928, only ten days before Portes Gil's inauguration. Both Calles and Portes Gil attended the meeting, as did several members of the cabinet, governors, and regional strongmen, including Aarón Sáenz Garza (Nuevo León), Bartolomé García

Correa (Yucatán), Pérez Treviño (Coahuila), and Adalberto Tejeda (Veracruz). The meeting produced an organizing committee with Calles as its chair. At the meeting, Calles asked all those in attendance to remain in their respective political offices through November 21, 1929, which barred them from the presidency.[12] This maneuver appeared to clear the way for Sáenz, the former head of Obregón's presidential campaign and the only one present who did not hold political office at that time. In Calles's mind, Sáenz's candidacy would reconcile the *obregonistas* to the existence of a civilian party structure. On December 2, a manifesto published in all major newspapers announced the formation of the PNR and invited all those loyal to the regime to join the new party.[13]

Just three days later, Calles committed a political gaffe that sidelined him from further formal involvement in the party's creation. Sensing the need to shore up *Laborista* support at a moment when the nascent PNR did not include any elements from the CROM or its political wing, the Partido Laborista Mexicano, he attended the ninth annual convention of the CROM in the Teatro Hidalgo in Mexico City. Just after Calles had given a conciliatory speech to the delegates, Morones launched a diatribe against Portes Gil. In particular, the CROM leader attacked the interim president for allowing the performance of a skit titled "El desmoronamiento de Morones" (The Coming Apart of Morones).[14] To Portes Gil and his supporters, Calles was guilty by association. As a result, the former president resigned from the organizing committee. He announced that he would "retire absolutely and definitively from political life and return . . . to the condition of the most obscure citizen who no longer intends to be—nor ever will be again—a political factor in Mexico."[15] In the long run, however, Calles's newest gambit increased his ability to maneuver as a seemingly nonpartisan and impartial senior statesman. His choice of residence reflected his intention of staying close to the center of power; in December 1928, he moved into a new, expensively renovated house in Colonia Anzures, just north of Chapultepec Castle.[16] Hence the popular adage *esta es la casa del presidente / pero él que manda vive enfrente* (this is the house of the president, but the one who rules lives over there).

Without Calles's participation, the organizing committee drafted a program and a set of statutes to be approved at the first PNR convention, scheduled for March 1929 in the city of Querétaro, a symbolic choice as that city had also hosted the Constituyente of 1916–1917. Committee members also traveled throughout the nation to invite the existing parties to apply for PNR affiliation, a status that would allow those parties to send delegates to the Querétaro convention and, hence, wield influence in the choice of the next president. The organizing committee succeeded in incorporating regional parties such as Garrido's Partido Radical Tabasqueño (Radical Tabascan Party), Portes Gil's Partido Socialista Fronterizo (Socialist Party of the Frontier), and the Partido Socialista del Sureste (Socialist Party of the Southeast), founded by Felipe Carrillo Puerto of Yucatán. This process illustrated the top-down nature of the PNR. From the beginning, it became a party controlled and organized by the governing elite.[17]

Reflecting a desire to give broad appeal to the new party, the organizing committee crafted founding documents that invoked the populist rhetoric of Calles's first years as president. As the draft program stated, "the PNR is the instrument of political action by means of which Mexico's great campesino and worker masses fight to keep the control of the public power in their hands; a control wrested from the landowning and privileged minorities through the great armed movement that began in 1910."[18] According to the Declaration of Principles, "the PNR . . . will endeavor to improve the situation of the . . . masses by enforcing Articles 123 and 27 of the constitution, as the party considers the working and campesino classes the most important elements of Mexican society."[19]

As a signal that the Declaration of Principles was not merely political rhetoric, Sáenz failed to obtain the PNR nomination at the Querétaro convention. Although Sáenz enjoyed the right political connections, his political views constituted a liability. A partner of the Calles family in the ownership of the El Mante sugar complex, Sáenz stood on the right of the PNR. His tenure as governor of Nuevo León had been marked by tax cuts, business deregulation, and other measures that favored the state's beer and steel industry. By the time of the convention, Sáenz and General Juan Andreu Almazán were working in tandem to ensure control over government contracts for road building and other infrastructure improvements.[20] For those reasons, Portes Gil and other leaders close to agrarian and labor interests opposed Sáenz's candidacy. This opposition put Calles in a bind, as he had apparently assured Sáenz of his loyalty and support. As a way out, the ex-president let PNR leaders know that he favored the presentation of two candidates at the convention to give the appearance of a democratic process. The second candidate turned out to be the ambassador to Brazil, Pascual Ortiz Rubio, an ex-general who had been out of the country on diplomatic service since 1923. Although a lack of available documentation precludes definitive conclusions on this matter, Ortiz Rubio was likely Calles's handpicked choice. In the end, Sáenz withdrew his candidacy, and Ortiz Rubio easily obtained the nomination.[21] Although Sáenz quickly proclaimed his loyalty to the party despite his defeat, the lasting legacy of the nomination battle was the formation of clientelist factions. In the words of political scientist Luis Javier Garrido, the party operated initially as little more than a "confederation of caciques."[22] In this club, which only imperfectly checked the ambitions of powerful generals, Calles's support for Ortiz Rubio had demonstrated his willingness to jettison allies for his political aims.

The Querétaro convention marked the triumph of Calles's strategy to construct a new political system in which he enjoyed power behind the scenes. One of his most trusted allies, Coahuila governor Manuel Pérez Treviño, became president of the new party, and another *callista*, Luis León, became secretary. Although Veracruz strongman Tejeda—an inveterate supporter of agrarian aims disappointed in the presidential choices—defected from the new party, other *callistas* headed up regional parties within the PNR. In a symbolic move that indicated the true hierarchy within the new party, León assigned Calles the first membership card issued by the PNR.[23]

However, Calles's strategy immediately faced a stern test. On March 3, 1929, the third day of the PNR convention, Pérez Treviño surprised the delegates with the news of a revolt headed by General José Gonzalo Escobar in Sonora. Under the banner of the "Plan of Hermosillo," a group of *obregonista* generals called for the overthrow of the Portes Gil administration as a supposed instrument of Calles. The Plan of Hermosillo dubbed Calles the "Judas of the Mexican Revolution" and accused the former president of waging a corrupt and repressive campaign to impose his will on the republic.[24] The Escobar Rebellion, which ultimately involved 28 percent of the Mexican army, thus primarily constituted an anti-Calles movement. As such, it lacked any ideological orientation. The *escobaristas* included traditional enemies of Calles such as the Yaqui commander and former Maytorena ally Francisco Urbalejo, along with *obregonistas* such as General Escobar himself. The Escobar Rebellion quickly seized the states of Sonora, Durango, Chihuahua, and Veracruz, among others, and it sought to enlist the help of the approximately twenty-five thousand *cristero* guerrillas in central and western Mexico.[25]

Within three months, however, Calles and his allies had vanquished enemies hampered by low-quality leadership and ill-defined political goals. Calles himself commanded the government troops as secretary of war, and he had the benefit of advance warning. Since Obregón's assassination, Calles had suspected prominent *obregonista* generals of plotting a revolt. Founded in 1914 by Carranza and greatly expanded during the Calles presidency, the Oficina de Servicios Confidenciales, or Office of Confidential Services, kept the *jefe máximo* well informed by means of intercepted letters and telegrams. In addition, one of the rebel leaders had made the mistake of inviting a Calles loyalist, General Abelardo Rodríguez, to join the uprising. Bolstered by infusions of weapons and ammunition from the United States, government troops pushed back the *escobaristas*. Focused on taking urban areas, the rebels were unable to coordinate a military strategy with the rural *cristeros*, who preferred to keep their guerrilla war away from the cities.[26]

The end came in Sonora in late May, when Almazán and Cárdenas defeated the last redoubts of the rebellion. The third military revolt against the government since 1920, this rebellion eliminated many of the last recalcitrant *divisionarios*. It left Calles, who himself had used the military to come to power, disgusted with the military officers. In a speech on May 22, 1929, he admitted that the revolution had thus far failed in political terms, and he called for the elimination of the military from political life.[27] Inside, the *jefe máximo* must have felt triumphant, as the defeat of the Escobar Rebellion definitively tipped the scales in favor of the *callistas* over the *obregonistas*.

The Escobar Rebellion highlighted the need for the resolution of the seemingly intractable *cristero* issue. It diverted federal forces from central and western Mexico and allowed the *cristeros* to go on the offensive. In May, a US intelligence report estimated eight thousand *cristeros* in the core area of the rebellion, including five thousand in Jalisco.[28] After the defeat of the Escobar Revolt, Portes Gil therefore began to bring the church to the negotiating table.

This diplomatic effort appeared as early as March 1929, when US Ambassador Dwight Morrow resumed the mediation efforts that had been interrupted by Obregón's assassination. Morrow knew that the clergy desired to resume religious services under a face-saving compromise, and he found Portes Gil more amenable to dialogue with apostolic delegate Leopoldo Ruiz y Flores than Calles had been. While the president would not agree to an amendment of the Calles Law, which required the registration of priests, he informed Morrow and Ruiz y Flores that he did not intend to destroy the Catholic Church. In May, Ruiz y Flores entered into direct negotiations with Portes Gil, and Calles and Morrow served as informal advisers. Morrow even drafted position papers for both sides that served as the basis of discussions.[29] Meanwhile, the army dealt the *cristeros* a crushing defeat in Jalisco, dispersing the rebels to neighboring states.[30]

This combination of diplomacy and military force finally brought the Cristero Rebellion to an end. On June 21, Portes Gil and Ruiz y Flores announced an agreement that ended the church's self-imposed ban on religious services, which had been in effect for almost three years. Although the anticlerical laws remained on the books, church bells once again tolled over Mexico, and soon thereafter, the *cristeros* put down their arms. The fact that Portes Gil had been able to find a solution where Calles had failed highlighted the benefit of the passage of time, which forced the Catholic bishops to come to terms with an anticlerical state they despised, as well as Portes Gil's considerable political stature.[31] Even though the agreement did not imply the conclusion of the church-state conflict, the end of the rebellion gave the government important breathing room at a time when the military budget consumed a third of federal expenditures.[32]

In the second half of 1929—a period that coincided with an extended hiatus in Calles's political role—Portes Gil revived land-reform policies. The trials and tribulations of the year since Obregón's murder had left Calles exhausted, and in July he departed for Paris in order to tend to his health. Portes Gil used the absence of the *jefe máximo* as an opportunity to step up a land-distribution program that had languished during Calles's last years in office. In all, Portes Gil distributed 2.5 million acres of land to more than one hundred thousand households, much of it while Calles was in Paris.[33]

The most significant political event during Calles's absence was the 1929 presidential campaign, an election that Calles had promised would be democratic and fair. In this campaign, PNR candidate Ortiz Rubio confronted José Vasconcelos, the former secretary of education and an opponent of Calles since the de la Huerta rebellion. A lawyer, Vasconcelos had joined Madero's movement in 1909, and he had spent most of the 1910s in the United States. As head of the National University (UNAM) and the Education Secretariat, successively, his ideas had greatly influenced the urban middle class. Vasconcelos promoted the vision of the "cosmic race," the fusion of indigenous and Spanish elements in a Catholic and mestizo identity. He sought to unify the Latin American nations against the United States, which he despised as godless and materialistic. Vasconcelos's ideas had inspired populists such as the Peruvian Víctor Raúl Haya de la Torre, the founder of the populist Alianza Popular Revolucionaria Americana (APRA, or American Popular Revolutionary Alliance). As a presidential candidate, Vasconcelos represented himself as a civilian nationalist who would rescue his country from the generals and the clutches of US imperialism. He also highlighted his intellectual connections to the *indigenismo* movement with references to preconquest mythology. He portrayed himself as a "civilizing Quetzalcóatl," a priest-king who would triumph over the bloodthirsty Huitzilopochtli, the god of war in whose name the Aztec emperors had sacrificed thousands of people. Vasconcelos's candidacy garnered widespread support, particularly among university students.[34]

Vasconcelos's popularity forced the PNR to pull out all the stops to help its colorless and relatively unknown candidate. Ortiz Rubio's presidential bid therefore turned into a marathon to advertise the new party as the authentic heir of the revolution, and the campaign featured six months of almost nonstop travel by the candidate. In this endeavor, Ortiz Rubio held up Calles as the defender of the principles of the revolution. In Tulancingo, Hidalgo, he announced that "Calles and [Portes Gil] are consolidating the conquests of the revolution," and in nearby Necaxa, Puebla, he praised Calles as a "good, sincere man dedicated to the [Mexican] people."[35] This propaganda campaign, however, was not enough, and widespread fraud marred Ortiz Rubio's triumph on November 17, 1929, by the official count of more than 1.8 million votes to 106,000 for his opponent.[36] In large part, this lopsided tally could be attributed to the suppression of the Vasconcelos vote in urban areas. Brutal repression played a role as well, as the killings of sixty *vasconcelistas* in Topilejo on the road from Mexico City to Cuernavaca demonstrated.[37] Ortiz Rubio's triumph marked the true beginning of the *maximato*, as the party (and Calles behind it) overshadowed the incoming president, whom they had helped elect.

The True *Maximato*, 1930–1932

Ortiz Rubio's tenure coincided with the worst years of the Great Depression, which followed the collapse of the stock market on Black Friday, October 29, 1929. The Great Depression led to mass bankruptcies and layoffs throughout the United States and Europe, drastically reducing demand for Mexican raw materials. It also caused the repatriation and deportation of hundreds of thousands of Mexicans and Mexican Americans in the United States, including many US citizens of Mexican descent. These displaced people swelled the ranks of the unemployed, which grew daily due to the lack of demand for Mexican exports. By 1930, Mexico, already hit by the slowdown of the late 1920s, experienced negative economic growth of 4 percent annually. The depression was a daunting challenge for any government—one that decisively contributed to Franklin D. Roosevelt's defeat of US president Herbert Hoover in the 1932 presidential election and the rise and triumph of the Nazi Party in Germany. In Mexico, the crisis led to a plummeting of government revenue, already down 7 percent from the beginning of the Calles presidency. Between the first and last year of Ortiz Rubio's tenure, federal revenue dropped 25 percent in real terms. The crisis was exacerbated by the decline of the peso, a currency buttressed by the country's silver export. While worldwide deflation kept prices in check for those spending dollars, marks, and pounds, Mexicans experienced rising prices for imported goods.[38]

The Great Depression greatly deepened the chasm between the official party rhetoric and Calles's own, increasingly conservative political views. The economic crisis contributed to a steady drift to the right in the political persona of the *jefe máximo*, who increasingly leaned on Ambassador Morrow and US investors in an effort to blunt the impact of the Depression. As a presidential candidate, Calles had wrapped himself in the *zapatista* banner and advocated land reform, and as president, he had confronted the United States in the oil controversy and over Nicaragua. The *jefe máximo*, on the other hand, opposed land reform and forged a cordial relationship with both the Hoover and the Roosevelt administrations. Only in the areas of education and the religious conflict did his rhetoric still resemble the firebrand populism of the early to mid-1920s.[39]

Ortiz Rubio's presidency therefore began under a dark cloud. In an ominous foreboding, the president became the target of an assassination attempt right after his inauguration on February 5, 1930. When the new president's Cadillac left the National Palace that afternoon, gunfire rang out. Of the six shots fired, one hit Ortiz Rubio's wife above the right ear and ricocheted to enter the president's right jawbone. The would-be assassin, twenty-three-year-old Daniel Flores, resisted all methods to make him talk, including torture and a faked shooting of his father. Nonetheless, public opinion implicated Gobernación Secretary Portes Gil and, to a lesser degree, Calles, who had become a default suspect for all politically motivated assassinations.[40] Whatever Flores's motives for the assassination attempt, the incident crippled Ortiz Rubio's resolve to be his own man as president. After his near death, he understandably became tentative and frightful, and his general health deteriorated.[41]

To a significant extent, this tentative demeanor reflected not only Ortiz Rubio's fear of his enemies and the consequences of the Great Depression but also the political weakness of a leader who had spent most of the prior decade as a diplomat in Germany and Brazil. Before taking office, Ortiz Rubio sought to build up a power base of his own, conscious that Calles was still in France. This attempt proved a mistake, as Portes Gil resisted all of Ortiz Rubio's efforts to construct a political base. Upon Calles's return from Paris in December, the partisans of the outgoing and the incoming president threatened to tear asunder the unity of the PNR. *Portesgilistas* and *ortizrubistas* battled over control of congress, a struggle that ended with a narrow victory for the former group and put an effective damper on Ortiz Rubio's power before he had even taken office. The congressional strife also highlighted Calles's prestige as the only leader capable of holding the nation together.[42] This period witnessed the rise of political operators such as Gonzalo N. Santos, who maintained close ties to both Calles's inner circle and the former obregonistas and served as crucial intermediaries between the legislative and executive branches, as well as between Calles and the governors. As a result of the influence of Santos and others, the congressional elections of 1930 swept in an anti–Ortiz Rubio majority. The first congress elected since Obregón's death, it was also the first in which most of the deputies and senators were loyal to Calles.[43]

Ortiz Rubio soon found himself besieged by a constant political crisis that forced him to rely on Calles; indeed, at no time did the *jefe máximo* wield greater influence than during his administration. Whereas Portes Gil had enjoyed a degree of independence from the *jefe máximo*, as witnessed by his revival of the land-distribution program while Calles was in Paris, Ortiz Rubio became forced to rely on Calles. Not only was congress in a defiant mood, but his government also resembled a game of musical chairs. Calles was personally involved in this game: In 1931 alone, he met twice with the cabinet without the president. Three days after the second of these meetings, on October 12, all four divisional generals in the cabinet—Juan Andreu Almazán, Joaquín Amaro, Lázaro Cárdenas, and Abelardo Rodríguez—resigned from their positions. This shakeup weakened not only Ortiz Rubio but also longtime Secretary of War Amaro. Many observers interpreted Calles's hand at work in Amaro's demotion to the directorship of the Colegio Militar, or Military College, a step that helped the *jefe máximo* assure himself of the loyalty of the only institution that could potentially threaten the dominance of the PNR. Indeed, Calles served a third term as secretary of war, which seemed to corroborate the impression that the changes had been designed to get rid of Amaro. In fact, however, Amaro had merely become a coincidental casualty in a larger power struggle. This power struggle also bore the marks of the personal ambitions of three divisional generals who had emerged as significant power brokers: future president Cárdenas, conservative agrarian leader Cedillo, and eventual presidential candidate Almazán. Despite the shakeup, the political crisis continued.[44]

In August 1932, when Ortiz Rubio had served long enough in office that a resignation would not trigger new elections under the constitution, Calles provoked his fall over a hospital-administration scandal that implicated the president's brother. The *jefe máximo* requested that no friend of his serve in the administration, a move that effectively blocked all prominent PNR politicos from service in the Consejo de Ministros. Ortiz Rubio then asked Puig, then chief officer of the Federal District, to draft his resignation letter. On September 4, 1932, three days after giving his last *informe* to congress, the president resigned from office.[45] Calles's heavy hand gave rise to the apocryphal story that Ortiz Rubio opened the newspaper one morning to learn that he had resigned.[46]

The ease with which the *jefe máximo* brought about the president's resignation represents the high-water mark of his influence in politics. Not surprisingly, observers ascribed dictatorial powers to Calles following Ortiz Rubio's removal. As US journalist Anita Brenner wrote:

> For seven years General Plutarco Elías Calles has loomed indestructibly in the Mexican picture, like a Toltec pyramid—huge, harsh, mysterious.

> His name adds naturally to the list of dictatorial gladiators that the world watches with mixed feelings, with its ancient admiration for the strong. He has been called a Mexican Mussolini, an Indian von Hindenburg, a Latin-American Lenin. . . . He plays a mighty game of chess, with other Cabinet Ministers, Generals, and Presidents as his pawns, capital and labor as his knights, and presumably his country as the queen and his own ambition as the king. He plays with calculation, always taking the offensive, against disunited forces moved by fundamental emotions. His favorite strategies are the stolen march and the ambush. The pieces are apt to jump themselves from one side to the other, and the object of the game is power. . . . If he loses, death may take him.[47]

As the Ortiz Rubio presidency illustrated, one important key to the *maximato* lay in Calles's ability to exploit economic difficulties and social unrest in order to sustain a perpetual political crisis that resulted in a high turnover in the Consejo de Ministros and the leadership posts of the PNR. His strategy of dividing the political leadership rested in large part on the fiscal difficulties of the national government and the constant challenges to both federal and state authorities by campesinos and workers unhappy with the broken promises of the revolution.

Yet a careful analysis of the Ortiz Rubio years reveals the limits of the power of the *jefe máximo*, who often followed trends rather than set policy. One good example is Calles's oft-cited 1930 comments discouraging further land distributions. By then, ongoing disputes about *ejido* land, declining productivity, and significant opposition to land reform in many states had convinced many other national politicians to back off the ambitious goal of returning land to the campesinos. That year, Agriculture Secretary, landowner, and Calles confidant Manuel Pérez Treviño seized upon a food crisis in which the volume of production had declined almost 25 percent as a pretext to halt further land distributions.[48] When Ortiz Rubio declared that further expropriations would be paid for in cash, this move effectively ended the land-distribution program, as the government had no such cash. On June 23, 1930, a reporter overheard Calles remarking that the agrarian program was not working and that radical change was necessary. Although food production rebounded the following year, land reform—a significant pillar of the PNR program—languished for the remainder of the Ortiz Rubio administration, a product of circumstance rather than Calles's edict.[49]

Regarding urban labor, the Ortiz Rubio administration showed initiative of its own. After years of relative complacency under Morones, industrial and mine workers once again took to the streets, demanding higher wages to make up for the loss in real income. In the north, the crisis of the mining sector and the influx of returnees from the United States produced a particularly acute situation. In Sonora, the predicament provoked a surge of xenophobia directed at the local Chinese population. When the state government took no steps to protect them, most of the Chinese left the country in fear of their lives. It was therefore not surprising that Ortiz Rubio's greatest achievement was the passage of the Ley Federal del Trabajo (Federal Labor Law) on August 28, 1931. This law expanded the purview of labor unions; it forced midsized firms to allow the establishment of unions; it codified the practice of asking foreign entrepreneurs to forsake the protection of their diplomatic representatives; and it established guidelines for the federal arbitration of labor disputes. Under Ortiz Rubio's direction, this law did not help workers to the extent that it promised, as the federal arbitration board declared most strikes "illicit" in view of the precarious economic situation. Nonetheless, the Labor Law would play an important role in the mass mobilization of the Cárdenas years and hence constituted a step toward the incorporation of the workers into the postrevolutionary state (figure 6.1).[50]

The *Maximato* in Decline, 1932–1934

What later appeared like the sudden demise of the *maximato* at the hands of Cárdenas and his followers constituted the culmination of a gradual process that began during the Rodríguez presidency. Twelve years younger than Calles, Rodríguez belonged to another generation—that of the *cachorros de la revolución*, or "cubs of the revolution." Leaders whose formative political experiences came in the revolution rather than in the *porfiriato*, this generation rose to military rank during the 1910s but did not number among the top brass at the time of the Sonoran triumph in 1920. Rodríguez's first political post came in 1912 as police chief of Nogales, and his opportunity to join the military arrived in March 1913, less than two weeks after the coup of Victoriano Huerta and the assassination of Francisco I. Madero. When the Sonora state government became one of only two to disavow the Huerta coup, Rodríguez joined the state's military forces as a lieutenant. He did not have any significant military victories to his credit but made the crucial decision early on to affiliate with Obregón and participated in the decisive battles of Celaya and León of 1915.

In July 1920, Obregón put Rodríguez in charge of a military expedition to Baja California in order to dislodge a rebel governor, Esteban Cantú. Within weeks, the expedition drove Cantú into exile in Los Angeles, launching Rodríguez on a trip to prosperity unparalleled among the other members of the Sonoran coalition, which had just assumed power at the national level.

Figure 6.2. Mexicans move past the Maximato *as Rodríguez asserts himself against Calles.* Courtesy of Archivo Casasola, Fototeca del INAH.

Over the next decade, Rodríguez became the unchallenged *cacique* of Baja California, and he served as governor from 1923 to 1929, a period longer than that of any other state governor since the beginning of the revolution. On repeated occasions, Rodríguez aided Calles and Obregón in their business endeavors, and in 1924 he gave financial assistance to the federal government in putting down the de la Huerta rebellion, which helped ensure that Calles and Obregón left him in his dual position as governor and military commander. As one US investor opined a few years after his tenure, he was the "best and most efficient governor Baja California has ever had."[51] Baja California had once been a sleepy backwater known only for the Tijuana and Mexicali brothels and casinos that served North Americans escaping the prohibition laws. Soon it became a bustling border state featuring booming fisheries, vineyards, and tourist resorts. Rodríguez himself got in on the act, joining US investors in founding Agua Caliente, the finest casino in Tijuana, and investing in wine making and agriculture.[52] In 1931–1932, he served as undersecretary of war before moving on to positions as secretary of industry, commerce, and labor, and, finally, secretary of war.

Although Rodríguez consistently espoused social reform—and particularly redress for the nation's poorest—he became one of the wealthiest members of the governing elite. He enjoyed close ties to investors in Southern California such as Wirt Bowman. Bowman felt so comfortable around Rodríguez that in October 1932 he wrote to the president in order to recommend the appointment of Abelardo's brother, Fernando, as governor of Baja California. After praising Fernando, he conceded "possibly he may take a few extra drinks like you and I do," in reference to the drinking problem that plagued Rodríguez and many others in the Mexican governing elite.[53]

Rodríguez's trajectory has led one historian to describe his time in power as the *maximato* on autopilot, a time during which Calles enjoyed the luxury of having a trusted friend in office.[54] Indeed, unlike Portes Gil and Ortiz Rubio, Rodríguez was one of Calles's friends and allies—the two even hailed from the same city. Nevertheless, the power of the *jefe máximo* began to dim during Rodríguez's reign. The president turned out to be more independent than Calles had imagined, using his friend's extended absences from the capital to make his own mark. Behind a façade of paying continued homage to Calles, Rodríguez and other politicians increasingly found space to oppose the influence of the *jefe máximo*.[55]

The idea that Calles's behind-the-scenes rule continued unabated during the Rodríguez presidency rests primarily on the continued rituals to honor the *jefe máximo* practiced by both Mexican politicians and US diplomats. On one of his trips to El Tambor, the entire cabinet, as well as several senators, deputies, and diplomats, saw Calles off at the Buenavista train station. The *jefe máximo* undertook the long voyage aboard the presidential train, and the secretary of war accompanied him all the way to Guadalajara.[56] Indeed, the power of the *maximato* rested as much on this exaggerated assumption shared widely by politicians and foreign diplomats as it did on real power. Not surprisingly, Rodríguez sought to install a different culture among his subordinates. In November 1932, he reminded the members of his cabinet of his sole authority over their actions, and ten months later, he stated that he, and not Calles, held the executive power of the nation.[57] In March 1933, he exchanged courteous notes with newly inaugurated US President Roosevelt, a ritual designed to emphasize the fact that Rodríguez was the head of state.[58]

Helped by an improving economic climate, President Rodríguez pledged to renew the reform drive interrupted by the crisis of the Ortiz Rubio years. His government promulgated the Código Agrario, or Agrarian Code, a body of legislation that united the disparate legislation on agricultural matters. He also resumed Portes Gil's effort to distribute hacienda lands to campesinos. Influenced by the new economic theory of John Maynard Keynes, which argued for consumer-driven growth anchored by deficit spending in times of financial and economic crisis, Rodríguez established a minimum wage indexed to the cost of living in each state. Finally, shortly before leaving office, the foundation of Petromex, a private company funded by a state subvention, created the first Mexican oil company large enough to compete with foreign investors and safeguard meeting the domestic demand for oil.[59] Over time, Rodríguez found out that he enjoyed far greater leverage than Ortiz Rubio. Much like Portes Gil, who had enjoyed political leeway when the *maximato* was still under construction and Calles spent five months in Europe, the new president participated in a system of shared government in which Calles played a primary role within the party and Rodríguez ran the executive.[60] Four months after he had taken office, the US military attaché observed that the president "is assuming more and more the responsibilities and decisions, which were formerly left to . . . Calles during the Ortiz Rubio administration" (figure 6.2)[61]

The case of Finance Minister Alberto Pani—a longtime Calles associate—demonstrated the attaché's point. In September 1933, Rodríguez's faith in Keynesian deficit spending (however modest given the situation of the treasury) clashed with Pani's belief in classical liberal economic policies. Moreover, Pani disagreed with the anticlericals in the cabinet over their harsh policy toward the church. The finance minister also made attempts to impede Rodríguez's businesses in Baja California.[62] Ordinarily, the president would have attempted to resolve the differences diplomatically. When Pani attempted to enlist Calles's help, however, Rodríguez asked for the finance minister's resignation. While Calles enjoyed a few leisurely days at a spa in Tehuacán (one owned by Rodríguez and his associates), the president forced Pani to resign, and he informed US Ambassador Josephus Daniels that he was "no Ortiz Rubio."[63]

While Rodríguez strengthened his own political position, Calles spent most of his time outside Mexico City—and some of it quite far away. Between 1932 and 1934, the *jefe máximo* vacationed for months at a time at his daughter Alicia's beach cottage in El Tambor, Sinaloa, and the president's ranch in El Sauzal, Baja California.[64] In El Sauzal, Calles also assisted with the growth of Rodríguez's vineyards, the first in Baja California.[65] Despite constant visits from politicians and diplomats, Calles could not keep close tabs on the political situation in the capital while at his redoubts in northern Mexico. Whenever he needed to be closer to Mexico City, Calles went to his new home in Cuernavaca, Morelos, a beautiful colonial city only one hour south of the capital. Located on what critics knew as "Ali Baba Street" or "Street of the Millionaire Socialist," the house lay among a stretch of palatial homes.[66] With justification, many Mexicans dubbed the wealthy politicos who inhabited those homes "robolucionarios," or robber-revolutionaries.

The travels of the *jefe máximo* owed in part to his deteriorating health. Calles had suffered from a rheumatic ailment since the winter of 1915, when he had

Figure 6.1. Railroad workers, a dynamic sector of the Mexican working class. Courtesy of Archivo Casasola, Fototeca del INAH.

spent many nights outdoors in subfreezing temperatures engaged in his faction's struggle against Pancho Villa and his allies. Over the years, the pain intensified, and Calles visited a variety of physicians in France, Germany, Mexico, and the United States hoping to find a cure. While therapeutic treatments and rest provided relief, the pain came back whenever Calles returned to work. Over the years, severe intermittent colic and insomnia added to these symptoms. It was not until 1932 that Mexican doctors discovered the nature of Calles's illness: a combination of arthritis, atherosclerosis, and chronic irritable bowel syndrome caused by his poor diet. Together, the *jefe máximo*'s ailments were due to far more than the natural aging process, and both the insomnia and the excruciating pain in his legs often forced Calles to the political sidelines. By the time of his diagnosis, when he was only fifty-five years of age, he felt like an old man. Nonetheless, instead of following his physician's advice to consume a low-fat diet rich in grains, fruits, and vegetables, Calles continued to eat meat and eggs and defied his doctor's orders to give up coffee, alcohol, and tobacco.[67] His health, as well as his second wife's succumbing to a brain tumor on November 25, 1932, increasingly distracted him from political issues.[68]

Beset by these personal issues, Calles soon found that the PNR in the Rodríguez era was not as compliant as he might have wished. The *jefe máximo* sponsored two important initiatives: extending the idea of no reelection to all political offices, including legislative seats, and eliminating the regional parties and organizations that made up the PNR. Since the former idea directly challenged the prerogatives of top leaders who represented the party in congress, it encountered considerable opposition among PNR deputies and senators. At an extraordinary party convention in the city of Aguascalientes, the delegates rejected Calles's plan. Nonetheless, the PNR ultimately bowed to the *jefe máximo*'s wishes, primarily because the no-reelection plan had proven to be popular. In March 1933, congress amended the constitution to forbid consecutive reelection at the federal and state levels. This measure strengthened the party by preventing congressional seats from becoming the sinecures of powerful bosses. In December of that year, the second national convention of the PNR in Querétaro ratified Calles's proposal to dissolve the party's constituent organizations. The disappearance of the regional parties and organizations that had once banded together to form the PNR had equivocal results. On the one hand, the reorganization strengthened the party, which boasted 1.3 million members by April 1934; on the other hand, these regional parties "colonized" the national PNR, which found itself unable to enforce its directives at the state level.[69]

The Querétaro convention had an even more important task before itself—one that defined the extent of the power of both Calles and Rodríguez. With presidential elections scheduled for July 1934, the PNR needed to nominate a candidate. By the summer of 1933, two generals loyal to Calles had risen to the top: Manuel Pérez Treviño and Lázaro Cárdenas. Of the two, Pérez Treviño more closely followed Calles's political views, and he had been mentioned as a possible candidate for interim president after the assassination of Obregón. A veteran *obregonista*, former president of the PNR, and a significant player in bringing about the downfall of Ortiz Rubio, Pérez Treviño appeared to enjoy the inside track for the nomination. Rodríguez, however, loathed Pérez Treviño, a former rival for the affections of the woman who was now his wife, and hence supported an alternative. A native of Jiquilpan, Michoacán, Cárdenas appeared as unlikely to break away from Calles's influence as Pérez Treviño did. In 1915, Cárdenas had joined the Constitutionalists, and he soon became an avid supporter of Calles. During the Obregón presidency, Cárdenas first distinguished himself as an able chief of military operations in the Isthmus of Tehuantepec. As governor of Michoacán, he had carried out an ambitious land-reform program that targeted the state's large haciendas, a policy that contrasted with Calles's reluctance to make further land distributions. During the *maximato*, Cárdenas had held various positions in the federal government.[70]

Although Pérez Treviño appeared favored, Calles threw his weight behind Cárdenas several months before the convention. The reasons for Calles's decision remain a subject of debate among historians, but his choice constituted more evidence that he followed rather than directed political currents within the party. Whether he supported Cárdenas following the advice of his son Rodolfo and politicians such as Gonzalo N. Santos, as some evidence suggests; whether he decided on a candidate with excellent ties to labor and campesino organizations to defuse the mounting popular protests of his era; or whether he realized that Pérez Treviño faced insurmountable opposition, he gauged the sentiment in the party and acted accordingly.[71]

At the same PNR convention, Calles suffered a significant setback in the formulation of the party's six-year plan, a setback that again highlighted his gradually declining influence. A Rodríguez loyalist headed the committee in charge of drafting the plan. Supporters of land reform amended the original draft in a direction more acceptable to campesino organizations within the party and less so for Calles, who had declared in 1930 that land redistributions had ended. Bolstered by the new plan, which contained enough guarantees for private property to suit his purposes, Rodríguez used it as his guiding program during his last year in office. Meanwhile, he kept adding to his wealth, moving beyond his base in Baja California to a national entrepreneurial presence. During his presidency, he invested in spas, particularly the famous Garci-Crespo of Tehuacán in the state of Puebla—the very spa that Calles frequented on occasion.[72]

The areas in which Calles continued to make his influence most felt were public education and relations with the church. In 1933, Education Secretary Narciso Bassols, a radical within the PNR and one of Calles's close allies, called for "socialist education" in the public schools. As understood by Bassols (but few others), socialist education constituted an aggressive rejection of religious education rather than the imparting of ideas of social justice, let alone the dialectic materialism taught in Soviet schools. Predictably, socialist education produced an outcry among devout Catholics already upset about a number of provocations at the state level. The Veracruz state government limited the number of priests to one per one hundred thousand inhabitants, and in Tabasco, Governor Garrido's "Red Shirts" staged public burnings of crucifixes and other religious imagery. In May 1934, as tempers flared, Bassols resigned from his post after withdrawing the proposal for sex education. The ongoing debate about public education highlighted the relative weakness of the state more generally and the *jefe máximo* specifically to effect the implementation of government programs at the regional and local levels.[73] The fervor of the debate revealed the importance of education as part of what the Mexican anthropologist Manuel Gamio labeled *forjando patria*, or the forging of the fatherland—an effort that involved the attempted imposition of an official national culture.

As a former schoolteacher, Calles knew that the resolution of the church-state conflict at the political level left the educational realm as the primary area of contest with the church, and he showed that he remained as anticlerical as ever. As he announced in Guadalajara on July 20, 1934, "the revolution is not over . . . It is necessary to enter into a new period, one I would call the period of the psychological revolution. We have to enter and take possession of the conscience of children and youths because they belong and should belong to the revolution. . . . [The revolution must] uproot the prejudices and form the new national soul."[74] As a result of this speech and ongoing efforts in congress to amend Article 3 of the constitution to require socialist education, a second Cristero Rebellion broke out in the fall of 1934. A far cry from the original rebellion, this second uprising by adherents of the Catholic Church nevertheless brought new bloodshed.

Although Calles believed that he could continue his informal role even with Cárdenas in office, the PNR nominee had other ideas. Desirous of achieving even greater independence of action than Rodríguez, Cárdenas embarked on the greatest presidential campaign tour witnessed thus far in Mexico. Between December 1933 and July 1934, he visited every state and every territory, stopping frequently to give campaign speeches and to become acquainted with the people over whom he was to rule. Unlike Calles, Cárdenas relished the opportunity to meet ordinary Mexicans and to listen to their concerns. During the campaign, his ability to connect with people from a variety of social backgrounds on a personal level demonstrated a charismatic personality that could renegotiate the terms that bound him to the party and Calles. Because Cárdenas campaigned practically unopposed—a testament to the incipient strength of the PNR machine—the purpose of this tour was to build an independent political base. Although the candidate gave every indication that he would continue to respect Calles's authority, he was even more determined than Rodríguez to avoid becoming another Ortiz Rubio.

The Rodríguez presidency therefore marked the beginning of the transition to a political landscape without Calles. Without detracting from Cárdenas's considerable political acumen, this analysis of the Rodríguez presidency demonstrates that Cárdenas came to power at an auspicious time. In December 1934, the *jefe máximo* was a tired, sick man older than his years, a survivor of a turbulent quarter century.

Without a doubt, any analysis of the *maximato* begins with Calles as its central figure. Calles met with members of the national government at his convenience, made and unmade governors, and even precipitated the downfall of one president he had picked, Pascual Ortiz Rubio. As the "*jefe máximo* of the Mexican Revolution" and the putative head of the "revolutionary family," Calles became the subject of a significant personality cult.

Nonetheless, the *maximato* was a system of shared governance—a unique political order at a time when authoritarian regimes arose in the rest of Latin America in response to the Great Depression.[75] The *jefe máximo* engaged in a complex interplay with other political agents such as the presidents, the leadership of the party he had helped create, and that party's political base. Rather than a dictator who imposed major policy decisions on weak puppet presidents, he was the arbiter of political life. Through an intricate alliance system that included members of the national government, legislators, the party leadership, and state governors, he undermined politicians he considered either incompetent leaders or unwanted rivals. He was also capable of exerting decisive influence in the executive branch, elections, and congressional debates. But he neither shaped the terms of most debates nor centralized decision making in his own hands. In particular, President Rodríguez made his own mark as a political leader and directed a period during which the *maximato* entered its terminal crisis.

Perhaps most important, neither Calles nor any of the presidents of the *maximato* controlled campesinos and workers the way they had intended. Mexico remained a weak state throughout the 1930s, and the negotiation of power remained fiercely contested at the regional and local levels. When President Cárdenas forged strong new alliances with worker and campesino organizations disaffected with the status quo under the *jefe máximo*, he had found the perfect formula to end the long Obregón-Calles era.

Notes

1. Plutarco Elías Calles, "Informe de gobierno del 10. de septiembre de 1928," in Plutarco Elías Calles, *Declaraciones y discursos políticos* (Mexico City: Cuadernos de causa, 1979), 167–68.
2. Jürgen Buchenau, *The Last Caudillo: Alvaro Obregón and the Mexican Revolution* (Chichester, UK: Wiley Blackwell, 2011).
3. Plutarco Elías Calles, "Informe," 167–68.
4. This attribution of the origin of the term is Abelardo Rodríguez's, in John W. F. Dulles, *Yesterday in Mexico: A Chronicle of the Revolution, 1919–1936* (Austin: University of Texas Press, 1961), 673.
5. See John W. Sherman, *The Mexican Right* (Westport, Conn.: Praeger, 1997), 18–19; Lorenzo Meyer, Rafael Segovia, and Alejandra Lajous, *Historia de la Revolución Mexicana*,

1928–1934: Los inicios de la institucionalización (Mexico City: Colegio de México, 1978); and Lorenzo Meyer, *Historia de la Revolución Mexicana, 1928–1934: El conflicto social y los gobiernos del maximato* (Mexico City: Colegio de México, 1978); Tzvi Medín, *El minimato presidencial: Historia política del maximato* (Mexico City: Era, 1982); and especially Rafael Loyola Díaz, *La crisis Obregón-Calles y el estado mexicano*, 3rd ed. (Mexico City: Siglo XXI, 1987).

6. With the help of new source material, this analysis builds upon my discussion of Calles's role in the *maximato* in Jürgen Buchenau, *Plutarco Elías Calles and the Mexican Revolution* (Lanham, Md.: Rowman and Littlefield, 2007), chap. 6.
7. For the achievements and shortcomings of the Calles administration, see Buchenau, *Calles*, chap. 5.
8. National Archives, College Park, Md. (hereafter NA), RG 165: Records of the War Department General Staff, Military Intelligence Division (hereafter MID), box 1665, 2657-G-657/5, Robert Halpin, G-2 report, Mexico City, Oct. 30, 1928.
9. Meyer et al., *Los inicios de la institucionalización*, 27–28. In his memoirs, Portes Gil claims that Calles did not play much of a role in his selection. Emilio Portes Gil, *Quince años de política mexicana*, 2nd ed. (Mexico City: Ediciones Botas, 1941), 29–30.
10. Alejandra Lajous, *Los orígenes del partido único en México* (Mexico City: UNAM, 1979), 394.
11. Luis Javier Garrido, *El Partido de la Revolución Institucionalizada: La formación del nuevo estado en México (1928–1945)* (Mexico City: Siglo XXI, 1982), 103–232.
12. Luis L. León, *Crónica del poder: En los recuerdos de un político en el México revolucionario* (Mexico City: Fondo de Cultura Económica, 1987), 294–96.
13. *El Universal*, Dec. 2, 1928.
14. *Excélsior*, Dec. 6, 1928; Plutarco Elías Calles, *Pensamiento político y social: Antología, 1913–1936*, ed. Carlos Macías Richard (Mexico City: Fondo de Cultura Económica, 1988).
15. *El Universal*, Dec. 8, 1928. The text can also be found in Fideicomiso Archivos Plutarco Elías Calles y Fernando Torreblanca (hereafter FAPEC), Archivo Plutarco Elías Calles (hereafter APEC), gav. 21, exp. 28, "Declaraciones del General Plutarco Elías Calles."
16. FAPEC, Fondo Plutarco Elías Calles (hereafter FPEC), serie 010901, exp. 23, inv. 658, "Casa de Anzures. Menaje de casa."
17. Garrido, *El Partido de la Revolución Institucionalizada*, 99–102.
18. FAPEC, FPEC, serie 010801, exp. 6, inv. 393, "Programa de Trabajo del PNR," vol. 1.
19. Quoted in Meyer et al., *Los inicios de la institucionalización*, 47.
20. Alex M. Saragoza, *The Monterrey Elite and the Mexican State* (Austin: University of Texas Press, 1988), 120–25.
21. Meyer et al., *Los inicios de la institucionalización*, 59–63.
22. Garrido, *El Partido de la Revolución Institucionalizada*, 103.
23. APEC, FPEC, serie 010100, exp. 12, inv. 12, Luis León to Calles, July 24, 1929.

24. Quoted in Lajous, *Los orígenes del partido único*, 55.
25. NA, MID, box 1665, 2657-G-657/8 and 11, G-2 reports, Mexico City, Feb. 21 and Mar. 5, 1929.
26. FAPEC, FPEC, serie 010802, exp. 1, inv. 395, "Rebelión Escobarista;" Joseph A. Stout Jr., *Spies, Politics and Power: El Departamento Confidencial en Mexico, 1922–1946*. (Fort Worth: Texas Christian University Press, 2012).
27. Elías Calles, *Pensamiento político y social*, 286–92.
28. NA, MID, box 1664, 2657-G-616/26, Gordon Johnston, G-2 report, May 8, 1929.
29. Amherst College, Dwight Morrow papers, series X, reel 17, Morrow, draft statements for Ruiz and Portes Gil, May 11 and June 13, 1929.
30. NA, MID, box 1664, 2657-G-616/30, Gordon Johnston, G-2 report, June 25, 1929.
31. NA, MID, box 1664, 2657-G-616/31, Gordon Johnston, G-2 report, July 3, 1929; David C. Bailey, *Viva Cristo Rey: The Cristero Rebellion and the Church-State Conflict* (Austin: University of Texas Press, 1974), 255.
32. Nacional Financiera, *Statistics on the Mexican Economy* (Mexico City: Nacional Financiera, 1977), 358.
33. Dulles, *Yesterday in Mexico*, 479.
34. John Skirius, *José Vasconcelos y la cruzada de 1929* (Mexico City: Siglo XXI, 1978).
35. FAPEC, APEC, gav. 58, exp. 51, inv. 4239, "Ortiz Rubio, Pascual (Ing.)," vol. 1.
36. Garrido, *El Partido de la Revolución Institucionalizada*, 110.
37. Alfonso Taracena, *Los vasconcelistas sacrificados en Topilejo* (Mexico City: Editora Librera, 1958).
38. Haber, *Industry and Underdevelopment*, 149–70; Nacional Financiera, Statistics on the Mexican Economy, 351.
39. Interview with Portes Gil in James W. Wilkie and Edna Monzón de Wilkie, *México visto en el siglo XX: Entrevistas de historia oral* (Mexico City: Instituto Mexicano de Investigaciones Económicas, 1969), 540–41; James W. Wilkie, *The Mexican Revolution: Federal Expenditure and Social Change since 1910* (Berkeley: University of California Press, 1970), 66–67.
40. Dulles, *Yesterday in Mexico*, 481–87; Pascual Ortiz Rubio, *Memorias, 1925–1928* (Morelia: Universidad Michoacana de San Nicolás, 1981), 215.
41. NA, MID, box 1664, 2657-G-605/328, Robert G. Cummings, G-2 Report, Mexico City, Sep. 13, 1932.
42. Meyer et al., *Los inicios de la institucionalización*, 105–45.
43. Gonzalo N. Santos, *Memorias*, 4th ed. (Mexico City: Grijalbo, 1986), 389–511.
44. APEC, FPEC, serie 010100, exp. 13, inv. 13, "Secretario de Estado Encargado del Despacho de Guerra y Marina," acta de nombramiento, Pascual Ortiz Rubio; Martha Beatriz Loyo Camacho, *Joaquín Amaro y el proceso de institucionalización del ejército mexicano, 1917–1931* (Mexico City: UNAM, 2003), 173–76; NA, MID, box 1664, 2657-G-605/314, G-2 report, Mexico City, Dec. 31, 1931.

45. Dulles, *Yesterday in Mexico*, 533–40; NA, MID, box 1664, 2657-G-605/329, Robert E. Cummings, G-2 Report, Mexico City, Sept. 5, 1932.

46. Michael C. Meyer, William L. Sherman, and Susan M. Deeds, *The Course of Mexican History*, 7th ed. (New York: Oxford University Press, 2003), 570. Another textbook correctly points out that this story is a "joke" or "legend." Douglas W. Richmond, *The Mexican Nation: Historical Continuity and Modern Change* (Upper Saddle River, N.J.: Prentice Hall, 2002), 271.

47. Anita Brenner, "Again General Calles Shows His Hand: Stern and Decisive, the Strong Man of Mexico Plays the Role of Dictator and Makes and Unmakes Presidents," *New York Times Magazine*, Sept. 18, 1932, 6–8.

48. Nacional Financiera, *Statistics on the Mexican Economy*, 107.

49. NA, MID, box 1662, 2657-G-561/10–12, Gordon Johnston, G-2 reports, Mexico City, Feb. 21 and June 6, 1930, and "Memorandum on the Mexican Agrarian Situation," Sept. 30, 1930.

50. Meyer, *El conflicto social*, 148–54.

51. Universidad Autónoma de Baja California, Tijuana, Baja California, Archivo General Abelardo L. Rodríguez (hereafter AGALR), Presidencia de la República, "Evans, W. B.," San Ysidro, Calif., Sept. 6, 1932.

52. José Alfredo Gómez Estrada, *Gobierno y casinos: El origen de la riqueza de Abelardo L. Rodríguez* (Mexicali: Universidad Autónoma de Baja California, 2002).

53. AGALR, Presidencia de la República, "Bowman, Wirt," Bowman to Rodríguez, Tijuana, Oct. 24, 1932.

54. See, for example, Meyer et al., *Los inicios de la institucionalización*, 158–87.

55. See also Barbara A. Kuzio, "President Abelardo Rodríguez (1932–34): From Maximato to Cardenismo" (master's thesis, Portland State University, 1996). Kuzio's thesis is based only on US archival sources.

56. NA, RG 59, 812.00/30040, Daniels to Secretary of State, Apr. 17, 1934.

57. Francisco J. Gaxiola, *El Presidente Rodríguez (1932–1934)* (Mexico City: Editorial Cultura, 1938), 94–96, 120.

58. AGALR, Presidencia de la República, Franklin D. Roosevelt to Rodríguez, Mar. 17, 1933.

59. Meyer et al., *Los inicios de la institucionalización*, 163–65.

60. Dulles, *Yesterday in Mexico*, 573.

61. NA, RG 59, 812.00/29828, Robert Cummings, G-2 Report, January 1933.

62. AGALR, Presidencia de la República, 325.81/61, Marte Gómez to Secretario de Hacienda, Sept. 30, 1932.

63. NA, RG 59, 812.00/29926, Daniels to Secretary of State, Sept. 29, 1933.

64. FAPEC, APEC, gav. 66, exp. 189, inv. 5010, Calles to Rodríguez, El Sauzal, Baja California, Mar. 29, 1933.

65. AGALR, Presidencia de la República, exp. 325.81/44; Plutarco Elías Calles to Abelardo L. Rodríguez, El Sauzal, Apr. 15, 1933.

66. For these terms, see Josephus Daniels, *Shirt-Sleeve Diplomat* (Chapel Hill: University of North Carolina Press, 1947), 60.

67. APEC, FPEC, serie 010901, exp. 46, inv. 681, "Elías Calles, Plutarco (Gral.), Reportes Médicos."

68. APEC, FPEC, serie 010901, exp. 32, inv. 667, "Elías Calles, Leonor. Datos clínicos."

69. Meyer et al., *Los inicios de la institucionalización*, 184–87; Garrido, *El Partido de la Revolución Institucionalizada*, 158–59.

70. Enrique Guerra Manzo, "La gubernatura de Lázaro Cárdenas en Michoacán (1928–1932): Una vía agrarista moderada," *Secuencia* 45 (September 1999): 131.

71. Arnaldo Córdova, *La política de masas del cardenismo* (Mexico City: Ediciones Era, 1974), 16–36.

72. Garrido, *Partido de la Revolución Institucionalizada*, 156–57; Abelardo L. Rodríguez, "A qué debe tender el plan de los seis años," *Del México actual* 11 (1933): 10; APEC, Archivo Abelardo L. Rodríguez (hereafter AALR), Presidencia de la República, Antonio Juárez to Rodríguez, El Riego, Pue., Nov. 11, 1933.

73. FAPEC, FPEC, serie 010806, exp. 44, inv. 624, "Papa Pío XI"; Dulles, *Yesterday in Mexico*, 560–61; Mary Kay Vaughan, *Cultural Politics in Revolution* (Tucson: University of Arizona Press, 1998), 77–136.

74. Quoted in Meyer et al., *Los inicios de la institucionalización*, 178.

75. Arnaldo Córdova, *La Revolución en crisis: La aventura del maximato* (Mexico City: Cal y Arena, 1995).

CHAPTER 7

Revolution without Resonance?

Mexico's "Fiesta of Bullets" and Its Aftermath in Chiapas, 1910–1940

Stephen E. Lewis

At first blush, a reassessment of the Mexican Revolution in the impoverished southern state of Chiapas would seem to be a dry, rather pointless exercise. After all, Chiapas has been geographically and politically marginal to Mexico for most of its existence. During the violent decade of 1910–1920, Chiapas was relatively calm for the first four years. When the revolution finally came to the state, it triggered very little of the popular mobilization experienced elsewhere in Mexico. When the fighting began to die down in 1920, the victors in Chiapas were not the colorful rebels celebrated in *corridos* and the mural art and film of the 1920s and 1930s but precisely those forces that *resisted* revolutionary reforms and reformers. Indeed, it was common throughout the twentieth century for historians, politicians, teachers, and others to remark—with some justification—that the revolution never arrived in Chiapas.

However, if we consider the Mexican Revolution as a thirty-year process, with the decade of violent destruction followed by two critical decades of postrevolutionary reconstruction, Chiapas becomes the ideal laboratory for the study of revolutionary actors, institutions, and outcomes. For precisely the reasons mentioned earlier—the state's geographic location, its marginalized, diverse, and impoverished population, its defiant and fiercely independent ruling class—Chiapas challenged revolutionary and postrevolutionary state and nation builders as much as any other Mexican state. This chapter explores four deceptively simple questions: Was there a revolution in Chiapas, a period of reforms, or neither? How did Mexico's "fiesta of bullets" and its aftermath affect ordinary *chiapanecos*? How successful was the postrevolutionary state at forging more secular, sober, modern Mexican citizens? Finally, just how important is the Mexican Revolution to the history of modern Chiapas?

Imported Revolution, Homegrown Reaction

On paper, at least, Chiapas was ripe for revolutionary violence in 1910. During the course of the nineteenth century, most indigenous people in the state lost their ancestral land due to various liberal land grabs and led precarious, miserable lives. Porfirian governors created an elaborate tax code meant to drive indigenous workers into the wage economy. Debt-labor contractors representing lowland planters "hooked" other indigenous workers into seasonal contracts through a process known as *enganche*. Most major plantations and ranches in the state featured company stores called *tiendas de raya*, as well as private, subterranean jails, and the owners' will was the law of the land.[1]

But the history of Chiapas suggests that misery and abject poverty do not necessarily a revolution make.[2] In 1911, just as the violence began to spread elsewhere in Mexico, ladinos (non-Indians) in highland Chiapas turned to the highland Maya as part of their interminable rivalry with lowland ladinos. Many of the indigenous people mobilized for war, led by Jacinto Pérez, a Chamula also known as El Pajarito. Once El Pajarito's movement got rolling, however, ladinos on both sides of the conflict (including the instigators) decided that mobilized Indians represented a greater threat than their ladino foes. The ladinos closed ranks and crushed El Pajarito's forces with the help of the federal army. For the next three years, while much of Mexico tore itself to pieces, there was no popular mobilization in Chiapas because the state's ladino ranchers and planters, whatever their differences, united in their fear that renewed violence would trigger a race war that might sweep them away.[3]

Chiapas remained calm until late 1914, when a Constitutionalist army led by Jesús Agustín Castro entered the state and imposed a series of reforms at gunpoint. Castro's most significant reform was his October 1914 Workers' Law (Ley de Obreros, also known as the Ley de Liberación de Mozos, or Peon Liberation Law). It represented the first federal attempt to regulate labor in Chiapas by ending debt peonage, *enganche*, and the *tiendas de raya*. The law also set minimum wages according to occupation and geographic location and created a corps of labor inspectors. It established rudimentary accident and disability insurance for workers, set a ten-hour day, and stipulated, vaguely, that rural proprietors establish schools for the children of their workers.[4] Two months later, Castro passed an anticlerical law that prohibited confession, legalized divorce, closed convents, restricted the celebration of mass to once a week, and confiscated all church property. A firm believer in central government, Castro intended to liberate the masses of mestizo and indigenous peasants and workers from the priests, *finqueros* (plantation owners), and ranchers, who had previously controlled their lives.[5]

Not surprisingly, these laws enraged the Catholic Church and many of the state's planters and ranchers, and soon they organized a resistance. Lowland ranchers and planters who called themselves Mapaches (raccoons) were led by a young law student named Tiburcio Fernández Ruiz. The Mapaches made common cause with their erstwhile enemies, the highland ladinos, led by Alberto Pineda. They fought the invading army to a draw over the course of the next six years. In this hard-fought civil war of attrition, the warring parties took pains not to mobilize Chiapas's rural masses, especially Indians. According to Jan Rus, the highland ladinos' political mutiny of 1911 had already been recast as a menacing Indian uprising, a "cautionary tale about the dangers of mobilizing and arming the 'semi-savage' Maya peasants."[6] Many highland Maya communities were caught between the *pinedistas* and the Constitutionalists. They were often pressed into service as guides, load bearers, cooks, and servants but only rarely as soldiers. According to Miguel Ordóñez, a Tzeltal from Cancuc, the Constitutionalists took men not to fight ("*tirar bala*") but rather "to care for the generals' women, to care for the horses and kill the bulls that the generals ate."[7]

For indigenous people, this hardly amounted to a revolution. Actively discouraged from taking a more direct role in the conflict, they still suffered its consequences as the warring parties passed through their towns and fields, wreaking havoc and destruction, stealing money, corn, chickens, and sheep, and raping and murdering at will.[8] The bloodletting abated somewhat in 1920, when Mexican president Venustiano Carranza's erstwhile right-hand man, Álvaro Obregón, rose against him in rebellion. The *obregonistas* made common cause with the Mapache resistance in Chiapas. Once Carranza's government fell, the Mapaches suddenly found themselves in control of Chiapas, and the Mapache leader, Tiburcio Fernández Ruiz, became state governor.

During the revolution's violent decade, most of Mexico experienced mass mobilizations that swept away or at least significantly altered the old political, economic, and social order. The popular character of the uprising left its mark on the 1917 constitution. This charter, which made provision for sweeping land reform, labor reform, and free, secular education, among other things, was arguably the most progressive in the world. In Chiapas, however, local counterrevolutionaries prevailed over those who had tried to impose a reform agenda from Mexico City. Governor Fernández Ruiz and other state politicians were subsequently able to blunt the reforms built into the document. To quote historian Thomas Benjamin, "Mapache reconstruction in the area of labor and agrarian reform was exactly that—the reconstruction or restoration of the Porfirian social order as much as possible."[9]

Chiapas marched to its own drummer until the mid-1930s. The state's politicians were either unwilling or unable to implement the reforms that most historians associate with the Mexican Revolution, and presidents Álvaro Obregón (1920–1924), Plutarco Elías Calles (1924–1928), and the three men who served at Calles's pleasure from 1928 to 1934 had little interest in compelling Chiapas to comply. Obregón's land-reform program targeted areas that had suffered significant rural violence during the revolution's destructive stage, especially Morelos and Chihuahua, but otherwise protected large haciendas; Calles eventually withdrew his support from land reform altogether and controlled labor through his domination of the Mexican state's official labor confederation, the Regional Confederation of Mexican Workers, or CROM.[10] Among the major reforms enshrined in the 1917 constitution, only Article 3, which promised free, secular education for all, was consistently supported at the federal level during the early postrevolutionary period. In Chiapas, however, even this modest effort to build schools, train teachers, teach literacy, and promote Mexican national unity rarely enjoyed the support of the state's political class.

Obregón created Mexico's Ministry of Public Education, or Secretaría de Educación Pública (SEP), in 1921, as soon as the revolutionary dust began to settle. The SEP expected federal teachers to teach literacy and other basic skills, of course, but it also charged instructors with "forging the fatherland" in unsettled, war-torn regions where armed locals demanded resolution of their long-standing grievances and where powerful governors, *caciques*, ranchers, and planters resisted federal intervention. In rural Chiapas, federal teachers served as "shock troops" by introducing federal reforms and institutions while also challenging local power brokers.

But the odds were certainly stacked against their success. The SEP was a fledgling, untested federal institution in the 1920s and early 1930s, and rural Chiapas was often a rough-and-tumble place ill suited for building schools. Lukewarm or nonexistent community support, as well as ethnic tensions, also vexed the SEP's teachers, who tended to be ladinos (non-Indians) who were monolingual in Spanish. Even under the best of circumstances, many teachers lacked the basic skills and training to succeed. The SEP was postrevolutionary Mexico's most important agent of social engineering, but in states like Chiapas, its impact in the 1920s and early 1930s rarely lived up to the lofty rhetoric of its directors in Mexico City (figure 7.1).

The SEP's shortcomings became especially glaring in indigenous communities. Its inspectors and teachers in Chiapas were unable and often unwilling to confront the structures and institutions that profited from the exploitation of

Figure 7.1. SEP rural schools were expected to have a theater (teatro escolar) *to stage patriotic celebrations and performances, but few communities in Chiapas had the resources to build one.* Courtesy of Archivo Histórico de la Secretaría de Educación Pública, México, D.F.

the indigenous people. In 1928, federal education inspector Eduardo Zarza enumerated the staggering political, economic, and cultural obstacles to SEP programs in the indigenous highlands:

> The following factors hinder, stagnate, and retard the progress of the schools and the effective involvement of the communities: enganche, which depopulates entire regions . . . the tenacious resistance of parents to send their children to schools; the indifference with which the municipal authorities in the pueblos, with few exceptions, view the schools sustained by the Federation . . . the economic state of the pueblos, which obliges many parents to submit their children to the tyranny of servitude; the dispersed settlement patterns of the inhabitants in indigenous regions, who live an autonomous and obscure life; the unrestricted use of alcohol; the lack of roads . . . which keeps pueblos largely incommunicado and makes commercial activity difficult and products costly; the participation of mestizos in governing indigenous pueblos, the former exploiting the latter due to their ignorance, to the point where parents pay them to keep their children out of school; the lack of hygiene and cleanliness which afflicts entire commu-

nities, causing epidemics that decimate their inhabitants; and other factors that one could mention.[11]

Into the 1930s, Chiapas was a state still characterized more by Porfirian continuity than by revolutionary change. Indigenous debt peonage continued to be practiced widely, even though it had been banned by the Constitution of 1917. The *tienda de raya* had also been outlawed by the constitution, but every major plantation in Chiapas had one. Land reform had been blocked. Ladino hoarders (*acaparadores*), operating with the blessing of the local authorities, installed themselves at the gates of San Cristóbal de Las Casas and commandeered indigenous goods at a fraction of their market value. Indian sellers who refused to go along with this scheme were often beaten and thrown in jail by municipal police. (This practice persisted into the 1960s, as illustrated by Rosario Castellanos's short story "Modesta Gómez," which she based on contemporary sources.[12]) Indians found in San Cristóbal after dark were arrested for "public scandals" (*escándalos en vía pública*) or alleged drunkenness. They were freed the next day but only after cleaning city streets and plazas.[13] As late as 1934, the reforms that we tend to associate with the Mexican Revolution had had no appreciable impact on the lives of the vast majority of *chiapanecos*.

Imported Revolution, Homegrown Reaction, Take Two

During the mid-1930s, authorities in Mexico City launched a second major effort to bring the revolution to Chiapas. Many historians believe that if a genuine revolution took place at all in Mexico, it happened during the six-year presidency of Lázaro Cárdenas (1934–1940). During the Cárdenas years, the SEP renewed its efforts to bring free, secular, primary schooling to all Mexicans, thereby at least partly meeting the promise enshrined in Article 3 of the constitution. In fulfillment of Article 27, the federal government redistributed roughly 48 million acres of land and recovered oil fields from US and British oil companies. The Cárdenas administration also sided with labor in most of its disputes with capital, upholding the spirit of Article 123. Cárdenas himself took special interest in the plight of Mexico's indigenous population and became the country's first (and only) self-declared *indigenista* president. Some argue that the Cárdenas administration was not in fact *revolutionary* because it merely upheld the terms of a constitution that had been written twenty years earlier. Nonetheless, it is also true that no Mexican president had done more for the downtrodden than Cárdenas, and because his successors after 1940 were generally uninterested in the plight of peasants, workers, and indigenous people, the Cárdenas presidency looms large as the apotheosis of the Mexican Revolution.

So, how did the *cardenista* agenda fare in Chiapas? Much of it hinged on federal teachers. Their grassroots efforts largely determined whether the communities they served would benefit from the land and labor reforms that Cárdenas brought to the state in the late 1930s. In December 1934, just as Cárdenas assumed office, Article 3 of the 1917 constitution was rewritten to stipulate that federal education "will be socialist and, besides excluding all religious doctrine, will combat religious fanaticism and prejudice."[14] Even if the meaning of socialist education was never very clear, a radicalized SEP worked with a populist federal government to lay the foundation for the modern Mexican nation-state during the Cárdenas years.[15]

Socialist education in Chiapas manifested itself through a variety of state- and nation-building campaigns. The SEP expected teachers to promote agrarian reform, enforce compliance with federal labor laws, unionize peasants and workers, and combat local exploiters like *enganchadores* and alcohol sellers. They were also expected to forge more secular, more sober, and healthier Mexican citizens. The ministry's textbooks became quite radical in the mid-1930s, celebrating mass mobilization, patriotism, and the class struggle. The SEP also aimed to substitute the cult of the saints with the cult of the state. In Chiapas, federal educators tried to supplant the sacred calendar, with its countless religious feast days, with a secular calendar featuring forty secular holidays honoring civic heroes, inventors, and important events like the massacre of workers at Río Blanco, Veracruz, in 1907, and France's Bastille Day.[16] The SEP's radicalized state- and nation-building project sparked fierce resistance from planters, ranchers, the Catholic Church, alcohol merchants, and the state governor. However, it won the acceptance, if not the full support, of mestizo communities that had previously regarded SEP schools with indifference.[17]

The fate of socialist education (and the entire *cardenista* project) rested largely on regional factors. Chiapas has a diverse topography, with peaks and valleys, pine forests, rain forests, jungles, and coastal plains. Several distinct indigenous ethnic groups live in the higher elevations and in the steamy lowland jungles and rain forests in eastern Chiapas. In very general terms, the indigenous people worked small plots of land and supplemented their incomes with seasonal stints on lowland plantations. Ladinos inhabited the valleys and coastal areas and were typically engaged in plantation agriculture. Due to space limitations, the following discussion of the fate of socialist education focuses on two strikingly distinct settings: the predominately indigenous highlands and the mostly ladino coastal lowlands (map 7.1).

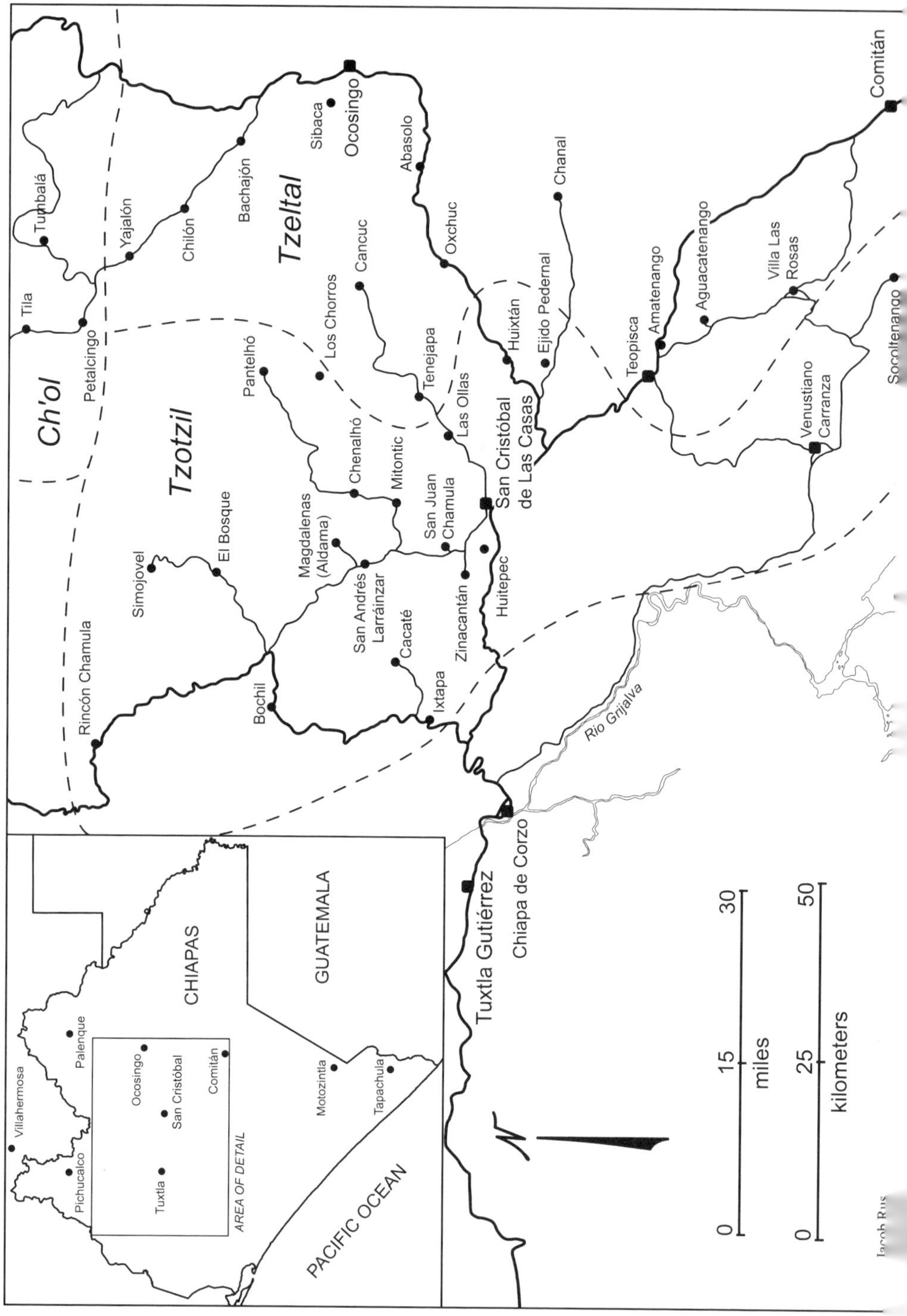
Ch'ol
Tzotzil
Tzeltal
Tila
Tumbalá
Petalcingo
Yajalón
Chilón
Bachajón
Sibaca
Ocosingo
Abasolo
Chanal
Oxchuc
Cancuc
Los Chorros
Pantelhó
Tenejapa
Huixtán
Ejido Pedernal
Las Ollas
Chenalhó
Mitontic
San Cristóbal de Las Casas
San Juan Chamula
Magdalenas (Aldama)
El Bosque
Simojovel
Rincón Chamula
San Andrés Larráinzar
Zinacantán
Huitepec
Cacaté
Ixtapa
Bochil
Teopisca
Amatenango
Aguacatenango
Villa Las Rosas
Venustiano Carranza
Socoltenango
Comitán
Río Grijalva
Chiapa de Corzo
Tuxtla Gutiérrez
0
15
30
miles
0
25
50
kilometers
N
CHIAPAS
GUATEMALA
PACIFIC OCEAN
AREA OF DETAIL
Villahermosa
Pichucalco
Palenque
Ocosingo
San Cristóbal
Tuxtla
Comitán
Motozintla
Tapachula

When Manuel Castellanos became education inspector of Chiapas's fifth zone in January 1935, he assumed administrative control of a vast area encompassing the central highlands and the lowlands of eastern Chiapas. The SEP barely had a foothold in the region. According to Castellanos, its schools and teachers were under siege by those who felt threatened by federal education's expanded social mandate:

> As enemies of the redemption of the Indian we have entire communities of landowners and their agents, manufacturers and sellers of *aguardiente* [cane liquor], and secretaries and municipal agents, who on some occasions are the instruments of the exploiters. Until now the Indian problem remains intact and insoluble . . . which is shameful for our country and represents a negation of revolutionary principles.[18]

Teachers were routinely threatened, beaten, shot at, and hauled to court, and schoolrooms were burned to the ground with some regularity. But Castellanos fought back with every means at his disposal. Backed by a reinvigorated SEP, Castellanos launched the first real challenge to the institutions of indigenous exploitation in the highlands.

Castellanos's achievements during his first year as inspector were impressive, as he labored tirelessly to improve school infrastructure. He inherited twenty-seven schools; seven months later, there were forty-four schools. While only sixteen of the schools were housed in buildings in January 1935, indigenous villagers had built thirty-four one-room schoolhouses—with woven-straw roofs and walls of mud and sticks—by July. During that same period the number of pit toilets jumped from three to thirty-four. The number of athletic fields more than doubled; the number of desks and benches almost tripled.[19]

Once the basic infrastructure was in place, schools in Castellanos's zone launched the first major public health campaigns seen in the region. In July and August 1935, teachers and local education-committee members shaved, deloused, and cleaned 687 indigenous children. Children and adults alike were vaccinated against smallpox in thirty-two communities, and campaigns against typhoid fever and malaria were conducted in every community where there was a school. All of the schools in Castellanos's zone had anti-alcohol committees, although Castellanos admitted that little could be done after they had been established since "the *alcoholeros* enjoy more guarantees and official support than the teachers."[20]

Castellanos then began attacking *enganche*, which instantly put him and his teachers at odds with local officials. As he told it, "The authorities are paid by the *enganchadores* and *alcoholeros* to help recruit people to go to the coffee plantations. For this reason they are from day one the determined enemy of the teacher who combats this kind of exploitation."[21] Castellanos also intervened to jump-start the federal agrarian-reform program, which had been stalled on all fronts in Chiapas, especially in the highlands. "This revolutionary promise has greatly disappointed the *campesinos*," he wrote, "with the exception of a few places where with a thousand sacrifices agrarian colonies and centers have been established." Indians had been swindled by unscrupulous agrarian-reform engineers or had been forcibly removed from lands they were soliciting. Others had been persecuted, incarcerated, and even assassinated, "all so that the campesinos might renounce the just rights that the Revolution has conquered for them and return to being submissive and resigned . . . to the yolk of servitude."[22] Given this degree of resistance, Castellanos managed to establish only a handful of agrarian committees. When major land reform finally came to Chiapas in the late 1930s, its effect was negligible in the highlands.

By early 1937, two years after he assumed his post, Castellanos began showing signs of disillusionment. His condemnations of ladino *enganchadores* and alcohol merchants are reminiscent of the reports he submitted two years earlier. However, his reports also suggest a flagging faith in the indigenous population. Gone was the sympathetic rhetoric of class exploitation, which was replaced by the familiar, denigrating language of civilization and barbarism. "They are excessively dirty since they never bathe themselves voluntarily," he wrote. "They do not cut their hair, and they neither wash nor change their clothes until they disintegrate. They believe blindly in their 'witches,' and their customs are truly savage."[23] Castellanos had been defeated, and so had socialist education in highland Chiapas. Faced with insurmountable political and cultural obstacles, SEP educators had been unable to introduce agrarian or labor reforms. Their efforts to promote sobriety, nationalism, and secular lifestyles had also failed. By the time *cardenismo* finally reached highland Chiapas, the SEP was already in willful retreat (map 7.2).

The panorama was more uplifting on Chiapas's Pacific Coast and particularly in the southern region, known as Soconusco. Here, Mexican and foreign investors had established coffee plantations beginning in the late nineteenth century. Article 123 of the 1917 constitution required rural proprietors to provide schools for the school-aged children of their workers. In the 1920s, the state government administered these schools. Very few were actually established, given the proclivities of the state government and the strength and economic clout of Chiapas's plantocracy. However, in January 1934, administration of these schools passed to the federal SEP; later that year, the SEP adopted socialist education. Efforts to force compliance with Article 123 therefore coincided

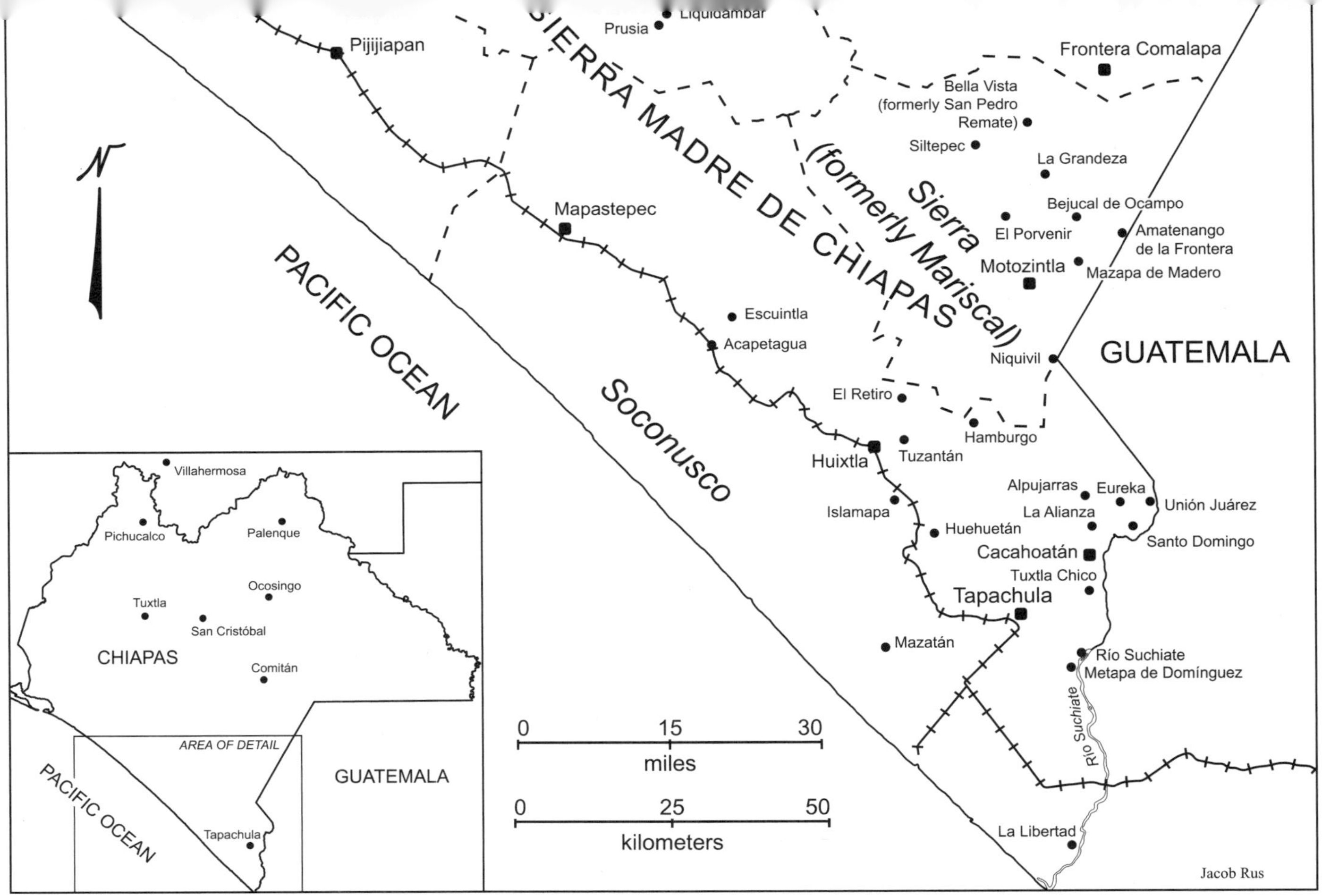

Map 7.2. Southern Chiapas, including Soconusco. Courtesy of Jacob Rus.

with the radicalization of the SEP and its teachers. Rural elites, who already resented the minimal costs associated with sustaining schools, reacted viscerally to the federalized Article 123 schools, which they rightly feared to be hotbeds of social mobilization.

For the federal government, the Article 123 schools represented the most direct means of intervening in the lives of workers on Chiapas's plantations. Teachers were expected to build a rural constituency *and* check the power of the state's planter and rancher class. Naturally, landowners resented the intrusion of a federal entity bent on scrutinizing labor practices, promoting federal unionization and agrarian reform, and monitoring the quality of life on their *fincas*. Article 123 teachers therefore found themselves in an unenviable position. Charged with implementing an ambitious social program and winning the sympathies of the workers, they still needed to draw their salaries from hostile planters.

Most planters initially resisted the Article 123 schools on legal grounds. The entire project derived from one sentence found in the revised Federal Labor Law (Ley Federal del Trabajo), which required proprietors to "establish and sustain elementary schools on behalf of their workers' children when their land is situated more than three kilometers from population centers, and only when the number of school-aged children exceeds twenty."[24] Recalcitrant planters and their lawyers scrutinized this sentence and subjected every word to rigorous analysis in search of loopholes. The ministry's attempts to force compliance through fines and threats of property confiscation were frequently met with well-prepared legal appeals. Many planters used their influence or bought off local authorities to evade payment. The education inspector from Comitán, P. Arturo Mota, complained that the SEP's fines had little effect on the *finqueros* and never resulted in the prompt payment of teachers' salaries. "The directors of the Public Credit Offices [Hacienda] do not initiate legal action so as to avoid difficulties with the planters, many of whom are the directors' friends or relatives," he noted. The SEP was equally frustrated in Soconusco. In 1936, Chiapas's director of federal education, Rafael Bolio Yenro, wrote that the toothless fines of the SEP had the same effect on the *finqueros* "as the League of Nations' sanctions have against the dictator Mussolini."[25]

Why were the plantation owners so determined to undermine the Article 123 schools? Simply put, the teachers became successful grassroots organizers. After the March 1934 federal Agrarian Code accorded resident debt peons the right to petition for land reform, teachers in Soconusco busied themselves preparing the paperwork for their communities. The SEP also expected them to organize workers into local branches of the federal Confederation of Mexican Workers (CTM). Needless to say, this campaign also placed teachers in direct conflict with powerful local interests. Some teachers, like the combative

Amadeo Tercero, rose to the task. In 1937, he attempted to form a Rural Workers Syndicate at El Retiro, the plantation where he taught. Tercero battled with the German plantation administrator, whom he accused of being "a member of a Hitlerian organization." The administrator threatened the unionizing workers and later attempted to derail the official registration process by offering bribes to the municipal agent and to Tercero himself. This battle Tercero won—at least temporarily. Shortly after official recognition of the syndicate, workers at El Retiro negotiated a collective-bargaining agreement with management.[26] However, the experience prompted Tercero to propose to the Mexican congress the complete nationalization and socialization of Soconusco's coffee plantations. In his words, "the wealth of the region is in the hands of French, English, Spanish, Italian, and predominately German capital." Tercero's plan would exclude "assassins, thieves, evildoers, and foreigners" from becoming industrial partners.[27]

As social activists, Tercero and other Article 123 teachers often left an impressive record in Chiapas. Statewide, in 1935 they shut down illegal *tiendas* de raya on thirty-four plantations and replaced them with consumer cooperatives. Ten teachers organized land invasions to present sluggish agrarian-reform officials with a fait accompli. Others called strikes to protest violations of the Federal Labor Law. Teachers up and down coastal Chiapas vaccinated students, conducted health campaigns against malaria, led reforestation projects, oversaw the repair of roads, organized sporting events, and combated alcohol vendors.[28] But they battled against insurmountable odds. By the late 1930s the Article 123 schools in Chiapas were in full retreat, but not before teachers had prepared communities for the major *cardenista* land expropriations that finally came to Chiapas in 1939 and 1940.

The Cardenista Offensive

Socialist education represented the first wave of the revolutionary offensive in 1930s' Chiapas. The second wave came in 1936, when that year's election enabled reformers to impose a new governor. Outgoing governor Victórico Grajales had been openly hostile to Cárdenas ever since the future president made a campaign stop in Chiapas in February 1934. Grajales, an ally of *jefe máximo* Calles, saw his political capital fall when Cárdenas defied Calles in June 1935 and exiled him to San Diego one year later. Cárdenas used this opportunity to purge *callista* governors throughout the country, but he decided to allow Grajales to finish out his term. Meanwhile, a *cardenista* coalition that included employees of the federal agrarian reform, education, forestry, and agriculture ministries, purged the state branch of the official party, the National

Revolutionary Party (PNR), and took other measures to ensure that their candidate, agronomist Efraín Gutiérrez, bested Grajales's handpicked successor in the PNR party plebiscite and in the general election. Grajales was not gracious in defeat. He apparently ordered a hit on Gutiérrez one night after his victory and promised never to recognize the outcome of the election. In response, President Cárdenas ordered the national senate to depose Grajales. Two days later the federal army closed down and occupied the state government offices in the state capital of Tuxtla Gutiérrez. The Cárdenas administration named an interim governor, and Gutiérrez was sworn into office in December 1936.[29]

President Cárdenas had managed to impose an ally as governor, but could he impose his agenda on Chiapas? In the highlands, where socialist education was already in retreat, powerful ladinos took immediate steps to block *cardenismo*.[30] They turned to Alberto Pineda, the general who twenty years earlier had led the defense of the highlands against a different type of federal intrusion—the top-down *carrancista* "revolution" of 1914–1920. Pineda took advantage of the fragility of the *cardenista* transition just days after the army deposed Grajales. Aware that the state PNR (now under *cardenista* control) would try to impose its own candidate in San Cristóbal's upcoming municipal elections, Pineda, the local police, and armed supporters broke into the local PNR offices, disarmed General Secretary Wistano Molina, and threw him in jail while Pineda registered himself as a candidate.[31] He won the election six weeks later. Because San Cristóbal either directly or indirectly controlled all of the indigenous municipalities in its district and named all municipal presidents, secretaries, and agents, Pineda was perfectly situated to obstruct *cardenismo* in the highlands.

As municipal president, Pineda blocked agrarian reform, refused to cooperate with the federal anti-alcohol campaign, and continued the age-old practice of using unremunerated native labor for public works projects in San Cristóbal. His agents treated federal teachers (especially women) with great hostility in the surrounding indigenous communities. In July, Pineda ordered his supporters to storm fifteen of the town's churches, which had been closed years earlier by the notoriously anticlerical former governor, Grajales. He handed over the keys to eight of the churches and urged his mob to smash down the doors of the other seven. Several federal soldiers guarding the churches were wounded by the mob's attacks.[32]

Citing Pineda's "antirevolutionary activities," "financial irregularities," and violations of state and federal law, Governor Gutiérrez asked the state congress to withdraw official recognition of the entire government of San Cristóbal de Las Casas.[33] On July 20, 1937, the federal garrison forced Pineda out of office.

Figure 7.2. Erasto Urbina, director of the Department of Indigenous Social Action, Culture, and Protection, addresses a crowd of indigenous workers in San Cristóbal de Las Casas, ca. 1938. Courtesy of Archivo General de la Nación, México, D.F.

One day later the state government named state legislator Isidro Rabasa to head a new municipal government.

Cardenistas finally controlled the highlands, and they operated actively for the next several months. They supported the SEP's sobriety campaigns and jump-started the agrarian reform process. Governor Gutiérrez's director of the Department of Indigenous Social Action, Culture, and Protection, Erasto Urbina, took steps to correct the abuses inherent in enganche by founding the Indigenous Workers' Union (Sindicato de Trabajadores Indígenas, or STI). Soon, the union claimed nearly twenty-five thousand members. The STI was Urbina's most tangible *indigenista* policy, and working conditions for its members improved immediately. However, it prevented genuine indigenous participation in its collective-bargaining agreements with planters and never once called a strike. Urbina also trained young, bilingual, indigenous men to serve as municipal secretaries and agents in the highlands. In many communities, these men replaced ladinos, who generally used their positions to sell alcohol and to trade in indigenous labor.[34]

Meanwhile, ousted municipal president Alberto Pineda did not go quietly into the night. He crafted a successful legal case alleging that Gutiérrez and the state government had violated Article 115 of the constitution, which guaranteed municipal autonomy. In March 1938, the Mexican Supreme Court ruled unanimously in his favor.[35] After an occasionally violent two-and-a-half-week struggle with local *cardenistas*, Pineda and his allies retook the municipal government. He immediately reversed *indigenista* legislation and tied up pending agrarian-reform requests. The official paper of the federal CTM in Chiapas lamented that Pineda had unleashed "a wave of persecutions against the organized workers and the members of agrarian communities."[36]

In early June 1938, Pineda decided to take action against Erasto Urbina himself, who not only directed the Department of Indigenous Social Action, Culture, and Protection but was also running for a seat in the state legislature (figure 7.2). On the night of June 11, as Urbina rode his horse across the central plaza in San Cristóbal, municipal policemen, who once again took orders from Pineda, shot and wounded him.[37] A roundup of Urbina's supporters followed the attack. Two days later Urbina himself was seized in the federal garrison, where he had taken refuge to care for his wound.

The attack on Urbina sealed Pineda's fate. Four days later, the national senate granted the state government the right to name a local government as it saw fit. San Cristóbal was placed under martial law by federal forces under Urbina's command. Technically speaking, *cardenistas* once again controlled the local government of San Cristóbal, but they accomplished little over the two remaining years of the Cárdenas presidency. Local opposition to socialist education, *indigenismo*, and agrarian, as well as labor, reforms simply became too great. In the highlands, confrontation had given way to accommodation.

Cardenismo fared much better along Chiapas's Pacific Coast, especially where Article 123 teachers had been organizing workers and preparing communities for agrarian reform. Cárdenas found a propitious moment to strike against ethnic German planters. A vocal opponent of fascism, Cárdenas supported the Spanish Republic's desperate struggle against Francisco Franco and his fascist allies, Hitler and Mussolini, in the Spanish Civil War (1936–1939).[38] In the late 1930s, local conditions also conspired against ethnic Germans. The deplorable state of the coffee industry forced many Mexican planters to sink into debt with German creditors. In May 1938, Mexico City's colony of *chiapanecos* warned that Soconusco was "controlled by German and Spanish latifundistas and capitalists, by Nazis and the Spanish Falange, who either own the land directly or loan money at usurious rates."[39] Nationalism, envy, and charges of unfair and exclusionary business practices had many *chiapaneco* politicians calling for the internment of Germans even before Mexico entered World War II.[40]

Land reform finally came to Soconusco in March 1939, a time when *cardenismo* was in full retreat in the highlands and a couple of years after the most dramatic land expropriations had taken place elsewhere in Mexico. Governor Efraín Gutiérrez chose a reactionary Mexican of German descent as his principal target: Enrique Braun. *Cardenistas* correctly identified Braun with the state's *callista* faction and with the murders of several strikers and union leaders on his plantations. Nearly half of the 7,988 hectares expropriated came from Braun's property. This land was used to create six collective-farming units known as *ejidos*.[41] What made this expropriation exceptional was not the quantity of land, which was quite modest, but the fact that Braun's plantations were among the most productive in Mexico. The expropriation was rich in symbolic meaning: It suggested the dawn of a new age, when powerful ranchers and planters in Chiapas would be forced to occasionally submit to federal control. Later in 1940, Gutiérrez and President Cárdenas would seize the moment and expropriate land from most of the remaining large coffee plantations in Soconusco and Mariscal.

Ironically, as the federal government moved in to seize some of the richest land in all of Mexico, the schools that had helped to make the moment possible went into decline. Chiapas's rural elite continued to hammer away at the radicalized Article 123 schools with a combination of legal appeals, influence, bribery, and intimidation; such were the "weapons of the strong." In the words of historian Alan Knight, these were "arguably, the most effective deterrents to the full implementation of the Cardenista project, and the surest guarantee that it would fail." [42] By using the "weapons of the strong," elite *chiapanecos* put the Article 123 program on the defensive until the SEP adopted a more moderate orientation. Most Article 123 schools were closed by the early 1940s, but not before teachers at these schools had initiated land-reform requests, incorporated workers and peasants into official unions, and performed various functions as labor inspectors and agents of an emerging nation-state.

Taking Stock in 1940

The year 1940 marked thirty years since Madero's fateful call to arms and twenty years since Mexico entered the "reconstructive" phase of its revolution. The Constitution of 1917 had been in place for more than two decades, calling for free, secular education for all, land reform for the landless, and a host of labor reforms. By any logical standard, 1940 would seem to be the appropriate year to determine whether Chiapas had experienced a revolution. And yet assessing the revolution in Chiapas at that moment is no easy matter. Even after six years of *cardenismo*, the revolution's impact was uneven, and many of the progressive achievements of the 1930s were quickly swept away. If the gains under Cárdenas had been truly revolutionary, should they not have stood the test of time?

Part of the reason for the rollback of *cardenismo* is that it began *before* 1940, largely at the behest of Cárdenas himself. Following the dramatic expropriation of foreign-held oil fields in March 1938, his administration adopted a more moderate course. Historians have debated for decades whether economic crisis and intense domestic and international opposition forced this reorientation or whether it simply reflected the president's conspiratorial state-building aims.[43] Whatever the case may be, the *cardenista* state had moved from mobilization to consolidation. This shift is clearly apparent in education policy. Beginning in 1938, the SEP made fewer references to class conflict and began withdrawing its most radical textbooks from circulation. The following year, the new director of federal education in Chiapas, Jacinto Téllez, initiated a demobilization campaign that targeted Amadeo Tercero and other activist Article 123 teachers. Téllez transferred Tercero to another school as punishment for attending meetings of peasants and coffee pickers and performing other tasks that had been expected of him in the mid-1930s.[44] Many teachers seemed bewildered by the SEP's ideological shift. Rubén Aguilar Pola, the Article 123 teacher at *finca* Realidad, wrote Cárdenas in May 1939 with a simple question: "Illustrious leader," he began, "with all due respect, what is the role of the rural teacher at this time? Should we follow the indications of the . . . director of federal education in Chiapas, or do we continue agitating on behalf of the masses?"[45]

Téllez continued to suffocate radical pedagogy in the state after 1940. In early 1942, he declared to his superiors in Mexico City that "it is urgently necessary to transfer out of this state federal teachers who are hardened communist agitators who neglect their true work as teachers . . . and simply dedicate themselves to agitating and unjustly disorienting the workers and peasants."[46] Most SEP teachers and inspectors had already fallen in line, like highland inspector Manuel Castellanos. In 1941, Castellanos's social campaigns consisted of combating alcoholism, witchcraft, poor hygiene, locust plagues, typhoid fever, religious fanaticism, homicides, and poor diets. This amounted to attacking the symptoms, not the causes, of a brutally impoverished lifestyle. Castellanos was clearly a far cry from the determined activist who had fought *enganche*, alcohol merchants, and corrupt mestizo municipal presidents in 1935 and 1936. No longer challenging the victimizers, he blamed the victims. In his October 1942 report, Castellanos strikes a detached, paternalistic, dismissive tone that harkens to an earlier age:

> Knowing that the Indians commit a great number of assassinations, especially due to witchcraft; that they are liars and attached to alcohol . . . that they are spiteful and obstinate in their passions; that they feel an innate

> hatred toward the mestizo . . . in other words, that the ethical principles that guide their lives are distinct from those that constitute the base of our civilization, I have recommended that all of the teachers in the zone use every means at their disposal to attend to the extremely important moral aspect of education, forming in said Indians feelings and habits that will make them more human.[47]

Meanwhile, the chief architect of *cardenista indigenismo* in the highlands, Erasto Urbina, used his control over the STI to launch his political career and tighten his grip on the highlands. His indigenous associates assumed leading roles in local labor unions and agrarian communities; he eventually coached them to penetrate their home communities' "traditional" hierarchies and take political control. Mexico's one-party state soon learned that it could control entire communities by co-opting a relatively small number of "traditional" leaders. In exchange, they kept the peace and provided votes at election time. The result was a new type of indigenous *caciquismo*, or bossism, that had profoundly negative consequences for the Chiapas highlands during the second half of the twentieth century.[48]

The Mexican Revolution did not mobilize, liberate, or "incorporate" the Tzotzil and Tzeltal Maya, and census data in 1950 showed that nearly thirty years of SEP programs had taught few to read. Especially distressing were the language and literacy figures in communities where the SEP had established rural schools *and* indigenous boarding schools. In Chamula and Huixtán, literacy rates in Spanish were only 2 percent and 15 percent, respectively; in Chenalhó, only 9 percent of the inhabitants spoke Spanish.[49]

If federal educators throughout Chiapas were in full retreat, what of the principal beneficiaries of the *cardenista* land expropriations of 1939 and 1940, the *ejidatarios* of Soconusco? Many *cardenista* institutions like the *ejidal* banks, marketing agencies, and cooperative societies that were designed to help small producers became transformed from tools of emancipation into mechanisms of control. By 1942 Soconusco's *ejidatarios* were angrily criticizing officials of the Ejidal Bank in Tapachula. That April, the Central League of Agrarian Communities wrote to President Manuel Ávila Camacho, complaining that coffee *ejidatarios* were still alienated from the fruits of their labors; those who formerly controlled production had been replaced by a new owner, "which calls itself the Bank."[50] Workers complained that they were still "slaves of capital" and not "free citizens" because the true beneficiaries of the Ejidal Bank were people "favored by the Bank, who benefit from the sweat and sacrifice of others."[51] *Ejidatarios* from the southern tip of Soconusco went so far as to claim that the bank's exploitation was "worse than that endured before the

Revolution."[52] *Ejidatarios* now had land, thanks to the *cardenista* expropriations, but their struggles continued.

The picture I have painted so far has been one of utter failure in the highlands, compromised victories in the lowlands, and a teaching corps that underwent a devastating ideological purge after 1940. Is there a silver lining to this story? In fact, there is. Letters and petitions suggest that the culture of schooling began to take hold, especially among mestizo communities that participated in the export sector and benefited most directly from the SEP's program of socialist education. The more popular textbooks, the radicalized and better-prepared teachers, the social campaigns, the sports festivals, and teacher support for land reform helped win mestizo support. Furthermore, literacy was becoming an increasingly important skill as the Mexican state began intervening in the lives of rural people as never before.

The statistical and anecdotal evidence of the popularity of SEP socialism among mestizos is especially striking in Soconusco's embattled Article 123 schools. A 1938 federal teachers' survey showed that a startling 90 percent of the Article 123 schools and teachers enjoyed the support of parents and workers. As in the rural federal schools, the initial popularity of the Article 123 schools was due to the broad social mandate of federal teachers. However, support for education continued into the 1940s and beyond, long after the days of teacher-assisted land and labor reform were over. Workers along the Pacific Coast demanded schools as a right of modern citizenship, even after it had become painfully apparent that the SEP was no longer committed to a populist agenda.

Assessing the revolutionary campaign to change the behaviors and worldviews of rural *chiapanecos* is more difficult. Some radical teachers claimed in the late 1930s that religious "fanaticism" was extinguishing itself. Even if we take these observations at face value and conclude that most rural *chiapanecos* underwent a gradual process of secularization during this period of study, which is likely, it is difficult to determine the extent of the SEP's role in the process. Rural health clinics, market forces, the mass media, and other trappings of modernity also exerted considerable secularizing tendencies.[53] The federal sobriety campaign was a more categorical failure. In Chiapas, the effort to end the manufacture and sale of alcohol in rural communities was an uneven, short-lived fight. Inspectors and teachers soon realized there was little point in combating interests that enjoyed the protection of the governor, the state PNR, municipal authorities, and the state police.[54] The SEP's campaign of cultural nationalism enjoyed a more lasting legacy in mestizo communities, especially after the divisive rhetoric of class conflict and anticlericalism gave way to a focus on social justice and nationalism. The culture of schooling itself had important implications for rural Chiapas. Communities that had shunned schooling came to embrace it; by 1940 their pleas for schools appropriated a discourse of popular nationalism and citizenship first introduced by teachers.

An Irreverent Conclusion

The foregoing discussion suggests that powerful, reactionary forces fought a successful *counterrevolution* that suppressed the popular, mobilizing, reformist tendencies of the Mexican Revolution in Chiapas until the mid-1930s. When the revolution finally arrived in the state, it had an uneven, fleeting, ambivalent outcome that hinged greatly on the ability of federal educators to organize and mobilize their communities. This prevented resolution of the state's most pressing problems, like the land issue and the persistent, institutionalized mistreatment of indigenous peoples. Elsewhere in Mexico, the institutions of the revolution preserved the social and political peace for roughly seven decades. However, these institutions either did not have an opportunity to develop in Chiapas or were so thoroughly corrupted that they exacerbated problems instead of solving them.

Fast-forward to the early 1990s, when Mexico's political leadership abandoned the constitutional provisions that authorized agrarian reform and protected communal landholding. In 1994, as Mexico officially entered the North American Free Trade Agreement (NAFTA) and its ruling party abandoned decades of economic nationalism, indigenous rebels in Chiapas, led by a former university professor, seized several small cities and issued a long list of denunciations. They called themselves *zapatistas*, after the revolutionary *caudillo* Emiliano Zapata, who never actually visited Chiapas during his lifetime. These neo-*zapatistas* reappropriated the revolutionary nationalism that the SEP and the national government had sacrificed at the altar of free trade. The *zapatistas* demanded land reform, democracy, and regional autonomy and challenged Mexican society to conceptualize a multiethnic nation. Even those indigenous peoples who did not participate in the armed revolt were proud that other *indígenas* had stood up for themselves and challenged a political and economic system that was manifestly unjust.[55] Perhaps it was fitting that on the dawn of Mexico's entry into the North American trading bloc, when its revolutionary institutions and policies were being abandoned, its marginalized population in its most marginalized state rose in arms to demand social justice and the rights of citizenship enshrined in the revolution's most important document, the Constitution of 1917.

Most historians believe that the Mexican Revolution is the most important event in Mexico's contemporary history. But is it the most important moment in the history of contemporary Chiapas? In a recent essay, Jan Rus argues that the state's real revolution came in the late nineteenth century, with the introduction of plantation agriculture in the lowlands. As Chiapas became a major producer of coffee, rubber, cacao, and bananas, the state's political, economic, and social life underwent tremendous changes. Among other things, seasonal stints on lowland plantations allowed the indigenous people to remain "indigenous," rooted to their land in closed, culturally conservative highland communities.[56] Moreover, just as the rise of the plantation economy exerted major, perhaps revolutionary, effects on Chiapas, so too did its collapse after 1970, when global commodity prices fell, federal support for agriculture diminished, and the economy went into a free fall. Seasonal work dried up, and the state's indigenous people began desperately looking for ways to feed their families. They turned to a Mexican state that was no longer committed to land reform and social justice. At roughly this time, Marxist mestizos from central Mexico took up residence in the Lacandón Rain Forest and began working in indigenous communities. One of these mestizos was Subcomandante Marcos, who eventually led the rebellion.[57]

Perhaps the *zapatistas* are a by-product and a synthesis of both the officially consecrated Revolution of 1910 and the sputtering demise of Chiapas's "revolution" in plantation agriculture. They took up arms in a state where postrevolutionary state and nation building was belatedly introduced, fiercely resisted, easily corrupted, and turned away and where life in indigenous communities became increasingly unbearable after 1970. Once they emerged from their forest hideouts, however, they drew freely from the repertoire of revolutionary symbolism and heroes, which were part of the official version of the Mexican Revolution taught in SEP schools throughout the country. They also invoked the legacy of popular struggle most clearly embodied by Zapata himself. Today, the *zapatistas* have carved out five autonomous zones in highland and eastern Chiapas that they call *caracoles*. In these regions, they still enjoy significant support in spite of more than eighteen years of overt, and sometimes covert, official hostility.[58] Arguably, then, the case can be made that for many *chiapanecos*, and especially the indigenous, the ongoing *zapatista* movement is much more relevant and "revolutionary" than the officially consecrated revolution that we are commemorating in this volume.

Notes

1. Jan Rus, "Coffee and the Recolonization of Highland Chiapas, Mexico: Indian Communities and Plantation Labor, 1892–1989," in *The Global Coffee Economy in Africa, Asia, and Latin America, 1500–1989*, ed. Steven Topik and W. Clarence-Smith (Cambridge: Cambridge University Press, 2003), 262–64, 267–72, 277–280; and Sarah Washbrook, " 'Una Esclavitud Simulada': Debt Peonage in the State of Chiapas, Mexico, 1876–1911," *Journal of Peasant Studies* 33(3) (July 2006): 395–401.

2. See, among others, John Tutino, *From Insurrection to Revolution in Mexico: Social Bases of Agrarian Violence, 1750–1940* (Princeton, N.J.: Princeton University Press, 1988 [1986]).
3. Thomas Benjamin, *A Rich Land, a Poor People: Politics and Society in Modern Chiapas* (Albuquerque: University of New Mexico Press, 1996 [1989]), 99–143; and Jan Rus, "Revoluciones contenidas: Los indígenas y la lucha por los Altos de Chiapas, 1910–1925," in *Mesoamérica* 46 (enero–diciembre de 2004): 68–71.
4. Archivo Histórico del Municipio de San Cristóbal de Las Casas (hereafter AHMSCLC), 1917, Tomo 2, Borrador de Circulares, 1917, signed by J. A. Castro, General de Brigada, Gobernador y Comandante Militar del Estado de Chiapas, Oct. 30, 1914.
5. Benjamin, *Rich Land*, 120–22; Prudencio Moscoso Pastrana, *El pinedismo en Chiapas 1916–1920* (México: Fray Bartolomé de Las Casas, 1988 [1960]), 18–34; Archivo Histórico del Estado de Chiapas (hereafter AHECh), Fondo Documental Fernando Castañón Gamboa, 1039.1, Circular Núm. 17, Gobierno Preconstitucional del Estado de Chiapas, signed by Oficial Mayor Santiago A. Vázquez, dated from Tuxtla, Dec. 29, 1915.
6. Rus, "Revoluciones contenidas," 70–71.
7. Calixta Guiteras Holmes, *Cancuc: Etnografía de un pueblo tzeltal de los altos de Chiapas, 1944* (Tuxtla: Gobierno del Estado de Chiapas e Instituto Chiapaneco de Cultura, 1992), 139.
8. Rus, "Revoluciones contenidas," 74.
9. Benjamin, *Rich Land*, 150–51.
10. Jürgen Buchenau, *Plutarco Elías Calles and the Mexican Revolution* (Lanham, Md.: Rowman and Littlefield, 2007), 125–28, 153, 159–60.
11. Archivo Histórico de la Secretaría de Educación Pública (hereafter AHSEP), Dirección de Educación Federal (hereafter DEF), Informes, 1652 (4763), Exp. 1778/1, Fo. 100, from Dir. de Ed. Fed. Eduardo Zarza to Jefe del Departamento de Educación Rural (hereafter DER), SEP, México, D.F., dated from Tuxtla, July 26, 1928.
12. Rosario Castellanos, *Ciudad Real* (Xalapa: Universidad Veracruzana, 1960).
13. AHMSCLC, various from 1920s and 1930s, including 1929, Tomo 2, "Correspondencia de fuera del distrito, Mayo de 1929," from Carmen Hernández to Gobernador del Estado, dated from San Cristóbal de Las Casas, Apr. 25, 1929.
14. Ernesto Meneses Morales, ed., *Tendencias educativas oficiales en México, 1934–1964* (México: Centro de Estudios Educativos, Universidad Iberoamericana, 1988), 44.
15. Excellent research on socialist education includes essays in Mary Kay Vaughan and Susana Quintanilla, eds., *Escuela y sociedad en el período cardenista* (México: Fondo de Cultura Económica, 1997); and Mary Kay Vaughan, *Cultural Politics in Revolution: Teachers, Peasants, and Schools in Mexico, 1930–1940* (Tucson: University of Arizona Press, 1997).
16. AHSEP, DER, Caja 1375 (236), Exp., 28, Fo. 1, "Calendario escolar para todas las escuelas primarias dependientes del Gobierno del Estado y de la Federación, para el año escolar de 1935," from Dir. de Ed. Pública Ángel M. Corzo and Dir. Fed. de Ed. Septimio Pérez Palacios, dated from Tuxtla, Jan. 3, 1935.

17. Stephen E. Lewis, *The Ambivalent Revolution: Forging State and Nation in Chiapas, 1910–1945* (Albuquerque: University of New Mexico Press, 2005), 81–98, 194–201.
18. AHSEP, DER, Caja 1332 (191), Exp. 8, Fos. 10–11, from Castellanos to López in Tuxtla, dated from Ciudad Las Casas, Apr. 6, 1935.
19. Ibid., Fos. 18–20, "Informe de julio i agosto," from Castellanos to Dir. de Ed. Fed. in Tuxtla, Sept. 10, 1935.
20. AHSEP, Dirección General de Educación Pública en los Estados y Territorios (hereafter DGEPET), Caja 5324 (304), Exp. 20, Fo. 8, from Castellanos to Dir. de Ed. Fed. in Tuxtla, dated from Ciudad Las Casas, Mar. 12, 1936.
21. Ibid., Fo. 19, from Castellanos to Dir. de Ed. Fed. in Tuxtla, May 11, 1936.
22. AHSEP, DER, Caja 1332 (191), Exp. 8, Fo. 11, from Castellanos to López in Tuxtla, dated from Ciudad Las Casas, Apr. 6, 1935.
23. AHSEP, DGEPET, Caja 5489 (2788), Exp. 42, Fos. 18–21, from Castellanos to Dir. de Ed. Fed., Feb. 23, 1937.
24. *Memoria relativa al estado que guarda el ramo de educación pública el 31 de agosto de 1934*, II, 52.
25. AHSEP, DGEPET, Caja 5352 (334), Exp. 3, Fo. 67, from Rafael Bolio Yenro to Secretario de Educación Pública, Dirección General de Educación Pública, Urbana, y Rural en los Estados, México, D.F., dated from Tuxtla, Mar. 4, 1936.
26. AHSEP, DGEPET, Chiapas, Caja 6130 (80), Exp. 3, Fo. 9, from Amadeo Tercero to Cárdenas, dated from Finca "El Retiro," Jan. 3, 1938.
27. AHSEP, DGEPET, Chiapas, Caja 6130 (80), Exp. 3, Fo. 10, "Proyecto de ley que se somete a la consideración del H. Congreso de la Unión para su estudio, tendiente a la forma que debe socializarse la riqueza en la región del Soconusco del Estado de Chiapas," from Dir. Escuela Federal Art. 123 Amadeo Tercero, dated from Finca "El Retiro," Dec. 15, 1937.
28. AHSEP, DER, Caja 1375 (236), Exp. 26, Fos. 16–18, from López to SEP, DER, México, D.F., dated from Tuxtla, Aug. 14, 1935; and Caja 1332 (191), Exp. 3, Fo. 16, Fo. 2, "Informe de labores del 3er. Bimestre, en la parte relativa a las Escuelas rurales y Artículo 123," from Inspector P. Arturo Mota to López in Tuxtla, dated Aug. 5, 1935.
29. Archivo General de la Nación (hereafter AGN), Cárdenas, Elecciones gobernador, Chiapas, 544.2/6, from Dip. Mario E. Balboa to Pres. de la República, dated from Mexico City, June 2, 1936; Benjamin, *Rich Land*, 193–94.
30. For a more detailed discussion, see Stephen E. Lewis, "El choque del siglo: Los coletos y el cardenismo, 1936–40," in *Chiapas: De la Independencia a la Revolución*, eds. Mercedes Olivera y María Dolores Palomo (Mexico: CIESAS, PROIMMSE-UNAM and CONECULTA-Chiapas, 2005), 73–95.
31. AGN, Cárdenas, Elecciones Chiapas, Municipales, 544.5/496, from María M. de Molina to Cárdenas, dated from Las Casas, Sept. 30, 1936; AHMSCLC, 1936–1937, from Wistano Molina to Juez de Distrito, Tuxtla, dated from Ciudad de Las Casas, Oct. 1, 1936.

32. AGN, Cárdenas, Elecciones Chiapas, Municipales, 544.5/496, various to Cárdenas.
33. *Periódico Oficial*, July 20, 1937.
34. AHMSCLC, 1937/2, from Secretario Gen. Salvador Gómez Oso and Secretario de Conflictos Nicolás Espinosa to Pres. de la H. Junta Central de Conciliación y Arbitraje del Estado in Tuxtla, dated from Ciudad Las Casas, July 15, 1937; AGN, Cárdenas, Conflictos obreros, 533.31, from Srio. Gen. del Sindicato de Trabajadores Indígenas Salvador López to Cárdenas, México, D.F., dated from Las Casas, Sept. 16, 1939; and Jan Rus, "The 'Comunidad Revolucionaria Institucional': The Subversion of Native Government in Highland Chiapas, 1936–68," in *Everyday Forms of State Formation: Revolution and the Negotiation of Rule in Modern Mexico*, ed. Gilbert M. Joseph and Daniel Nugent (Durham, N.C.: Duke University Press, 1994), 277.
35. AHMSCLC, 1938/2, minutes of extraordinary session of H. Ayuntamiento Constitucional de Ciudad de Las Casas, dated from Ciudad de Las Casas, May 8, 1938, 1–2; AGN, Cárdenas, Elecciones Chiapas, Municipales, 544.5/496, various, including telegram from Pineda to Cárdenas, dated from Las Casas, July 23, 1937; and telegram from Ciro Coello G., Regidor Primero, Ayuntamiento Constitucional de Cd. Las Casas to Cárdenas, dated from Las Casas, Apr. 13, 1938.
36. "Alberto Pineda Ogarrio, Enemigo del Movimiento Sindical," in *Alborada*, Tuxtla, May 14, 1938, 1.
37. AGN, Cárdenas, Elecciones Chiapas, Municipales, 544.5/496, from Erasto Urbina to Cárdenas, dated from Las Casas, June 12, 1938.
38. Friedrich E. Schuler, *Mexico between Hitler and Roosevelt: Mexican Foreign Relations in the Age of Lázaro Cárdenas* (Albuquerque: University of New Mexico Press, 1998), 55–59.
39. *Colonia Chiapaneca*, Revista Anual de sus Actividades, México, May 1938, 21.
40. "Alemanes y Japoneses en Chiapas serán concentrados a Perote, Ver.," *El Sur de México*, Tapachula, May 11, 1942, 1.
41. Braun's brother Fernando also lost land. "Cómo fue hecha la repartición de tierras en el Soconusco" in *Chiapas Nuevo*, Tuxtla, Mar. 23, 1939, 4.
42. Alan Knight, "Cardenismo: Juggernaut or Jalopy?" *Journal of Latin American Studies* 26 (1994): 100.
43. These arguments are discussed in Knight, "Cardenismo."
44. AHSEP, DGEPET, Chiapas, Caja 6130 (80), Exp. 3, Fo. 41–46, from Sindicato de Trabajadores de la Enseñanza de la República Mexicana, Delegación XII de la Sección VII, to Téllez, Tuxtla, dated from Tapachula, May 15, 1939.
45. AGN, Cárdenas, 534.5/172, from Rubén Aguilar Pola, Maestro Rural Art. 123, Finca "Realidad," to Cárdenas, dated from Tapachula, May 27, 1939.
46. AHSEP, DEF, Chiapas, Caja 5581 (3530), Exp. 9489/2, Fos. 2–3, from Téllez to Lic. Roberto T. Bonilla, Sub-Secretario de Educación Pública, México, D.F., dated from Tuxtla, Jan. 16, 1942.

47. Ibid., Exp. 4482/29, Fo. 69, from Castellanos to Téllez in Tuxtla, dated from Ciudad Las Casas, Oct. 1, 1942.

48. Rus, " 'Comunidad Revolucionaria Institucional,' " 267.

49. Jorge A. Vivo Escoto, "Geografía económica y demográfica de Chiapas," *Boletín de la Sociedad Mexicana de Geografía y Estadística* (enero–junio 1959): 237–45.

50. AGN, Ávila Camacho, Ejidos, Exp. 703.4/238, from Liga Central de Comunidades Agrarias de la República, México, D.F., to Presidente, México, D.F., dated Apr. 8, 1942.

51. Ibid., from Rosendo Morales and others to Presidente, dated from Cacahoatán, July 15, 1942.

52. Ibid., from Pres. del Comité Ejecutivo de la Liga Central de Comunidades Agrarias de la República Lic. Luis Ramírez de Arellano to Presidente, dated from México, D.F., July 28, 1942.

53. Alan Knight, "Revolutionary Project, Recalcitrant People: Mexico, 1910–1940," in *The Revolutionary Process in Mexico: Essays on Political and Social Change, 1880–1940*, ed. Jaime E . Rodríguez O. (Los Angeles: UCLA Latin American Studies Center Publications, 1990), 230.

54. AHSEP, DEF, Chiapas, Caja 5298 (280), Exp. 2, Fo. 13., from Dir. de Ed. Fed. Rafael Bolio Yenro to Dir. Gral. de Ed. Primaria Urbana y Rural en los Estados Celso Flores Zamora, dated from Tuxtla, Jan. 16, 1936.

55. See, for example, Marián Peres Tsu, "A Tzotzil Chronicle of the Zapatista Uprising," in *The Mexico Reader: History, Culture, Politics*, ed. Gilbert M. Joseph and Timothy J. Henderson (Durham, N.C.: Duke University Press, 2002), 655–69.

56. Jan Rus, "Repensar la Revolución Mexicana en Chiapas: ¿Fue la Revolución el fenómeno social más trascedental para el siglo XX en Chiapas?" in *La Revolución mexicana en Chiapas un siglo después*, ed. Justus Fenner and Miguel Lisbona (Mexico: PROIMMSE-UNAM and Gobierno del Estado de Chiapas, 2010), 491–47.

57. See, among others, Nick Henck, *Subcomandante Marcos: The Man and the Mask* (Durham, N.C.: Duke University Press, 2007); and Nicholas P. Higgins, *Understanding the Chiapas Rebellion: Modernist Visions and the Invisible Indian* (Austin: University of Texas Press, 2004).

58. On autonomy and the Caracoles, see, among others, Richard Stahler-Sholk, "Resisting Neoliberal Homogenization: The Zapatista Autonomy Movement," in *Latin American Social Movements in the Twenty-First Century*, ed. Richard Stahler-Sholk, Harry E. Vanden, and Glen David Kuecker (Lanham, Md.: Rowman and Littlefield, 2008), 113–29.

CHAPTER 8

Back to Centralism, 1920–1940

Carlos Martínez Assad

Introduction

In this era of change, of a profound review of our history, we have to ask ourselves once again about the actions of the victors and the vanquished, the former consecrated in officially sanctioned history, and the latter still seeking their place in it. All of them come together, however, to demonstrate again the richness of Mexican history, which can reveal the existence of several truths as opposed to a single truth. My purpose here is to relate the other side of the story of the period that has been defined as *cardenismo*, when Lázaro Cárdenas headed the country's government between 1934 and 1940.

To be precise, *cardenismo*'s legacy lasted longer than just that period. The expropriation of the British and US oil companies strengthened Mexico's sovereignty when the country later had to successfully deal with pressure from abroad, particularly from the United States. It is not an exaggeration to state that it was not until the fourth decade of the twentieth century that Mexicans fully understood the meaning of nationalism.

When General Cárdenas took office as president, he was firmly convinced that to achieve a lasting peace, he had to anchor his administration in a sweeping social-justice program on behalf of the most beleaguered: the workers and peasants. His activism became as vast as his energy. Moreover, just as he forged a broad consensus that allowed him to implement extensive land distribution and award significant concessions to wage earners, he also had to face the discontent, disagreements, and dissidence of those who distanced themselves from his project and who contrasted it with their own cultural values, points of views, and histories produced in the various Mexican regions, particularly in the north and south.

Cárdenas's administration faced difficulties prompted by profound causes rooted in poverty, in established practices of domination, in ignorance, and in the urgent desire to find reasons for the hope that Mexico's elites denied the people. He took office with two very clear commitments: reinforcing presidentialism to avoid crises like the one the country had just gone through with the Calles-dominated *maximato* that Calles put together after the 1928 assassination of Álvaro Obregón[1] and advancing political centralization that, according to precedent, would guarantee the order that would allow the country to develop.

Central Mexico versus the Regions

Relations between Central Mexico and the regions had in practice been a tense, informal link in Mexico's history. This is expressed colloquially with a sense of identity in the saying "Outside of Mexico City, everywhere is Cuautitlán," alluding to the existence of two great spaces; the country's capital and its rural areas. The "center" meant domination, and the regions, the subordinate party to the relationship, because generally the big decisions that have given the country historicity have been made in Mexico City.[2] Various regimes coincided in seeking political centralization as a means to integrate the country and keep it peaceful. The Porfirio Díaz regime (1876–1880 and 1884–1911), or *porfiriato*, put mechanisms in place that allowed it to rather successfully exercise strong centralism until the outbreak of the revolution swept them away. An institutional order had to be designed based on the 1917 Constitution to again achieve a centralized political authority. That is why Mexico's postrevolutionary presidency had the aim of achieving this key element for exercising power.

In apparent contrast to the federalist system, which by law gave autonomy to the states, the 1917 Constitution reinforced centralism, and President Cárdenas gave it the dimensions that it has had since then. That was in the state's interest, but in practice it eliminated the possibility of forming regional power structures headed by local strongmen (known in Mexico as *caciques*).[3] The senate was created to give each of the states representation in congress; it is supposed to be the seat of geographical representation that the deputies do not necessarily have because, although they are elected in a specific state, their links to a political party have more weight.

Mexican legislation does not formally stipulate a dichotomy between the center and the regions. National geographical-spatial and political-legal, economic, and social distribution is alluded to in constitutional norms based on the categories "federation," "the states," and "the municipalities," establishing an operational interrelationship among these three levels of government. This tripartite system functions above all to define the operational basis for public administration. This can clearly be seen in Article 18 of the constitution, which stipulates that "The governments of the Federation and the states will organize the penal system in their respective jurisdictions . . . State governors, subject to stipulations by local legislation, will have the ability to come to accords with the federation."

There is, then, a certain ambiguity in the use of the concept "federation," which refers both to the federated states and to the central government, linked to the power of the president, something not clearly defined in the constitution or the law. Things become even more complicated if we consider that for a long period, the president was also the one who governed the country's capital, delegating its organization to another public official. He was, then, both the president and the virtual governor of Mexico City's Federal District because he had the authority to appoint the governor or regent according to his own interests and alliances. It was only after 1997, when the multiparty system put in place legislation that finally allowed the election of the head of the Federal District by popular vote, that the centralism exercised by the president diminished.

In the twenty-first century, the tension between central Mexico and the regions appears likely to be resolved in a different way due to the new assertiveness of state governments, even though the prevailing political culture continues to give enormous weight to the decisions made in the national capital.

The Centralization of the State

Mexico is a representative, democratic, federal republic. The free, sovereign states have accepted belonging to a federation ruled by the principles enshrined in the constitution. Coming to that determination became a difficult task since the nineteenth century was marked by clashes between regional federalists identified with liberalism on the one hand and centralists, most of the time conservatives, associated with privilege, on the other. Neither the federalists nor the centralists were absolute in defining themselves. For these reasons, both tendencies exhibited a certain ambiguity that made precise definitions rather difficult. The problem became more complex with the use and abuse of concepts that do not have the same meaning in the law and in reality because the 1917 constitution stipulates a federal regime, but the actual political practice is that of a centralist regime. It has often been said that legal Mexico does not necessarily correspond to the real Mexico, which has a tendency toward centralization even though it cannot be identified precisely as a centralist republic. This inclination in Mexico corresponds to the extralegal attributions acquired by the executive, which took faculties away from the other two branches of government, the legislature and the judiciary.

The recent regional historiography has produced new themes that suggest

Figure 8.1. In the 1920s, Mexico City enjoyed a vibrant night life. Courtesy of Archivo Casasola, Fototeca del INAH.

that the state began to centralize political authority after 1917. Regional research projects, linked to what has been called historic revisionism, have shown that the relationship between the central government and the regions was not homogeneous; on the contrary, it has emphasized the differences more than the similarities.[4]

However, those who have had power and wanted to keep it used every possible tactic and strategy to achieve their ends. Thus, the tendency to centralize functions, particularly the reinforcement of executive authority, could be considered as a national and even a necessary propensity in Mexican history. Porfirio Díaz's highest aspiration was to hold the reins of everything happening all over the country. He achieved that in part when he obtained the support of his political bosses and of the governors loyal to him.

Nevertheless, a nation with the profound geographical-cultural differences of Mexico became wide open for having far-flung regions with their own difficult links and aspirations that had little to do with the integrating idea of "the nation." Real separatist movements, frustrated attempts at secession, and the rivalries between the states and the capital were the consequence of affronts and resentments, the expression of a fragile sense of unity. Even federalism was neutralized for fear of localism exacerbated by private interests. The sovereignty of the states remained in the 1824 constitution but was restricted in practice.[5] The states believed they did not receive enough from the federal government, and the federal government did not believe it had the states' support in dealing with the needs of the nation.

The Mexican Revolution was the product of profound social causes and political realities. One of these was the power that the president had managed to accumulate after numerous moments of instability that had to be dealt with by giving more authority to the executive. In *The Spirit of the Laws* Montesquieu concluded that "Political freedom only exists when power is not abused; but experience constantly shows us that all men invested with authority abuse it . . . To prevent that abuse, it is necessary, because of the nature of things, for power to limit power."[6]

Clearly, this is his argumentation about the need to delimit the spheres of the three branches of government (the executive, the legislative, and the judicial) as the basis of freedom and the theory of the separation of powers. However, the country's tradition of *caudillismo* imposed the presence of regional figures as the leaders of the social and political process during the Mexican Revolution.[7] The rivalries that nourished that movement were expressed among the *caudillos*, who were interested in power but not very attentive to a consideration of the theory of checks and balances, regardless of whether it had been a concern during the creation of the federal republic in 1824.

After the fall of Díaz, the armed struggle, and the rise of the *caudillos*, the quest for institutionalization became the most important goal. This is demonstrated by the formulation of the 1917 constitution and, later, the rise of Álvaro Obregón. A political crisis broke out when he was assassinated in 1928. The centralization achieved earlier by the *porfiriato*, which the revolution shat-

Figure 8.2. In the 1920s, sex appeal emerged as a marketing technique. Courtesy of Archivo Casasola, Fototeca del INAH.

tered, necessitated new controls over regional *caudillos* and local strongmen. Therefore, Plutarco E. Calles created the *maximato* and imposed his will as *jefe máximo*. For historian Arnaldo Córdova, however, this did not mean that he had the absolute powers that have been attributed to him because he was actually only the "arbiter of groups."[8] This period fostered the emergence of many figures who dominated their regions with fear and guns and eliminated anyone who did not approve of their methods. During the *maximato*, a political game was established in which loyalties and support were exchanged for greater power.

For regional leaders to remain in good standing with the national government, they had to support it in return for more autonomy regardless of their origins and institutional performance. The traditions of local-strongmen-based regimes were reinforced in this political period, counterposed to the creation of a single party that operated as an umbrella for the broad spectrum of revolutionaries. The most noteworthy cases, because of the power they represented in their respective regions, are Tomás Garrido Canabal in Tabasco, Adalberto Tejeda in Veracruz, and Saturnino Cedillo in San Luis Potosí.

Veracruz, under Adalberto Tejeda's domination, explains how an entire stage in the organizational structures of workers, mainly rural laborers, advanced to the point of proposing an organization independent of the central state. Although the rank and file took many initiatives in this case, they recognized Colonel Tejeda as their main leader. Furthermore, this became possible only due to the fact that Veracruz was the port of entry for many European socialist and anarchist intellectuals, who were interested in an ideological conquest of the Americas.

In Tabasco, Garrido Canabal demonstrated the contradictions between the power of regional and central governments. The state's vast forests and waterways, with the country's largest rivers, the Grijalva and the Usumacinta, created lands that lent themselves particularly well to plantation agriculture. Its most important products (logwood, bananas, and cacao) were traded by companies partnered with the United Fruit Company. All of this allowed its isolation from the political center of the country and its exceptional economic autonomy.[9]

Strongman Saturnino Cedillo's control in San Luis Potosí contrasted with these two progressive states because it was based on traditional agriculture, which utilized the labor of peasants who developed during the breakup of the hacienda-based economy with a very specific form of property ownership called "military agricultural colonies." Although Cedillo's influence was very strong in the most economically deprived areas, it extended throughout the state. The relationships he established with his followers were faithful renditions of a family-based patronage system combined with cronyism.[10]

These were the last links severed in the transition marked by President Lázaro Cárdenas's break with *jefe máximo* Plutarco Elías Calles in 1935. This opened the road to the political centralization that has existed in the country since then despite Mexico's being, in law, a federal entity.

Creating a Single Party

Building the National Revolutionary Party (PNR) was one of the main achievements of Calles. The PNR incorporated the local political forces by attracting the parties built around personal interests. The project recognized the "autonomy" of the parties in each of the states with regard to local matters and established geographically based representative bodies like municipal committees. However, in addition, the National Leadership Committee would include a representative from each local party and function through a National Executive Committee (CEN).[11]

The *maximato* clearly became interested in establishing channels of communication to forge a close relationship with the hundreds of regional parties. Naturally, the CEN was also very paternalistic when it declared that antagonisms among the local parties should be avoided.

However, the proposal did not satisfy everyone. For example, the Veracruz leader Adalberto Tejeda, former minister of the interior under President Calles, in addition to twice being governor of Veracruz, insisted that the simple unity of these groups did not guarantee any social reforms and proposed to the *jefe máximo* that "representatives of the workers and peasants be appointed to the leadership of the new party."[12]

A less committed but more adroit reaction was that of Garrido Canabal in Tabasco; he systematically refused to dissolve the Tabascan Radical Socialist Party. The PNR had to accept that this local grouping, along with the Socialist Party of the Southeast, the Socialist Party of Quintana Roo, the Confederation of Socialist Parties of Oaxaca, and the Socialist Party of the State of Mexico, could continue to use their own emblems alongside that of the national party's green, white, and red symbol. Other parties did the same to slowly integrate themselves into the national party.

These local issues were clearly linked to the presence of regional strongmen who controlled their territories, and many more of them existed although they were not as powerful as those already mentioned. Some of these were Agustín Arroyo Cházaro in Guanajuato, Saturnino Osornio in Querétaro, Emilio Portes Gil and Marte R. Gómez in Tamaulipas, and Carlos Riva Palacio in the State of México.[13]

Arnaldo Córdova concludes that "the strength of the PNR was in its local groups. Its congenital weakness: the lack of discipline and the arbitrary way they acted. This was not a party. It was the guesthouse of a group of little local bosses, who, from time to time, would seek out a favor from the center."[14]

However, before it took root nationwide during the 1929 campaign, the PNR was able to put engineer Pascual Ortiz Rubio, Calles's candidate, in the presidency. His most important opponent, José Vasconcelos, in the end also helped in this endeavor by maintaining an anti-Calles discourse that, as is well known, earned him the hostility of local authorities loyal to the *jefe máximo*. This was reinforced by the uprising headed by generals Francisco Manzo and Pablo Escobar that same year, dampening the optimism about the country's political future as sparked by the PNR's creation.

Vasconcelos's federalist proposal was certainly interesting; he was probably correct when he proposed changing the federal regime and eliminating the constitutional recognition of states and replacing it with a free and sovereign republic organized as a "republic of independent, confederated municipalities" with the "municipality as the cell of political sovereignty within the vast organism of the Hispanic-American continental homeland."[15]

Around this same time, Luis Cabrera jumped in with an argument against the fantasy of a municipal structure by saying, "We have been wrong in creating that institution before educating our peoples." Moreover, he took advantage of the opportunity to make a strong criticism of federalism:

> There is no sovereignty of the states, nor have we ever had a federal republic, nor can we have one, nor is it a good idea to have one. . . . State sovereignty has always been a falsehood and has only served for the center to elude responsibilities or to facilitate creating the space for strongmen with which the top *caudillos* pay their lieutenants.[16]

For Cabrera, federalism was purely theoretical. On the eve of designing his six-year plan in late 1933, Calles took up the idea that the regional political parties should submit to the leadership of the PNR's CEN, probably because concern was increasing over the mounting lack of discipline among the political forces close to the party that did not fully accept its policies.

Interestingly, one of the most debated, conflictive topics at the PNR's second convention, at which changes in the bylaws and its six-year plan were to have been approved, was the issue of dissolving the regional parities. Despite a structure that gave so much importance to municipal delegates, the PNR was becoming a centralized organization with a vertical structure that probably indicated that this was the only way of achieving national integration and strengthening the postrevolutionary government.

When Cárdenas took office as president on November 30, 1934, he expressed concern about this very issue when he complained about

> [t]he country's economic situation; the problems from one end of the republic to the other; the neglect of many of our towns; the criminal apathy of many authorities and lack of interest in resolving the fundamental problems put on the agenda by the Revolution; the attitude of those who, calling themselves revolutionary, actually have conservative criteria; the lack of understanding of military commanders who ignore the social ends of our Revolution; the enormous vested interests of individuals acting on the stage of national politics . . . [17]

The new president understood and gave particular importance to strengthening the executive branch, using the idea of Calles's "arbitration." He made this very clear during the crisis of June 1935, when he reaffirmed himself as the "constitutional president of the United States of Mexico" and reiterated that he represented the thinking of the government of the republic and held the "responsibility as head of the Executive branch of the Nation with the legal right of fulfilling the post for which I was elected by my fellow citizens."[18] Under the aegis of the institutions and using language based on the law, Cárdenas outlined a new way forward that emphasized political centralism as necessary for carrying out the mission of integrating the country and dismantling the regional political forces that had held power. He was able to do this as a result of the support he got from the masses, that is, from the workers' movement, his fundamental ally, and the peasantry, both part of the state apparatus.

Cárdenas consolidated his government on the basis of two institutions that became fundamental for his regime: the executive and the official party. Almost at the end of his term, Cárdenas wrote the following in his notebook: "In the government, a single political force must stand out: that of the president of the republic, who must be the only representative of the democratic sentiments of the people."[19] From that perspective, it was logical that the more powerful regional strongmen like Tejeda, Carrido Canabal, and Cedillo were kept away from power by the use of intelligent maneuvering, even though in the latter case it was accomplished perhaps rather polemically because of Cedillo's rebellion. However, he also put an end to other local-strongmen-based regimes like that of Saturnino Osornio in Querétaro and eliminated the official immunity of a good number of governors whose political dealings were very traditional and opposed Cárdenas when he took away their previously existing privileges.

But during his administration, criticisms were raised that were echoed more and more over the years due to the metaconstitutional functions that the president acquired. Mexico finally seemed to find the tranquility it needed to continue with the organizational process that extended throughout the land and to all of its social classes, even if the prevailing idea was that of centralization, so distant from federalism.

Federalizing with Centralization

Organizing the sectors in the Mexican polity was a fundamental strategy of the Cárdenas regime; undoubtedly workers and peasants were its major focus, although it also paid attention to employers. Toward the end of his six-year term, when the PNR morphed into the Party of the Mexican Revolution (PRM) in 1938, Cárdenas organized it into four sectors: workers, peasants, middle classes, and the military.

From Carranza's time, precedents already existed of employers joining the National Business Chamber and the Employers Federation, which brought together as many as 1,157 industrialists. Early labor legislation led to federal regulation under Article 123 of the constitution, establishing the principles that would guide relations between capital and labor from Ortiz Rubio's brief presidential term on. Even from the time of the Abelardo L. Rodríquez administration, the electrical industry was federalized, while the Federal Electricity Commission was created in 1937.

The official discourse appealed to federalism in the rhetoric of uniformity, which interrupted the particular development of the peasants' and workers' organizations that had emerged in various regions and states. From the time of its leader, Luis N. Morones, the powerful Revolutionary Confederation of Workers of Mexico (CROM) had already encountered resistance from workers' organizations that refused to join it. Litigation took place between local unions that for different reasons did not join and preferred to stand alone. This was the case of the longshoremen affiliated with the Central League of Resistance of Tabasco, which always refused to join the CROM. It is true that this was partially due to the animosity between Morones and Garrido, who maintained absolute control over his apparatus. However, the workers linked the defense of their workplaces to their resistance when the CROM brought in the longshoremen from Veracruz to work on banana shipments.

In the end, the important thing to point out is that the organization of resistance leagues in Tabasco and in Yucatán did not obtain recognition on the national level as a model, regardless of the fact that it has been said that the PNR did take them into account when Calles organized its structure.

The Cárdenas group soon accepted that the alliance with the workers was fundamental, and its support became decisive when Cárdenas shook off Calles's tutelage in 1935. The General Confederation of Workers and Peasants of Mexico (GCOCM) came out cautiously for Cárdenas and offered to continue fighting to defend workers' rights. Also, at the urging of the Mexican Electrical Workers' Union (SME), the most combative unions agreed to sign the Pact of Solidarity and the constitution of the National Proletarian Defense Committee in response to the need to create a national worker-peasant organization.[20]

The working class became key to the Cárdenas administration's course of action and participated in the new design of government policies. Cárdenas counted on the strength he gained from workers and peasants. The workers were organized into a single union confederation in 1936: the Workers' Confederation of Mexico (CTM) amid a consensus forged by Vicente Lombardo Toledano on labor's side and an alliance between the PNR and the Communist Party of Mexico.

Organizing the peasants was more complicated because they served as the rank and file of the revolutionary armies, but they also became a pillar of the regional or local strongmen, who resisted accepting institutionalization. In addition, the peasants were also fundamentally influenced by leaders like Saturnino Cedillo, who also threw the support of several agrarian community leagues to Cárdenas, which later came together to form the Peasant Confederation of Mexico (CCM) in 1936.

However, a very significant precedent to this form of organization had been the creation and influence of the National Peasant League (LNC), which became the country's most important agrarian force during an intense period of agrarianism. The LNC was a group that emerged in the state of Veracruz in 1929 during Tejeda's second term as governor. Tejeda had been given the decided support of agrarian leader Ursulo Galván, who turned out to be an occasional ally of the communists, with whom he broke when his friend Guadalupe Rodríguez, a fighter for a communist ideal that did not conform to the party line, was shot by the government during the 1929 revolt.[21]

The important point here is that the government considered peasants a threat when they autonomously organized and when the national government did not control them. That is why, from the start of his administration, Cárdenas asked his followers with influence in the countryside, like Graciano Sánchez and Saturnino Cedillo, to build agrarian community leagues in each state so that they could later be unified in a single national organization. The president began to be concerned about the national influence of San Luis Potosí strongman Cedillo because, when the CCM was created, a bizarre discussion took place when the participants were asked to choose between Cedillo and Cárdenas as national leader of the peasants. The *cardenista* leaders had a hard time but finally managed to get this title bestowed on the president.[22]

The work to unify the peasantry had to continue and concluded only in 1938, when the states that still had not held their unification congresses did so: Tabasco, Yucatán, Oaxaca, and the territory of Quintana Roo. The National Peasant Confederation (CNC) was founded on August 28, precisely at the time that Cedillo had already staged an armed uprising in San Luis Potosí and was fleeing from the Mexican army. It was obvious that Cedillo was a fly in the ointment of the plan to create the government-controlled confederation because of his influence on the peasants his entire life.[23]

Cardenismo's Regional Campaign Lags

After the assassination of Obregón on July 17, 1928, the country was splintered. Nonetheless, Calles, together with his other supporters, pushed forward a project leveraged by the PRN. Years of serious disagreements concerning the implementation of a reform agenda followed in the *maximato*. After that, Cárdenas was able to turn the situation around and create a solid government, pushing to one side the governors and regional strongmen in order to achieve stability and a transition toward building institutions.

The most influential of these were men whose participation during the revolution put them into prominent positions but who were an impediment to Cárdenas's program and his quest for centralism, just as the Díaz government had aspired to. Many were not even well known, but among the best recognized (because of their activism) are the aforementioned Garrido Canabal, Tejeda, and Cedillo. They stand out more than others because of their long tenure in government positions and the power they wielded in their areas of influence. They demonstrated the country's heterogeneity and cultural diversity: Just the three of them represented a constellation of modernity and traditionalism, an ideology of the dominance of the whites (*criollos*) and indigenous peoples, of deserts and great rivers, of Catholicism and anticlericalism.

However, Mexico was crisscrossed by as many political and social movements as its regions. It was difficult to find a unifying axis that, with all of their contradictions, the followers of Garrido, Tejeda, and Cedillo could agree upon. That made them more important and confronted them with the centrality of the state that Cárdenas was ready and willing to build, thrusting to one side anything that might hinder his objective. Inside any political circumference, only one center of power can exist, and Cárdenas decided to be that without ceding an inch until the crises of 1937 and 1938.

In the first years of the Cárdenas administration, governors who believed they still had the privileges of the old political bosses were pressured by the president to leave their posts after the June 1935 crisis, when, historians agree, Cárdenas shook off the influence of Calles.[24] However, all over the country different leaders and even bandits did whatever they wanted. I have found more than twenty local warlords between 1935 and 1938 whom Cárdenas, according to the press, pursued for different reasons, almost always linked to agrarian disputes. Among them are Lauro Rocha, Domingo Máximo, José de Jesús Padilla, Cura B. Cabral, Jesús Macías, Ramos Lares, Miguel Luna López, Plutarco Ramírez, Pedro Ibarra, Manuel Barraza, Angel Martín del Campo, J. Cruz López, Jesús Rodríguez Uribe, J. Peralta, Manuel Rodríguez, Villa Michel, Celestino Murillo, Jesús González (El Coto), Pablo Tejeda, Jesús López, and Buenaventura Cabral.

Three cases exemplify the different actions the peasants carried out and demonstrate the way Cárdenas dealt with their demands; from the resolution of these conflicts emerge many of the traits of the political system and the methods he used to satisfy and channel its agrarian policies.

Upheaval in Jalisco

In the early *cardenista* years, Jalisco was governed by Everado Topete and Sebastián Allende. The Mexican Peasant Confederation accused the former of being an enemy of the "peasant class" and the latter of committing "outrages against the peasants because of the links he had with Jalisco's hacienda owners, from whom he took money."[25]

The conflicts, which became very wide ranging, involved agrarianists and small landowners, while rural teachers tended to support agrarian reform. The weapons of the powerful were wielded by white guards and, on occasion, by officers from the federal army.[26] Some authorities even convinced the agrarianists to respect small landholding as an important part of Cárdenas's policy. Using precedents like these, the members of the Union of Small Landholders asked the military to return their lands and also give them the lands occupied by the agrarianists.[27]

One important conflict was the agrarianist invasion of the mescal plantations and mills that prevented the workers from milking the sap from the agave plants.

> The National Chamber of Commerce declared that the requests presented to the Agrarian Department and the civilian authorities to recuperate control of these lands and the mescal plantations and mills had been useless. For this reason, the closure of the tequila factories is imminent, which will leave 800 families without work and sustenance, in addition to the fact that the owners will stop paying their taxes.[28]

The petition concluded with the withdrawal of the agrarianists from the Tequila region because they accepted that the restitution of the land to its legitimate owners had been the result of the peaceful intervention of the military authorities.

These movements with their modern characteristics, where employers and workers accepted and resolved their differences with the mediation of legal bodies, contrasted with the agitation and rebellions that plagued the rest of Jalisco during the Cárdenas period. Among the more than twenty local warlords I was able to locate, one of the most bothersome for the government was Lauro Rocha because of his large following. Also, his ranks included several other leaders, each of whom headed his own trained group of rebels. Rocha called himself the "Supreme Head of the Movement to Reconstruct Jalisco." Outstanding among his actions was the assassination of the head of the San José de Gracia[29] *ejido*.[30]

Rocha had many sympathizers, as demonstrated by the numerous actions they staged and the fact that the rebels were able to elude the army, supply themselves with weapons, and take refuge among the population. Even though the acts committed against hacienda owners and their families could have had religious or even criminal motives, they were marked by the conflict over the land, as exemplified by the *ejido* members' assassination of the son of the owner of the La Soledad hacienda.[31]

When Rocha was killed in his hideout at Villa de Guadalupe Hidalgo, the army found fifty handmade bombs, thirty-six weapons, and more than ten thousand rounds of ammunition.[32] Jalisco's problems were far reaching; a fight between two groups of agrarianists in Tamazula led to a bloody brawl that left numerous people injured[33]; representatives of the Huichol tribe of San Andrés Cohamiatla requested that the Agrarian Department send specialists to survey and specify which land belonged to them after neighboring landowners seized the property.[34] A rebel group headed by Plutarco Ramírez took possession of the La Higuera hacienda in the municipality of Tuxpan and created from it several *ejido* members' homes, an *ejido* headquarters, local store, and also took merchandise and money.[35] Peasants from Autlán, El Grullo, and El Limón petitioned the nation's president for justice because their lands had been invaded by armed agrarianists. In addition, the city halls of Chapala and Talpa were violently occupied by men on horseback.

Some attribute these actions to amnestied *cristeros*,[36] and others to political causes stemming from Col. Manuel Medina Chávez's "peacekeeping" mission to contain the many groups of rebels. For these reasons, ten thousand peasants represented by their agrarian communities petitioned the president to honor the 16th Cavalry Regiment for its "peacekeeping" efforts.[37] Did the 16th

Cavalry intervene to support land reform? If so, did it do so with the support of Cárdenas? Yes.

In the midst of this upheaval in Jalisco during these years, agrarianists, rural teachers, bandits, and small landowners were cut down in the crossfire between those who struggled vigorously for the agrarianists' demands, those who wanted to stop them, and the groups involved in the second Cristiada movement, which took innumerable lives in those years.

The Veracruz Radicals

Veracruz, considered one of the most radical states in the 1930s, also boasted the most militant leaders of Mexico's interior: Adalberto Tejeda, Úrsulo Galván, Heriberto Jara, and others. A long tradition of agrarian struggle and peasant organizations tinged with the leftist movements of the moment took place during the Cárdenas era. As early as 1923, the League of Agrarian Communities had been formed; it had distanced itself from the National Agrarianist Party, whose principles did not seem radical enough for rural Veracruz residents. In fact, there soon was a distancing between President Obregón and Tejeda, which increased during the rebellion of Adolfo de la Huerta in 1923.

By 1927, the leaders of Veracruz had proposed creating a National Peasant League, the first national organization to bring together peasant groups from all over the country. In the 1930s agrarian congresses in different parts of the state sought to unify these agricultural workers and to bring them in line with PNR corporatism. This idea would be taken up again by Cárdenas's centralization. For example, with this perspective, the Organizing Committee of Peasant Unification convened an agrarian convention on March 18, 1937, to form the League of Agrarian Communities of the State of Veracruz when it had actually been created fourteen years earlier. But the Cárdenas strategy, a project of corporate control above all, persisted. The objective was to form leagues in all states until a national convention could be called to form the National Peasant Confederation, which, organizers explicitly stated, would be a part of the PNR.[38]

For this reason, the intention of the Veracruz activists became clear when they criticized the actions of General Heriberto Jara, head of the state's military zone, when he "tried to impose the leaders of the peasant organization . . . on the group of Tejeda fanatics headed by former Deputy Carolino Anaya, who is receiving orders from Paris, France, from Colonel Adalberto Tejeda." One newspaper article accused Jara of wanting to be the next presidential candidate and, tangentially, blamed Governor Miguel Alemán for favoring this anti-Cárdenas movement.[39]

An even more discordant note from the unification congress came from Vicente Lombardo, secretary of the CTM, founded only a year before in 1936, who in the opening ceremony of his confederation's fourth congress declared, "It will not naturally be the peasantry of our country that is called upon to unify the proletarian forces, unfortunately for all of us, given its backwardness, its ignorance, its division, its lack of class consciousness."[40]

Only the *ejido* executive committees of Veracruz had the courage to respond to Lombardo: "The peasantry remains backward because the Revolution has not paid enough attention to it," and "We peasants are in a process of unification that had been neglected, but we united, perhaps because of our ignorance, to defend our rights more effectively, to improve our collective living conditions, to find better methods for cultivating and using the land, to recover our tools to work the land, to ask for dams for irrigation, and not to participate in politics."[41]

The situation was by no means uncomplicated: The peasants, in this case from Veracruz, felt distanced from the political project and continued to be pressured by the different groups that used the state of Veracruz as a battlefield. Emilio Armenta was a well-known warlord who, heading two hundred armed men, laid waste to the environs of Tlapacoyan. Among other things, the Armenta brothers attacked the Villa Rica hacienda in Misantla and torched several small hamlets. The cries of "Long live Calles!" and "Long live Christ the King!" had still not been silenced.[42]

Armed groups continued to strike at different towns. Gangs of fifteen to fifty men rustled cattle, stole crops, murdered peasants, and raped rural women. Confusion often obscured where the violence came from, but it is a fact that the large landowners, threatened by land distribution, armed their own defense groups. At the same time, the Veracruz agrarianists had turned over their arms to the government on different occasions. It had been Cárdenas, in fact, who, as minister of war under President Pascual Ortiz Rubio, had carried out a widespread campaign of disarmament. Rumors circulated, however, that as late as 1937 Heriberto Jara, head of the military zone, had given the peasants arms in order to establish guerrilla bands.[43]

The civil war in Spain strongly influenced peasants and workers' organizations to form militias. The League of Agrarian Communities of Veracruz asked the president to transform the rural defenses into "peasant militias with obligatory service." In their request, they argued that "the undeniable enemy of the workers is fascism." For that reason, they requested that the peasants be "fully armed" and that this policy include urban workers. Clearly Cárdenas considered the proposal unacceptable because of the ideological effects of suggesting the creation of "workers' militias," "artisan's militias," or "revolutionary student militias."[44]

Despite the denunciations of white-guard activities, as soon as General Jara left his post as head of the Veracruz military zone and Cárdenas replaced him with General Manuel Monge, the "red guerrilla bands" began to be dissolved a few months later. Journalists linked to the Cárdenas administration argued that the peasants had made bad use of the weapons and utilized them to commit crimes.[45]

La Laguna, or Modernization

The agrarian struggle of these same years in La Laguna, one of the most revolutionary regions, located in the states of Durango and Coahuila, was very different. Peasant activity became decidedly agrarian in orientation, encouraged by leftist groups and organizations very close to *cardenismo*, and this mobilization led to the regime's longest agrarian project. Linked to a modernization process because of the vast swaths of irrigated land and crops used for export, the revolution had established a clear dividing line between large landowners and the peasants, many of whom were followers of Pancho Villa's army.

In 1930, peasant unrest began leading landowners, very much despite their traditional instincts, to propose certain agricultural measures that favored their interests but also included concessions to the peasants. They suggested forming *ejido* districts outside the cultivated areas, which would be benefited by irrigation from the Nazas and Aguanaval rivers. In 1936, according to the Ministry of Agriculture and the National Agrarian Commission, they distributed 21,640 hectares among 2,318 *ejido* members, although it was not mentioned that only 5,600 hectares (barely 20 percent) were cultivable.

Problems continued despite the fact that in 1934 President Abelardo L. Rodríguez created two *ejido* districts in the region. Faced with what historian Joe Ashby has characterized as "physically capitalist" exploitation because these agricultural units utilized irrigation, modern techniques, and machinery and paid the laborers a wage, the agitation continued.[46]

The landless rural population expressed its discontent in two ways: making their demands with weapons in hand and presenting appeals for land distribution. Gangs committed various bloody acts. Then, the minister of war, General Andrés Figueroa, found it necessary to travel to La Laguna and use different strategies to pacify the peasants in the region. One leaflet distributed among them proposed that the rebels accept an amnesty by "turning in all their weapons and ammunition in exchange for a safe conduct pass that would protect them on returning to their homes so they could do honorable work with dignity, as many have already done."[47]

Francisco García accepted the amnesty and turned in his weapons together with the twenty-three men under his command, their horses, saddles, and ammunition.[48] In contrast, warlord Trinidad Mora, considered invincible in the Western Sierra Madre Mountains, remained mobilized until he was killed in an armed clash,[49] although Federico Vázquez continued to command a party of armed rebels.

On the other hand, the struggle to divide up the 75 haciendas ranging from 1,000 to 10,000 hectares each, the 19 haciendas of over 10,000 hectares, and the 3 that comprised 100,000 hectares, many of which belonged to foreign individuals or companies, continued to spur rural activism. In July 1935 a strike broke out among the workers of the Manila Hacienda in the municipality of Gómez Palacio. Owners Hermosillo and García came to an agreement with the Maclovio Herrera Union, while those who belonged to Librado Rivera's union requested that the hacienda be "attached" because the cotton and alfalfa crops had to be harvested. Many other agrarian groups expressed their solidarity, among them those from the Lujan and El Castillo haciendas.[50]

The singular thing about these struggles is that they included union negotiation, and the president even commissioned Vice Minister of the Interior Agustín Arroyo Cházaro to go to La Laguna to conduct talks between employers and workers to end the conflicts in late January 1937. Arroyo Cházaro's arbitration did not take place, though, because the property-line disputes between those who were dividing up the land into lots and the *ejido* leaders had finally been resolved. However, measures like state-government regulation of the payment for the seventh day of work[51] and the firings of more than four hundred workers were the sparks that prompted 104 CTM-affiliated unions representing almost twenty thousand workers to call for a general strike.

Initially scheduled for May 26, 1936, the general strike was postponed twice. Cárdenas himself had to go to La Laguna, and on July 27, he arrived in Torreón to try to solve the conflict among the various stakeholders. However, the strike broke out on August 18, and to avoid confrontations, federal forces moved into the area and disarmed the agricultural workers; the CTM demanded that the president provide an explanation. On August 29, Cárdenas decided to definitively take matters into his own hands and, from Mexico City in a meeting with the union confederation, declared that the La Laguna region was "the richest in the country," that in recent years hacienda owners had made profits of more than 300 million pesos but had invested only 17 million pesos, and that he therefore had come to the following conclusions: (1) The land would be distributed among all of the region's workers, who would not have to present written requests for land; (2) the government would provide the implements the workers needed to cultivate the land; (3) temporary workers would leave the region as soon as possible with the support of the army and public officials, which would force the nonunion workers to leave; (4) employers would respect the collective-bargaining agreements and would employ only unionized workers; and (5) a commission would be sent to ensure that the waters of the Nazas River would be better utilized. Importantly, the secretary of agriculture at the time, Cedillo, disagreed with this vast distribution of land.

This was the first step toward the government's definitive solution. On October 6, 1936, it decreed the expropriation of three-quarters of all of the land in La Laguna, setting the stage for a broad national polemic about the policy of expropriation, earlier established by Article 27 of the 1917 constitution.

The End of a Process

Of the three strongest men in the defiant regions, President Cárdenas had rid himself of both Garrido Canabal, who left the cabinet after the 1935 crisis, and Tejeda, whom he had sent to head a mission to the Spanish Republic. The only one left was Cedillo. This San Luis Potosí strongman held the post of secretary of agriculture, although he did not agree with the expropriation in La Laguna, which he only learned about from the press. It was actually Francisco J. Múgica, then secretary of communications, who did the work of distributing the land, a job that corresponded to that of the secretary of agriculture. Cedillo had already clashed with the president (e.g., on October 17, 1936, he had been required to be present to provisionally turn over his family's own ranch of 6,582 hectares in Palomas, San Luis Potosí. This was the week before the expropriation in La Laguna). Thus, a secretary of agriculture was put in a curious position when he was given thirty-one days to vacate his own land because it had been expropriated.[52]

The disagreements with Cárdenas became evident, and rumors began circulating from the Left, grouped around Vicente Lombardo Toledano, stirring up passions and making Cedillo look like the instigator of a plot against the president. Cornered and without realistic alternatives, he had to resign from the cabinet on August 15, 1937.

On March 18 of the following year, after a complicated process involving British and US oil companies, the president expropriated the country's oil resources. The response resulted in almost complete support from the populace; however, among those expressing their disagreement was Cedillo, who made his views known. Toledano then insisted that Cedillo had an understanding with the foreign companies, an allegation that has never been proven, and even of his having direct contact with the Nazis, for whom Mexico's oil was important. But the most serious issue for Mexico was that the countries whose companies were seized refused to buy Mexican oil. The break in relations between Mexico and Britain caused consternation in the US State Department, but the United States contributed to the boycott by suspending its purchase of silver from Mexico, which at that time came to 30 million dollars a year.

Cedillo's resignation was a harsh blow to him, but he had fulfilled his aspirations: From a first-blush revolutionary and San Luis Potosí rancher, he had later taken a national post with enormous responsibilities. Several things had come together to make him a rebel if we take into account his past as a revolutionary combatant. His Potosí militias provided substantial support to the government in various conflicts, above all during la Cristiada. Also, Cedillo became a governor who fought against the local oligarchy and promoted the CCM, thus becoming an armed defender of institutionalization. Finally, he served as a member of Cárdenas's cabinet in opposition to Calles, with whom he had also been linked.

Conclusion

In 1938, three events reinforced the centralist design of the Cárdenas regime, in which, he liked to say, the executive played a prominent role: Cedillo's disappearance from the scene and, with him, that of the only important regional alternative remaining from the past; the unification of the agricultural workers in the CCM and the creation of the Party of the Mexican Revolution; and the nationalism that spread throughout the country after the expropriation of the oil companies on March 18 of that year.[53]

Cárdenas held the destiny of the country in his hands, and his governmental agenda now emphasized the change that was indispensable for the party that had ushered him into the presidency. The PNR had been designed in a way that was not appropriate for the country's new political and social circumstances. Its organization had matured, but after almost ten years, its internal disparities and problems had become obvious. The party's mediation had been important in the consolidation of institutions and had managed to put several personalist considerations to one side.

However, despite the dissolution of regional parties, some local branches continued to use the regional emblems alongside that of the PNR. In general, the PNR's national character was indisputable, and it became the party's most tangible expression resulting from the revolution. The PNR supervised local elections, any one of which became national reference points for strength and discipline.

However, the PNR did foster the emergence of leaders who exercised new mediating functions between the party apparatus and the regions. This was a new generation of strongmen with political clout, although with less territorial reach than that of the powerful leaders who came out of the revolution.

Just as the PNR was one of Calles's ideas, so in 1937 Cárdenas felt the need to create the Party of the Mexican Revolution (PRM) a year later. The necessity for a strong state and the similarity to the situation nine years earlier meant that the government imposed the party on society. The president used the strength of his office to establish an organization in which peasants and workers each formed their own groups. He also believed that, together with the military and public employees, they would make up the four sectors—workers, peasants, middle classes, and the military—that would contribute to the strengthening of state policies.[54]

The contribution of *cardenismo* to the centralist regime was that it changed Article 49 of the constitution to allow the president to request that congress grant him the authority to issue laws. Cárdenas believed that these extraordinary powers, which undermined the activities of the legislature, were unfortunate but that this reform was not very profound; consequently, the president increased his ability to legislate within certain limits, contravening the spirit of federalism.

Another proposal from the executive amended Article 94 regarding the judiciary, suppressing the lifetime appointment of supreme court and superior court justices. The official report written by President Cárdenas's secretary, Ignacio García Téllez, declared the following:

> Without disregarding the advantages of judicial officials remaining in their posts for life, it was nevertheless necessary to prevent that permanent status from making the judicial branch rigid since it is its responsibility to administer justice precisely at a time when a complete ideological transformation was taking place . . . [With this measure, the government sought] to create opportunities for the systematic renewal of the judges and for taking advantage of the new values forged in the social struggle.[55]

Historians also state that the executive managed to maintain the spirit of the 1917 constitution in relation to the concept of the "free municipality."[56] Cárdenas did not accept the proposal to eliminate elected city councils and replace them with administrative councils appointed by the governors, "something that can be allowed only if complete anarchy reigns, so much so as to be equivalent to the demand that the federal government intervene to take over state goventment."[57] Additional instances of increased centralization arose when dissidents challenged Cárdenas. For example, the regime did not explain why it stripped governors of their official immunity, sometimes at moments of grave risk, as in the case of Mateo Hernández Netro, who was involved in Cedillo's San Luis Potosí rebellion. Another case was that of Lastra

Ramírez, when Garrido Canabal was being tried in court the public opinion when Ignacio Garciá Téllez, the presidential secretary, declared the following:

> Different people, usurping the functions of municipal authorities, of the state legislature, and of the Organizing Committee [of the party], tried to declare victory in the elections by themselves, forgetting that the sovereignty of the people is exercised through the procedures which the Constitution stipulates. And, what is more, they tried to make the federal Executive the sole interpreter and absolute judge of the electoral results; they did all of this without thinking not only that the invitation to the president of the Republic to exercise a competency not attributed to him by the Constitution was illegal but also that it was illegal to attempt to disregard the competencies stipulated by the law of the duly constituted legislatures, which are the bodies with the faculty of deciding on the elections of the head of the Executive.[58]

The Cárdenas position, written by García Téllez, implies that the executive had not yet accepted the capability of being an arbiter, which he had constructed throughout his six-year term, particularly if one is aware of the numerous electoral and postelectoral conflicts, mainly regarding gubernatorial elections. Often the president would have to intervene to resolve litigation of this sort, as well as disputes between workers and employers, agrarian conflicts, and so on.

The sovereignty that was being built implied, on the other hand, the president's neutrality in choosing the PRM's presidential candidate. Cárdenas even asked the cabinet ministers who were going to run for office to resign six months before the election to guarantee that the people's decision would be respected and that the state would not be compromised. However, it is almost impossible to accept the idea that President Cárdenas did not influence the PRM's decision to nominate Manuel Avila Camacho as its presidential hopeful.

After 1940, federalism in Mexico took on another dimension, which eventually declined because of the modifications of *cardenismo* to the political system. The institutional and social acceptance of the power of the executive was a determining factor in reorganizing the country after the Mexican Revolution because it put an end to the excesses of *caudillos* and achieved the participation of all of the regions into one nation.

Notes

1. The period between 1930 and 1935 is called the *maximato*, which began with the assassination of Álvaro Obregón, when Plutarco Elías Callas acted as the *jefe máximo*, or "top boss," trying to hold many of reins of power during the brief administration of Emilio

Portes Gil, Pascual Ortiz Rubio, and Abelardo Rodríguez. The *maximato* came to an end in the first few months of the Lázaro Cárdenas administration.

2. A fundamental book—particularly the introduction and conclusions—for understanding the regions' involvement in this process is Thomas Benjamin and Mark Wasserman, *Historia regional de la Revolución Mexicana: La provincia entre 1910–1929* (Mexico City: Consejo Nacional para la Cultura y las Artes, 1996).
3. The term *caciquismo* is limited to traditional Mexico with a strong indigenous presence, but it is actually broader and refers to a constellation of regionally and locally based powers centered in local strongmen. Historians have discussed twentieth-century *caciquismo* to differentiate it from the kind that became functional for Mexico's political system in the era of the Institutional Revolutionary Party (PRI).
4. Carlos Martínez Assad, ed., *Estadistas, caciques y caudillos* (Mexico City: UNAM Press, 1988).
5. See many examples in the work compiled by Josefina Zoraida Vázquez, *El establecimiento del federalismo en Mexico (1821–1827)* (Mexico City: El Colegio de Mexico, 2003).
6. Constitución política de los Estados Unidos Mexicanos comentada (Mexico City: UNAM, 1985), 119.
7. *Caudillismo* is the political system characterized by those who led armies during the nineteenth century to win power. The word *caudillo* is often used to describe people with the gift and capacity for command, even above the law. It is closely linked to the term *caciquismo* (see note 3). During the Mexican Revolution, Obregón became known as the *caudillo* par excellence, and Zapata was called the "*caudillo* of the South."
8. Arnaldo Córdova, *La politica de masas del cardenismo* (Mexico City: Editorial Erov, Serie Popular, 1974), 42.
9. Carlos Martínez Assad, ed., *El laboratorio de la Revolución: El Tabasco garridista* (Mexico City: Siglo XXI, 1979).
10. Dudley Ankerson, *Agrarian Warlord: Saturnino Cedillo and the Mexican Revolution in San Luis Potosí* (DeKalb: Northern Illinois University Press, 1984).
11. Luis Javier Garrido, *El partido de la Revolución institucionalizada: La formación del nuevo estado en Mexico (1928–1945)* (Mexico City: Secretaria de Educación Pública, 1986), 101.
12. Ibid., 104.
13. Arnaldo Córdova, *La revolución en crisis: La aventura del maximato* (Mexico City: Cal y Arena, 1995), 214.
14. Ibid., 298.
15. Ibid., 79.
16. Ibid., 195.
17. Lázaro Cárdenas, *Apuntes, 1913–1940, Obras*, vol. 1 (Mexico City: UNAM, 1972), 22, and Córdova, *La política de masas del cardenismo*, 40.
18. Carlos Martínez Assad, "La formación del nuevo grupo en el poder y la ruptura Calles-Cárdenas," in *Casa del tiempo* 10 (Mexico City: Universidad Autónoma Metropolitana, June 10, 1981).

19. Córdova, *La política de masas del cardenismo*, 44.
20. Samuel León, "Alianza de clase y cardenismo (junio de 1935–febrero de 1936)," *Revista Mexicana de Ciencias Politicians y Sociales* 89 (Mexico City: Universidad Nacional Autónoma de México/Facultad de Ciencias Politicas y Sociales, July–September 1977).
21. For this historical figure and what happened in his state, see Roman Falcón, *El agrarismo en Veracruz: La etapa radical (1928–1935)* (Mexico City: El Colegio de Mexico, 1977), and Romana Falcón and Soledad García, *La semilla en el surco: Adalberto Tejeda y el radicalismo en Veracruz, 1883–1960* (Mexico City: El Colegio de México, 1986).
22. Carlos Martínez Assad, *Los rebeldes vencidos: Cedillo contra el Estado cardenista* (Mexico City: Fondo de Cultura Económica/Universidad Nacional Autónoma de México, 1990).
23. Carlos Martínez Assad, Friedrich Katz, et al., *El camino de la rebelión de general Saturnino Cedillo* (Mexico City: Oceano, 2010).
24. Arnaldo Córdova deals with the *maximato* exhaustively in his *La revolución en crisis*.
25. *Excélsior* (Mexico City), Dec. 22, 1936.
26. The white guards were militias formed in the haciendas to face down the agrarianists, who wanted to take over the land. As such, the guards represented a counterrevolutionary interest.
27. *Excélsior* (Mexico City), May 29, 1937.
28. Ibid., June 18 and 21, 1937.
29. For details about what happened there, which exemplifies what was going on in different parts of the country, see the classic book by Luis González, *Pueblo en vilo: Microhistoria de San José de Gracia* (Mexico City: El Colegio de Mexico, 1968).
30. The *ejido* is the form of land tenure created by the revolutionary armies to favor the peasantry. It was the basis for agricultural development under the postrevolutionary regime.
31. *Excélsior* (Mexico City), Nov. 10, 1935.
32. Ibid., Jan. 8, 1937.
33. Ibid., Aug. 7, 1936.
34. Ibid., Oct. 20, 1936.
35. Ibid., Nov. 24, 1936.
36. Between 1926 and 1929, groups of Catholics, called *cristeros*, mainly in Central Mexico, staged armed rebellions against the secular government to prevent the state from advancing its regulation of civilian life. They organized with the support of the Catholic Church, which withdrew as the Cristiada struggle progressed.
37. *Excélsior* (Mexico City), Feb. 19, 1938.
38. Ibid., Mar. 19, 1937.
39. Ibid., Mar. 13, 1937.
40. On this same idea, see my interview with Valentín Campa of the Mexican Communist Party in Carlos Martínez Assad, ed., *El camino de la rebelión de general Saturnino Cedillo*, 159–70, and Excélsior (Mexico City), Apr. 3, 1937, 16–17.
41. *Excélsior* (Mexico City), Apr. 30, 1937.
42. Ibid., Jan. 10 and 26, 1936.

43. Ibid., Mar. 13, 1937.

44. Ibid., November 1938.

45. Ibid., Mar. 1, 1937.

46. Joe Ashby, *Organized Labor and the Mexican Revolution under Lázaro Cárdenas* (Chapel Hill: University of North Carolina Press, 1967).

47. *Excélsior* (Mexico City), June 17, 1936.

48. Ibid., July 2, 1936.

49. Ibid., July 20, 1936.

50. Ibid., July 7 and 8, 1935, and *El Machete* (Mexico City), Aug. 3, 1935.

51. A substantial gain of the workers' struggle was the mandatory paid day of rest once a week for both men and women. This had been a demand by many social movements in the early twentieth century.

52. For information about this local strongman, see Dudley Ankerson, *El caudillo agrarista: Saturnino Cedillo y la Revolución mexicana en San Luis Potosí* (Mexico City: Gobierno del estado de San Luis Potosí, Instituto Nacional de Estudios Históricos de la Revolución Mexicana, 1994).

53. Jonathan Brown and Alan Knight, eds., *The Mexican Petroleum Industry in the Twentieth Century* (Austin: University of Texas Press, 1979); David E. Cronon, *Josephus Daniels in Mexico* (Madison: University of Wisconsin Press, 1960); Lorenzo Meyer, *Mexico and the United States in the Oil Controversy, 1917–1942* (Austin: University of Texas Press, 1977).

54. For other studies of the *cardenista* period, see Adrian Bantjes, *As if Jesus Walked on Earth: Cardenismo, Sonora and the Mexican Revolution* (Wilmington, Del.: Scholarly Resources, 1998); Lyle C. Brown, "Cárdenas: Creating a Campesino Power Base for Presidential Policy," in George C. Wolfskill and Douglas W. Richmond, eds., *Essays on the Mexican Revolution: Revisionist Views of the Leaders* (Austin: University of Texas Press, 1979), 101–36; Luis González, *Los días del presidente Cárdenas* (Mexico City: El Colegio de México, 1981).

55. México, Secretaría de Gobernación, *Seis años al servicio de México, 1934–1940* (Mexico City: Talleres Gráficos de la Nación, 1940), 3–4.

56. The Mexican Constitution of 1917 stipulates that the third level of government after the federation and the states shall be the municipality, allowing for the administrative organization of towns and localities as the bodies of government closest to society.

57. México, Secretaría de Gobernación, *Seis años al servicio de México, 1934–1940* (Mexico City: Talleres Gráficos de la Nación, 1940), 5.

58. Ibid., 6.

CHAPTER 9

The Mexican Revolution

One Century of Reflections, 1910–2010

Thomas Benjamin

Introduction

Few countries cultivate history with such enthusiasm as Mexico.
LUIS GONZÁLEZ Y GONZÁLEZ

As the opening epigraph to this chapter suggests,[1] the Mexican Revolution was one of the titanic revolutions of modern history. It was a jumbled combination of several popular uprisings that destroyed a prolonged dictatorship and gave rise to significant political, social, and economic reforms. It was complicated, inspirational, and terrible. Many hundreds of thousands of Mexicans took up arms in their country between 1910 and 1920, and more than one million lives were lost to violence, famine, and epidemics. The human and physical destruction that took place in Mexico was appalling. There was a profound need from the beginning to make all of this meaningful and redemptive, and Mexicans have been doing this for one hundred years. Approximately one hundred years later, Mexicans and others are celebrating the revolution and its heroes.[2] We need to recognize, however, that the remembered and historicized Mexican Revolution has always been in a state of flux.[3]

The events that began in 1910 and 1911 were immediately defined as la Revolución. The Mexican Revolution has been reported and chronicled, filmed and photographed, novelized and illustrated, researched and analyzed almost without end. It has been remembered and commemorated, glorified and contested, politicized and mythologized. For one century Mexicans and quite a few aficionados of Mexico have given great significance and diverse meanings to the Mexican Revolution.

The first bibliography of the revolution, which appeared in 1918, listed some eight hundred books, pamphlets, manifestos, and documents. A second bibliography in 1931 more than tripled the relevant number of publications.[4] In the mid-1960s the US historian Stanley R. Ross warned that the number of books and articles about the Mexican Revolution was threatening to reach "truly torrential levels."[5] Dirk Raat's annotative bibliography in 1982 listed studies written not only in Spanish and English but also French, German, Italian, Portuguese, Russian, Japanese, and Chinese.[6] In the following decades not only were there more and more histories of the revolution, but more of them were also better and better. Given the quantity and quality of such literature, we are compelled to ask, why has there been such enduring interest in the Mexican Revolution?

There is, in fact, no fully satisfactory answer to this question. We human beings seem to have a compulsion to give meaning to the past and, as a result, the past gives meaning to our individual lives and collective identities. "The past has been a living past," noted J. H. Plumb, "something which has been used day after day, life after life, never-endingly."[7] All peoples and societies have done this, and we moderns have surely overdone it. Consider the enormous attention given to the French Revolution for more than two centuries.[8] Mexican historians and intellectuals have long noted that their culture is particularly attached to, preoccupied with, and even burdened by the past. Some intellectuals and pundits have complained that Mexico has remained in the shadow of the Mexican Revolution far too long.[9] This view has merit, but I wish to focus on how Mexicans have reflected the light and shadows of the revolution. Today it seems much more appropriate for commentators like me to praise the revolution than to bury it.

What follows is a brief excursion through one century of memories, myths, and histories. The emphasis here is on how Mexicans have made sense of, given meaning to, and represented their revolution. Any brief survey such as this is risky business. This subject is, after all, a vast, complex, and incomplete story. Its contours are ragged and often undefined. Interpretative trends are fraught with countertrends and outliers, all of which have been controversial. With these warnings, let us proceed.

Inventing the Revolution: The 1910s

Mexican revolutionaries carried on an uninterrupted discourse of memory during the 1910s. Writing about the revolution as a historical event begins with the revolution itself. Politicians, journalists, intellectuals, and other scribblers wrote about contemporary events and put them in historical perspective. These *voceros de la Revolución*—spokespersons or mouthpieces of the revolution—wrote proclamations, articles, pamphlets, and books trying to make sense of it all and, more important, influence the course of events. In order to triumph, one has to convince.[10]

Although factionalism emerged from the beginning, the various and often opposing *voceros* defined the events of the 1910s in remarkably similar and enduring ways. What began in 1910–1911 was not another political brawl or petty revolt but a genuine revolution on a great and historical scale. This revolution became historicized, presented as the third stage of an ongoing revolutionary tradition in Mexico that began with the insurgency in 1810 and the reform in the 1850s. The revolution, finally, was reified, meaning that revolutionaries portrayed these events as a conscious entity, a historical force destined to forge a better Mexico regardless of the resistance of reactionaries or the errors of particular revolutionary leaders and movements. One *vocero* wrote in 1911, "The Revolution continues its march, slow but sure, devastating and imposing."[11] When conceived in this manner, the inexorable revolution must achieve its inevitable triumph. This Mexican Revolution, the revolution with these fundamental characteristics, was the one that politicians speechified, artists represented, and writers eulogized for a century.[12]

With the first revolutionary victories in 1911, revolutionary factionalism emerged, as did contentious narratives. The supporters of Francisco Madero began to define the revolution, as did Madero's former allies and new opponents. Following the overthrow and assassination of Madero, the Constitutionalist movement, led by Venustiano Carranza, redefined the ongoing revolt. Once again, former allies and new opponents, the supporters of Francisco (Pancho) Villa and Emiliano Zapata, provided their own interpretations of the uprising.[13] The *villistas* and *zapatistas* attracted urban intellectuals—"city boys"—who wrote revolutionary plans and propaganda. *Zapatista* and *villista voceros* portrayed Carranza as the false leader who betrayed the revolution. These and other political movements inspired and produced popular ballads—*corridos*—that sang their praises.[14]

Revolutionary leaders and some (staged) events were extensively photographed and filmed. The photojournalist Agustín Victor Casasola established his own newsphoto agency in 1912, hired five hundred photographers, and purchased the images of others to portray events in Mexico. Beginning in 1921 Casasola began a long family tradition of publishing and reprinting albums of annotated photographs. The *Historia gráfica de la Revolución*, writes John Mraz, was a "fundamental resource for constructing a nation in a largely illiterate country devastated by a cataclysmic revolution."[15] Only a few dozen of these images, from the hundreds of thousands of photographs created in the 1910s, became iconic and influential. These precious few, particularly those of Zapata and Villa and their soldiers and *soldaderas* (camp followers), remain powerful reflections of the revolution. Mexican films of the revolution appeared during the 1910s as well. Salvador Toscano's *La historia completa de la Revolución* arrived as early as 1912. Pancho Villa signed an exclusive contract with Chicago's Mutual Film in 1914. The fictional *The Life of General Villa* (1914) and others that followed helped created the Villa myth in both the United States and Mexico. "Villa's relationship with the moving image," writes Andrea Noble, "is the stuff of legend."[16]

The *carrancistas* attracted many "city boys," that is spokespersons, journalists, and intellectuals. As a result, they published the most newspapers in the country and sent the most essays to foreign papers, magazines, and journals. Consequently, a deluge of articles, pamphlets, and books poured from *carrancistas'* typewriters and presses from 1913 to 1920. "The triumph of the Constitutionalist cause, as with all good causes," noted the *vocero* Guillermo Mellado, "was driven by the incomparable force of justice." Alfredo Aragón's 1916 tract, *A las Armas*, portrayed the *villistas* as reactionaries, the *zapatistas* as bandits, and the Carranza Constitutionistas as the reformers.[17] The Carranza government also produced postage stamps honoring revolutionary martyrs and heroes, including Carranza himself.[18] "Every revolution tends to worship its leaders, and Carranza, the first of the revolutionary Caesars," noted Mexico's Nobel laureate, Octavio Paz, "was a forerunner of the so-called 'personality cult,' which is merely a euphemism for modern political idolatry."[19]

These contemporary accounts by bitter enemies, nevertheless, still shared the view that this momentous revolution was genuine, historic, and inevitable. Still, much of the writing about the recent revolution, according to a University of California professor in 1919, "has been by way of propaganda for one side or other of the combatant forces." A Mexican jurist writing in the same year argued that "as civil strife grows fiercer, those who narrate political events adhere more tenaciously to the idea that history is a tribunal, in order that they may lay the blame and curse of history upon their adversaries." Seven decades later Gloria Villegas Moreno, one of the best scholars of revolutionary historiography, reminds us that, from the start of the armed struggle, writing was "an integral part of the confrontation."[20]

Remembering the Revolution: The 1920s–1930s

Revolutionaries in the 1920s and 1930s remembered and revered the Mexican Revolution but in very different and quite divisive ways. They spoke and wrote about it, illustrated and painted it, commemorated it, and built monuments to it in order to shape Mexico's collective memory, to gain political legitimacy and advantage, and to encourage and promote social justice and reform. Presidents Álvaro Obregón (1920–1924) and Plutarco Elías Calles (1924–1928) declared that the revolutionary conflict was concluded but that the revolution itself continued through government, reconstruction, and reform. The remembered revolution remained divisive for some time. By 1923 Madero, Zapata, Carranza, and Villa—and many other revolutionary heroes—were dead.[21] In the 1920s and 1930s the notable revolutionary movements of the 1910s were transformed into fractious and opposing personal cults by surviving veterans and supporters. The Pro-Madero Group, according to its founding statement in 1920, formed in order "to create a sentimental and patriotic cult for the memory of Señor Madero."[22] The anti-Madero Antonio Islas Bravo, on the other hand, referred to the rancorous *maderistas* as pious members of the "Perpetual Veil of Madero."[23] The members of these revolutionary cults commemorated their particular anniversaries, wrote their memoirs and chronicles, and memorialized their heroes in monuments. A pervasive regionalism accentuated these divisions among revolutionary factions past and present. "In all of the sierras and valleys of Mexico," recalled the Taxco silversmith William Spratling in 1932, "each region has its own revolutionary hero" (see table 9.1)[24]

Successive governments during these decades turned to the revolution for legitimacy and began an effort to unify revolutionaries in the present and from the past and to heal the wounds of memory. One of the conceptual tools of this unification is the metaphor of the *familia revolucionaria* (revolutionary family), which invited former opponents and enemies to come together on behalf of

Table 9.1. Revolutionary Martyrs: Dates of Their Sacrifice and Posthumous Titles

November 19, 1910	Aquiles Serdán: "The Martyr of the Revolution"
February 22, 1913	Francisco Madero: "The Apostle of Democracy"
April 10, 1919	Emiliano Zapata: "The Apostle of Agrarianism"
May 20, 1919	Venustiano Carranza: "The First Chief of the Revolution"
November 26, 1919	Felipe Angeles: "The Humanitarian of the Revolution"
July 20, 1923	Francisco Villa: "The Strong Arm of the Revolution"
January 3, 1924	Felipe Carrillo Puerto: "The Saint of the Proletariat"
July 17, 1928	Álvaro Obregón: "The *Caudillo* of the Revolution"

a greater purpose. Miguel Yepez Solórzano, an alderman in the Mexico City government, demanded the "solidarity and cohesion of the Social Class, which steers the Mexican Revolution."[25] In 1925 Juan Sánchez Azcona complained in the press that the "schisms of the Revolution" undermined the legitimacy and power of the revolution and its government.[26] This became clearly visible that same year when Mexico's lower house of congress, the Chamber of Deputies, proposed to write the name of Francisco Madero "in Letters of Gold" on its Wall of Honor. This tradition of official recognition and honor of national heroes began in the 1820s. The congressional resolution on behalf of Madero in 1925 passed the chamber, but *zapatista* veteran (and Deputy) Antonio Díaz Soto y Gama protested: "We are still here now, many *zapatistas*, enemies of *maderismo*" (see table 9.2)[27]

Some of the most enduring representations of the revolution appeared in the public murals of the 1920s and 1930s. These were part and parcel of a Mexican cultural renaissance that began with the revolution. Intellectuals created the Popular Mexican University in 1912, providing free lectures in Mexico City to workers and housewives. Beginning in 1921, the new national Department of Public Education (Secretaría de Educación Pública, SEP), promoted a national literacy campaign, sent "missionary teachers" to native villages, and

Table 9.2. In Letters of Gold: Revolutionary Leaders Honored on the Wall of the National Congress

1925	Francisco Madero
1929	Álvaro Obregón
1930	Felipe Carillo Puerto
1931	Aquiles Serdán
1931	Venustiano Carranza and Emiliano Zapata
1936	Belisario Domínguez
1954	The Legislative Martyrs of 1913
1966	Francisco Villa
1976	Lázaro Cárdenas
1984	Francisco Múgica
1993	Vicente Lombardo Toledano
2000	Ricardo Flores Magón

created thousands of small libraries throughout the country. The muralist movement of the 1920s and 1930s produced public frescoes and paintings that celebrated peasant, worker, and indigenous Mexico. It has been proclaimed as "the greatest revolutionary art of this [the twentieth] century.[28] Painters and graphic artists formed open-air art schools and collective workshops. The Popular Graphic Arts Workshop (Taller de Gráfica Popular, TGP), established in 1937, produced thousands of remarkable linoleum and woodcut prints.[29] This cultural revival, as well as the policies of some national and state leaders, became rabidly anticlerical. The alleged fanaticism of the church was presented in art and literature as anathema to the ideals of the revolution and the needs of the Mexican people.[30]

Political radicalism, cultural nationalism, and revolutionary art attracted the attention of many American—and European—political activists, journalists and writers, artists and photographers, and other aficionados in the 1920s and 1930s. The pages of the *New Republic, Nation, New Masses, Liberator, Survey*, and the *Christian Century* examined and admired the revolution and its aftermath. Mexico lured Katherine Ann Porter (in 1920), Jean Charlot (1921), D. H. Lawrence (1923), Edward Weston and Tina Modotti (1923), the mysterious B. Traven (1923), John Dos Passos (1926), Malcolm Cowley (1930), Leopold Stokowski (1931), Sergei Eisenstein (1932), Graham Greene (1938), and others. Ernest Gruening, editor of the *Nation*, and Frank Tannenbaum, an Austrian-born New York intellectual and historian, wrote important histories of the revolution that are still consulted and reprinted in the United States and Mexico.[31] Journalist Carleton Beals, Stuart Chase, and others wrote broad surveys of Mexico that were illustrated by Diego Rivera.[32] Tannenbaum dedicated *Peace by Revolution* to Diego Rivera and had it illustrated by Miguel Covarrubias. In 1933 the *New York Times* referred to "the present enormous vogue of things Mexican."[33]

The assassination of president-elect Álvaro Obregón in 1928, believed by many Mexicans to be the indispensible *caudillo* of the revolution, posed a considerable threat of destabilization, revolt, or worse. Seeking to hold together a fragile coalition of *obregonistas* and *callistas*, President Calles called again for the unification of all "revolutionaries." A new National Revolutionary Party (PNR) was formed in 1929 "in accordance with the plan of unification and organization of all the elements of the Revolution from the Maderista beginning to the present."[34] Emilio Portes Gil, president of the PNR, a few years later asserted that the "collective and impersonal interpretation of heroes" had become a "doctrine of state."[35]

The PNR, as a political institution and an instrument of revolutionary propaganda, encouraged the solidarity and cohesion of all Mexicans, particularly

Figure 9.1. "Cárdenas Speaks!" Cover from the book of the same title (1940). Private collection of the author.

"revolutionaries." Brutal politicking and violence, as well as symbolic gestures, naturally compelled the unification of the revolutionary family and the new national state. Major revolts and rebellions among dissident factions or, to put it more accurately, revolts and rebellions against the national government occurred in 1920, 1923–1924, 1927, 1929 and 1938–1939. Revolts had the political benefit of categorically separating, in the words of Calles, "the false and the genuine revolutionaries."[36]

The Chamber of Deputies placed more names "in Letters of Gold" after Madero. The 1931 resolution to add the names of both Venustiano Carranza and Emiliano Zapata was controversial but also an important symbolic step forward. The resolution noted that both were genuine revolutionaries who struggled for the well-being of Mexico despite being enemies until death. As a journalist at the time noted, "The enmity and distance that the vicissitudes of politics provoked between Madero and Zapata, between Zapata and Carranza, between Carranza and Obregón, matter not."[37] This newfound official unity became visible in the PNR's annual *Nationalist Calendar* for the year 1935. A line drawing for November 20, "Day of the Revolution," pictured an idealized portrait of the revolutionary family, including Felipe Angeles, Carranza, Obregón, Calles, and President Lázaro Cárdenas. The Monument to the Revolution, a massive triumphal arch in Mexico City, was completed in 1938. Created to shape memory, this monument is grand and austere. The monument's revolution was designed to celebrate the people's revolution. The architect directed no attention to any of the revolutionary martyr cults. The official proposal stated that this monument "will not be erected to the glory of specific heroes, martyrs, or caudillos." Moreover, "there will be no names or portraits of persons. It will glorify, in the abstract, the secular work of the people"[38] (see figure 9.1).

Novelists and short-story writers, on the other hand, created a very different representation of the Mexican Revolution. These storytellers emphasized violence, cruelty, and chaos. Mariano Azuela, in his classic 1915 novel, *Los de Abajo* (The Underdogs), referred to the revolution as a hurricane because of its indiscriminate power. One of his characters proclaimed, "You ask me why I am still a rebel? Well, the revolution is like a hurricane: if you're in it, you're not a man . . . you're a leaf, a dead leaf, blown by the wind."[39] In many of these novels the protagonist was the revolution itself. "Thousands of men ceased to be men," noted Berta Gamboa de Camino, "[they] were transformed into irresponsible instruments of something omnipotent."[40] Martín Luis Guzmán, in *El águila y la serpiente* (The Eagle and the Serpent, 1928), found considerable ignorance, corruption, cynicism, and death in the revolution. In the 1930s novelists showed empathy for *zapatista* and *villista* soldiers yet still presented the revolutionary era as brutal and largely senseless. Gregorio López y Fuentes's novels of the 1930s explored the suffering and struggles of peasants and Indians, which the Mexican Revolution did little to ameliorate.[41] His classic agrarian novel of the period, *Tierra* (Land), narrated the revolution from the bad days of Porfirio Díaz to the assassination of Zapata from the perspective of everyday *zapatistas* (see figure 9.2). One finds in these novels, José Luis Martínez wrote in 1960, an ideological indifference and even disenchantment.[42] This stark and

Figure 9.2. "Land: The Agrarian Revolution in Mexico." Cover from the novel of the same title (1933). Private collection of the author.

realistic pessimism on the part of storytellers has been explained by literary critics as the artistic musings of educated urbanites regarding their unknown but exotic compatriots who participated in these events.

In the 1930s, the few Mexican movies about the revolution were based on some of these same novels and themes. As in the novels, the Mexican Revolution of these films accentuated violence and chaos. The outstanding films of Fernando de Fuentes, *El compadre Mendoza* (*Compadre Mendoza*, 1933) and *Vámonos con Pancho Villa* (Let's Go with Pancho Villa, 1935), as John Mraz notes, "emphasize the pain and torment, rather than the transformations" of the revolution.[43] These films also made little effort to disguise the bloody struggles among revolutionary factions. The revolution portrayed in the Mexican cinema in the 1930s was not only capriciously destructive but also self-destructive. Perhaps in reaction to this painful realism, Mexican filmmakers in short order began to produce films that romanticized life and customs in rural Mexico before the revolution. *Allá en el Rancho Grande* (1936) and *La Adelita* (1937), for example, were popular and profitable. This ranchero genre proliferated in the 1940s and 1950s because, Carlos Monsiváis notes, audiences were enchanted with "comedies and dramas that revolved around the idea of a paradise lost."[44]

The remembered Mexican Revolution remained contentious throughout the 1920s and 1930s despite the many calls for and efforts at healing and concord. These contested memories and grudges, in fact, have never completely disappeared in Mexico. The bitterness of factionalism, however, increasingly gave way to the idea of a great revolution that was both heterogeneous and inclusive.

Unifying the Revolution: The 1940s–1960s

The post–World War II period was something of a golden age for what came to be viewed as the official history of the Mexican Revolution. It was not until 1951 that a single-author history of the revolution, one patronized and published by the government party (now called the Institutional Revolutionary Party, PRI) appeared in print. The schoolteacher and historian Alberto Morales Jiménez published his *Historia de la Revolución Mexicana* as a result of a national competition for the best "integrated, clear, and precise idea of the development of the principal events of the Mexican Revolution."[45]

Official history, however, has an interesting and perhaps unexpected heritage. Veterans of the revolution, as well as politicians, officials, and bureaucrats in the 1930s, sought to unify the revolution retrospectively. José T. Meléndez edited a history of the revolution that comprised essays on the key movements

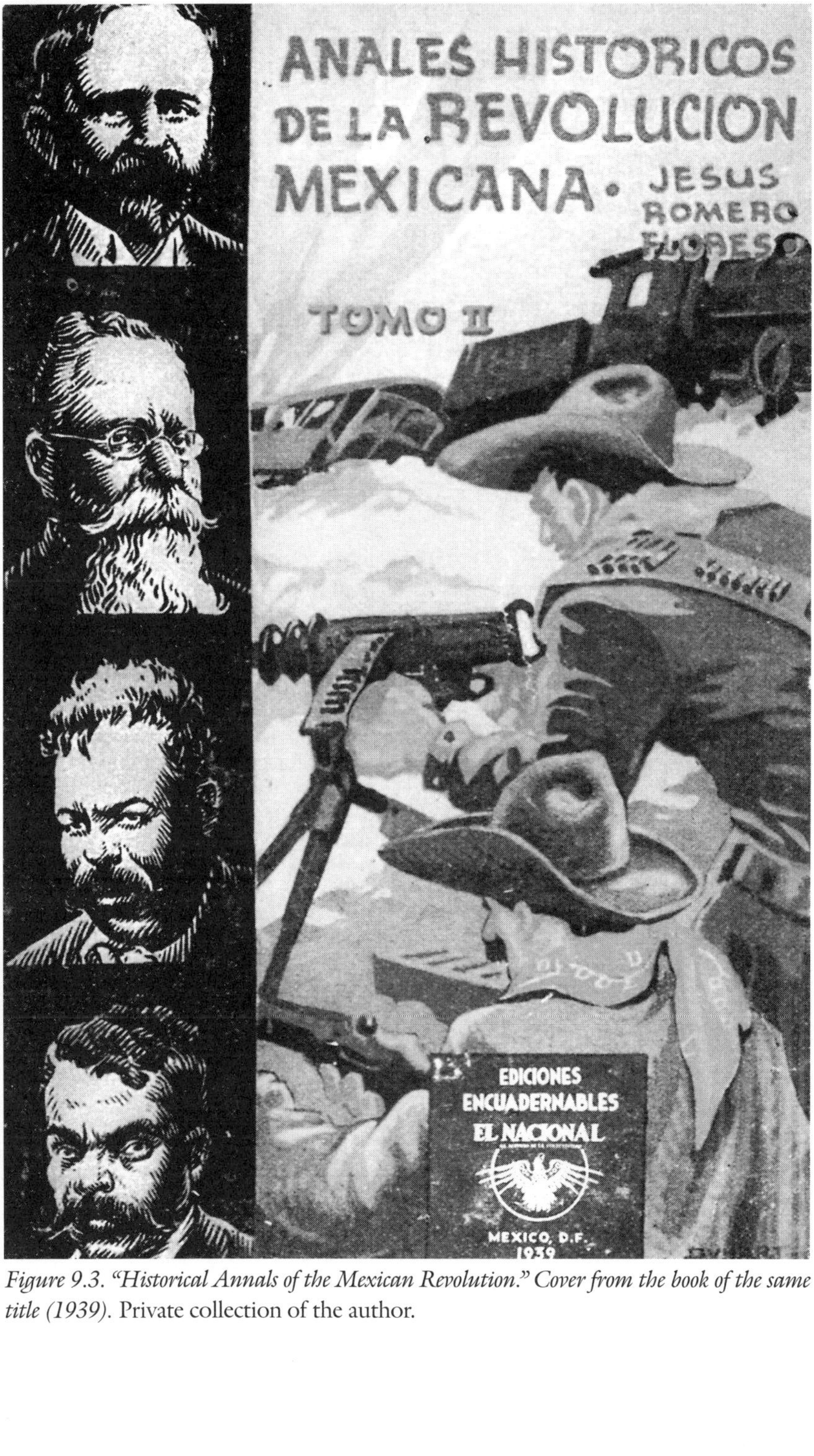

Figure 9.3. "Historical Annals of the Mexican Revolution." Cover from the book of the same title (1939). Private collection of the author.

and leaders written by former partisan *voceros*. In the prologue, Dr. Ramón Puente, a former *maderista* and *villista*, wrote that Madero, Zapata, Carranza, and Villa together "became a conglomeration of blood, of destruction, of greatness and heroism, and of the heterogeneous confusion that will secure a better future."[46] The key concept that began appearing in the 1930s and 1940s was that of *una revolución integral*, that is, complete and unified. Jesús Romero Flores, a veteran of the revolution and head of the Department of History in the National Museum, reinforced this notion in his four-volume *Anales históricos de la Revolución Mexicana* in 1939. The cover of his second volume showed drawings of Madero, Carranza, Villa, and Zapata (see figure 9.3).[47] In 1945 SEP published the first collection of historical documents and manifestos. It is proper to remember the ideas of all of the revolutionary heroes, the editor emphasized. "At times, that body of thought seems incomplete, at others, contradictory. But it is the origin, the base, and the force of the Mexican Revolution."[48]

Although the party and the state published many of these books, this history is not so much official propaganda as the reflection of a new consensus in official, intellectual, and national culture. We might refer to it instead as the corpus of the revolutionary vulgate, that is, the popular and populist version of the revolution. The typical intellectual of this period was both an employee and a critic of the revolutionary party or state.[49] This perspective appears in the pages of the PNR's newspaper, *El Nacional Revolucionario*, beginning in 1931, and among the membership of the Union of Revolutionary Writers and the Association of Revolutionary Veteran Schoolteachers.[50] It sometimes had a touch of socialism, as in José María Bonilla's *Individualismo y Socialismo* (1944), and more often one of simplicity and naïveté.[51] These histories were frequently illustrated by prints from the Popular Graphic Workshop.[52] In 1953 the national government established the National Institute of Historical Studies of the Mexican Revolution (INEHRM), which published scores of histories, biographies, and testimonies.[53] These books, as well as the speeches of politicians, epitomized what later came to be known as the "myth of the revolution."

Popular history and official rhetoric became first fatigued, then phony, and finally ridiculous. In the mid-1940s a number of Mexican intellectuals debated in the pages of *Cuadernos Americanos* whether the Mexican Revolution—as an agent of serious reform—was dead. In 1960 Daniel Cosío Villegas commented that a common attitude among today's old-time revolutionaries "is a tendency to proclaim to high heaven the virtues of the Mexican Revolution and to bury as deep as possible its faults."[54]

More impressive than the proliferation of official and popular histories was the remarkable professionalization of history in Mexico beginning in the 1940s. More and more Mexican historians and increasingly professional historians researched and wrote scholarly histories of the Mexican Revolution. Teams of historical scholars produced volumes of documentary collections and bibliographies that historians have relied upon for decades.[55] This generation organized and modernized the historical archives in Mexico. The professionalization of history in Mexico in the 1940s was marked by the establishment of the Institute of Historical Investigation at the National Autonomous University of Mexico (UNAM); the Department of Historical Investigation within the National Institution of Anthropology and History (IHAH); and the Center for Historical Studies by El Colegio de México. Only six state universities operated in 1940, but by 1961 twenty-four, one for every state in the Mexican federation, were enrolling students. These institutions of higher learning, as well as others in time, trained historians in rigorous seminars and programs, produced quality historical journals, and published more and more historical scholarship.[56]

The best historians of this time were genuinely inspired by the revolution but opposed to sectarian and official history. One of these was José T. Valadés, a former communist activist.[57] In the 1940s Valadés researched and reevaluated the discredited "Old Regime," the Porfiriato. In his multivolume history, he found aspects of the regime and of its era both to commend and to criticize. During the 1960s he published his acclaimed two-volume biography of Madero and his remarkable ten-volume history of the revolution. Valadés, as most historians of his generation, found his sources in the public documents of the revolutionary era.[58] The next generation would delve into not only the archives but also the private and bureaucratic papers of the revolutionaries and their regimes.

Valadés stated that he opposed both "monolithic" and "pessimistic" history (which I understand to mean ideological and antipatriotic history). He favored histories that were good in themselves and good for Mexico.[59] Manuel González Ramírez in 1955 stated that "factional passions are still alive," but he and others sought to put all of that behind them. In the introduction to his four-volume sources of the revolution, González Ramírez noted that his collection in particular and the study of the history of the revolution in general no longer needed to be confined by any "rigid factional points of view."[60] The Seminar of Modern Mexican History at El Colegio de México in the 1950s and 1960s, led by Daniel Cosío Villegas, produced the nine-volume *Historia moderna de Mexico*, truly a scholarly tour de force.[61] Isidro Fabela, Jesús Reyes Heroles, Jesús Silva Herzog, Luis González y González, Moisés González Navarro, and many more Mexican historians wrote superb histories of the *porfiriato* and the revolution. Their histories represented the best of Mexican erudition and scholarship.[62] More and more professional historians from the United States and Europe devoted their academic careers to researching and writing about the Mexican Revolution. The Mexican government in the 1950s began to translate many of these histories and studies in the journal *Problemas agrícolas e industriales de México* without regard to any political or ideological point of view. Javier Garciadiego referred to Charles C. Cumberland's two histories of the revolution as a "classic work about our revolutionary period."[63]

During the 1960s, veterans of the revolution met every August to offer their support to the president during what came to be known as the "Breakfast of Revolutionary Unity." These old revolutionaries, the "spent cartridges of the revolution," declared their fidelity to the revolution and to the government. "Our struggle was an authentic revolution," declared the featured speaker at the 1966 breakfast, Gen. Baltasar R. Leyva Mancilla. "It was not a rampage of factions or political maneuvering for personal aggrandizement." Historians acknowledged the factional struggles but emphasized that these divisions, this heterogeneity, made the Mexican Revolution greater than the sum of its heroes and movements. This kind of history became known in Mexico as *historia de bronce* (history of bronze), a reference to the type found in commemorative speeches and civic monuments.

Revising the Revolution: The 1970s–1980s

This evolving synthesis of the revolution came under fierce assault in the 1970s and 1980s. John Womack Jr. reported little change in how historians viewed the Mexican Revolution from 1959 to 1969. Not quite ten years later David Bailey wrote about a "wave of change in scholarly interpretations of the Revolution." The new revisionism, he continued, "has already altered the field, and clearly there is more to come. Specialists are sharply divided over its merits, and probably the only common ground left is to acknowledge that there is less agreement today about the nature and meaning of the Mexican Revolution than at any time since scholars first turned their attention to it more than fifty years ago."[64] Bailey recognized a revolution within the historiography of the Mexican Revolution.

Both Womack and Bailey focused almost entirely on academic history, the books and articles of professors. The rapidly increasing professionalization of history in the universities of Mexico, the United States, and many other countries produced not simply a new generation of historians but also more historians than had ever existed. Many, like me, were graduate students who were researching and writing their dissertations. Professional historians invaded this field of study and subdivided it not unlike the way that leaf-cutter ants dissect their fibrous prey. These historians brought new theoretical perspectives, methodological approaches, and vigor to the study of the revolution. They scoured the archives in Mexico and elsewhere as never before. They examined the Mexican Revolution from above and below, within and without, and from the center to the many peripheries. "Even the specialists," wrote Bailey in 1978, "find themselves overtaxed to read—and sometimes to locate—the books, articles and dissertations that pour forth not only in Mexico and the US but also in a half-dozen other countries."[65]

The term *revisionism* was widely adopted in reference to disenchantment with the Institutional Revolution, which was then projected back on the revolution of 1910–1920. As much as historians from the 1940s to the 1960s sought to put the discordant pieces of the Mexican Revolution together, revisionists in the 1970s and 1980s took it apart year by year, faction by faction, and region by region. In its place arose the idea of a powerful national state acting as the political arm of a battered but revitalized Mexican business class and a new so-called revolutionary and bureaucratic elite. The business of the Mexican Revolution was business in both the present and the past. This revisionist onslaught did not appear all at once but emerged and intensified over several years.[66]

The five stages of revisionism are criticism, disillusionment, radicalism, righteousness, and ridicule. We see the first serious signs of intellectual criticism of the institutional revolution in the 1940s and 1950s. Disillusionment closely followed in the late 1950s and early 1960s. The Mexican Revolution, to contemporary eyes, appeared conservative, complacent, and corrupt compared to the Cuban Revolution. A radicalism born of anger arose as the national government employed violence against dissident workers, peasant leaders, and protesting students. The shooting of protesters at the Plaza of Three Cultures in Tlateloloco (Mexico City) in October 1968 crystallized, it seemed at the time, the political and moral bankruptcy of the regime and the revolution it claimed as its heritage and inspiration. The Mexican "system," it appeared, had failed, and a fundamental reordering of just about everything was necessary. When this did not happen, the enfants terribles rewrote Mexican history from root to branch with an unwavering conviction that they were right and that their predecessors were either intellectually deluded or disgraceful lackeys.[67]

Ridicule of the revolution was best expressed in the cartoons and caricatures published in papers and, especially, on the covers of magazines. On the fiftieth anniversary of the founding of the revolutionary party in 1929, the cover of the weekly *Proceso* showed a couple celebrating their golden wedding anniversary. "La Señora" appeared as a prosperous if rather gaudy mature woman wearing jewelry inscribed with the letters PRI. "El Señor," in contrast, had clearly been dead for some time, a skeleton in tattered clothing with two bandoliers. The message is clear: The government party had become a member of the nouveau riche, while her partner, the Mexican Revolution, had been dead for decades but remained unburied.[68]

Marxism and neo-Marxism influenced a considerable portion of the new revisionist history. This was not new in Mexican historiography, but it became nearly dominant in the 1970s. The Mexican Revolution was no longer viewed as a triumph over agrarian feudalism by nonideological peasants and workers. Instead, the revolution was guided by a bourgeois capitalist ideology that promoted Mexican capitalism. Popular uprisings changed rulers in Mexico but only upgraded the national bourgeoisie. The postrevolutionary state appeased the masses with populist politics and mild reforms. Arnaldo Córdova provided the theoretical model for this new Marxist history, while other historians worked out the details.[69]

Another, parallel trend in revisionist history was a focus on the local and regional origins, processes, and outcomes of the revolution. The new regional history confirmed Frank Tannenbaum's notion that "a true history of the Revolution would detail the little obscure movements as they developed and gathered force and importance in localities, fought their battles and disappeared, to come to the surface again in another place."[70] Histories of Morelos, Chihuahua, Sonora, Michoacán, Tlaxcala, Puebla, Tabasco, Chiapas, and Yucatán—and other states and localities—proliferated.[71] As Allen Wells has written, when the regional study is successful, "it transcends its circumscribed locale by not losing sight of the political dimension, of the power relations that tie local society and culture into the larger contexts of the region, the nation and the international economy."[72]

The writing of regional histories of the revolution outlived revisionism and continues today as strong as ever. Political biographies and histories of leaders and their movements remain unconfined by ideological or methodological trends. Over the past three decades we have new and very well-researched accounts of Venustiano Carranza, Emiliano Zapata, Felipe Ángeles, Álvaro Obregón, Plutarco Elías Calles, and others.[73]

Whether ideological or regional, political, social, or economic, the new revisionism emphasized, more than anything else, the failure of the popular rebellions to transform Mexico and the triumph of the new state and its elites. In 1973 French historian Jean Meyer portrayed the revolution as a string of atrocities and suffering inflicted on the Mexican people by revolutionary regimes. For Ramón Eduardo Ruiz in his 1980 history, the revolution was simply a "Great Rebellion." In his influential 1986 essay Womack distilled the revolution into little more than a struggle for power. "For all the violence this is the main historical meaning of the Mexican Revolution: capitalist tenacity in the economy and bourgeois reform of the state."[74]

In the 1970s and 1980s, teams of Mexican historians produced more megahistory projects in the tradition of the *Historia moderna de México*. Daniel Cosío Villegas and Luis González launched the massive *Historia de la Revolución Mexicana, 1910–1960*. Nearly twenty volumes were written by a number of different historians; some of these were in the revisionist vein, some were not, but nearly all were first-rate histories of the revolution.[75] Pablo González Casanova was editor of *La clase obrera en la historia de México*, a seventeen volume multi-authored history of the working class. Enrique Semo was editor of the *Historia de la cuestión mexicana*, a thirty-two volume, multiauthored history of agrarian relations in Mexico from 1800 to 1982.[76] The smallest but most innovative of these kinds of projects involved the selection and publication of the stories told by everyday Mexicans who recalled the events and conditions of the revolutionary era. Guillermo Bonfil Batalla directed the three-volume *Mi pueblo durante la Revolución*.[77]

Impressive new syntheses of the Mexican Revolution appeared in the 1980s in the middle of the onslaught by historians of the revisionist generation. Friedrich Katz, Han Werner Tobler, François-Xavier Guerra, Alan Knight, and John Mason Hart researched and wrote histories of considerable merit and quality. Katz, an Austrian-born historian who taught at the University of Chicago since 1971, wrote a diplomatic history that was also a penetrating account of the revolution itself. Tobler, a Swiss historian, covered the most ground in his detailed narrative, which began the story in 1876 and ended it in 1940. Guerra, a French historian, focused primarily on the *porfiriato* and its modernist assault on traditional Mexican communities and culture. Knight, an English historian, following the direction begun by Tannenbaum, wrote about a popular revolution in all of its regional and local variations. Hart, a University of Houston historian, provided the most sophisticated class analysis of a revolution that was not only nationalist but also anti-imperialist.[78] All of these histories in their own way counter the primary revisionist claim that the revolution was a fraud and not a real revolution.[79]

Friedrich Katz contributed another significant history in this category, a book not published until the late 1990s. His numerous articles, chapters, and essays about Francisco Villa and the *villista* movement published in the 1960s, 1970s, and 1980s revised and corrected the hoary tradition that *villismo* was little more than social banditry.[80] Decades of research and writing led to his masterful *Life and Times of Pancho Villa*, published in 1998, a biography, regional history, and, at the same time, surely one of the best studies of the Mexican Revolution.[81]

Deconstructing the Revolution: The 1990s–2000s

The course of memory, myth, and history of the Mexican Revolution over many decades reminds me of Jorge Luis Borges's story "The Garden of the Forking Paths."[82] In Borges's garden, all possibilities coexisted simultaneously. In the contemplative garden of the Mexican Revolution, successive forking paths produced factional and partisan, official and popular, national and regional, and revisionist histories—none of which were mutually exclusive. These multiple and often contradictory memories, myths, and histories of the revolution remain alive and well today. These well-worn forking paths and new ones continue to make the Mexican Revolution a subject of enduring interest and controversy.

Contemporary events and developments in Mexico in the 1990s, as before, shaped popular and scholarly attitudes toward the revolution. The technocratic and neoliberal government of President Carlos Salinas de Gortari (1988–1994) pursued a series of reforms to move modern Mexico out of the shadow of the revolution. The redefinition of Articles 27 and 130 of the Constitution of 1917, regarding land reform and the Catholic Church, as well as Mexico's commitment to the North American Free Trade Agreement (NAFTA), led to widespread protests that the Mexican Revolution had been abandoned by the government and the ruling party. The new national history textbooks that appeared in 1992, lambasted for overvaluing the economic modernization of the *porfiriato*, reinforced this perception.[83] The *zapatista* rebellion in Chiapas in 1994, an indigenous uprising that adopted the symbols and ideas of the Mexican Revolution, produced a new respect for the revolt.[84]

A new cultural history of the Mexican Revolution began emerging in the 1990s, influenced by contemporary events in Mexico and international intellectual trends. It embraces two broad propositions. The first examines the problem of popular and lower-class historical agency in the origins, processes, and outcome of the Mexican Revolution.[85] Of course, we have been here before. The revolution has long been defined and explained as a popular revolution. Two generations of social historians in Mexico have been writing "history from below." Most everyday Mexicans who went to revolution and war were illiterate and therefore produced few historical records. New cultural historians, then, face considerable challenges in their attempts to recover the voices, intentions, and actions of the multitudes without history. Their methods, study of oral tradition, local and regional history, and reading sources against the grain are by no means new. Attention to deconstructing lower-class identities in order to better understand popular mobilization and action is new. Peasant and worker identities, formerly defined primarily in class and economic terms, are now examined as cultural creations influenced by space, ethnicity, religion, gender, and discourse.[86]

Where revisionists once portrayed the postrevolutionary state of the 1920s and 1930s as a powerful instrument that successfully tamed the masses, recent cultural histories provide more nuanced views. The postrevolutionary state was not so autonomous or powerful, and, as a result, popular demands and organizations were woven into its very fabric. The hacienda system was dismantled, and land was redistributed on a massive scale; peasant villagers eagerly embraced and supported rural schools, and communities throughout Mexico fiercely defended their local traditions and rights. Peasants and workers took advantage of revolutionary openings and sometimes cooperated with state and national political leaders and sometimes stood in their way. Radical anticlericalism and socialist education floundered on the reefs of popular opposition.

The second proposition of the new cultural history assumes that the Mexican Revolution itself was a cultural construction, an invention of popular and elite discourse and representation. Historians have begun to deconstruct the revolution, that is, to study how Mexicans remembered and represented the rebellion in texts, rituals, images, and monuments. My book *La Revolución* examines the largely forgotten speeches, articles, pamphlets, and books of the *voceros* of the revolution. Samuel Brunk's history considers how Mexicans—villagers as well as writers—created the myth of Zapata. John Mraz, studying photographs and cinema, argues that visual culture was particularly significant in understanding how Mexicans remembered the revolution and constructed their national identity.[87]

There are more studies like these and more to come. Indeed, we are just beginning to unravel to the threads of memory and myth in modern Mexican history. Scholars are reexamining the Mexican Revolution and its reflections in formal and popular arts, fiction, drama, sports, religion, and commemoration. Indigenous participation in and memories of the revolution, based on native-language texts and oral tradition, are starting to be sorted out. We are beginning to see studies of how the revolution was portrayed in radio programs and television series.[88] In short, here at the conclusion of this chapter, we should recognize that scholars today are really just beginning to research and understand the interrelated nature of memory, myth, and history with respect to the Mexican Revolution.

Conclusion

If one thinks of the Revolution from the ideas outlined in this essay, it's clear that it constituted a movement seeking to reconquer our past, assimilate it, and make it live in the present.
Octavio Paz

Historians prefer a coherent narrative order that achieves some kind of closure. This chapter, however, must leave things unresolved. The story of memory, myth, and history of the Mexican Revolution cannot yet attain narrative closure because this past remains hostage to the ever-continuing desires and demands of the present. Not only are Mexicans and aficionados of Mexico pursuing new approaches to the revolution of 1910–20, but they also continue to remember, reconsider, revere, and at times refute the revolution. Mexicans, like the revolution mentioned by Paz, prefer to assimilate their past and make it live in the present.

Notes

1. Luis González y González, "La pesada herencia del pasado," *Diálogos* (Julio–Agosto 1981): 35.
2. Moisés Sáenz in 1929 made the distinction "between the Revolution with a capital letter and revolutions with a small letter." Sáenz quoted in Ramón Beteta, "The Moving Forces in Mexican Life," in *The Mexican Revolution: A Defense* (Mexico: DAPP, 1937), 8.
3. A considerable portion of this chapter is based on my book La Revolución: Mexico's Great *Revolution as Memory, Myth and History* (Austin: University of Texas Press, 2000).
4. Ignacio B. del Castillo, *Bibliographía de la Revolución Mexicana, 1910–1916* (Mexico D.F., 1918), and Roberto Ramos, *Bibliographía de la Revolución Mexicana* (Mexico, 1931).
5. Stanley R. Ross, "Historia Política: La Revolución Mexicana," Historia Mexicana 15(2–3) (1965–1966): 426. The five-volume *Fuentes de la historia contemporánea de Mexico* (Mexico: El Colegio de Mexico, 1961–1962) lists nearly fifty thousand books, pamphlets, documents, and articles.
6. W. Dirk Raat, *The Mexican Revolution: An Annotated Guide to Recent Scholarship* (Boston: G. K. Hall, 1982). Also see W. Dirk Raat, "La revolución global de México," *Historia Mexicana* 32(3) (1983): 422–48.
7. J. H. Plumb, *The Death of the Past* (Middlesex, England: Penguin, 1969), 11.
8. See E. J. Hobsbawm, *Echoes of the Marseillaise: Two Centuries Look Back on the French Revolution* (New Brunswick, N.J.: Rutgers University Press, 1990).
9. See, for example, Héctor Aguilar Camín y Lorenzo Meyer, *A la sombra de la Revolución Mexicana* (Mexico: Cal y Arena, 1990).

10. A Mexican senator borrowed this phrase from Miguel de Unamuno, in Senator S. Díaz, "México, una Nación históricamente viable," in *Conferencia Nacional de Análysis Ideológico sobre la Revolución Mexicana* (Mexico: Partido Revolucionario Institucional, 1985), 182.
11. T. F. Serrano, *Episodios de la Revolución en México* (El Paso, 1911), 307.
12. In 1932 Rafael Ramos Pedrueza wrote, "The Revolution lives an intense, profound, sorrowful and sublime life," in *Sugerencias Revolucionarias para la Enseñanza de la Historia* (Mexico: Universidad Nacional de México Autonoma, Sección Editorial, 1932), 34.
13. There were also *magonistas, vasquistas, orozquistas, convencionists*, and many other revolutionary movements and factions on the national stage and in the provinces and localities.
14. See Samuel Brunk, *The Posthumous Career of Emiliano Zapata: Myth, Memory, and Mexico's Twentieth Century* (Austin: University of Texas Press, 2008). Todd Downing, in *The Mexican Earth* (New York: Doubleday, Doran, 1940), told the story of the revolution through the words and images of revolutionary corridos.
15. John Mraz, "Photographing Mexico," *Mexican Studies/Estudios Mexicanos* 17(1) (2001): 196. Also see his excellent *Looking for Mexico: Modern Visual Culture and National Identity* (Durham: Duke University Press, 2009). Today the photographs of Casasola and other Mexican photographers are archived in the enormous collection of the Fototeca Nacional in the city of Pachuca, Hidalgo.
16. Andrea Noble, *Mexican National Cinema* (London: Routledge, 2005), 51. Also see John Mraz, "Representing the Mexican Revolution," in *Photography and Writing in Latin America* (Albuquerque: University of New Mexico Press, 2006), 21–39; and Alexandra Jablonska and Juan Felipe Leal, *La Revolución mexicana en el cine nacional, 1911–1917* (Mexico: Universidad Pedagógica Nacional, 1997).
17. Guillermo Mellado, *Tres Etapas Políticas de Don Venustiano Carranza* (Mexico, 1916). Aragón's chart of Mexico's political parties is found in Benjamin, *La Revolución*, 64–65.
18. José L. Cossio, *Album histórico postal de la República Mexicana, 1856–1956* (Mexico: Dirección General de Correos, 1956).
19. Octavio Paz, *El laberinto de la soledad y otras obras* (New York: Penguin, 1997), 176. This essay was first published in 1950.
20. Herbert Ingram Priestley, "Mexican Literature on the Recent Revolution," *Hispanic American Historical Review* 2(2) (May 1919): 286; T. Esquivel Obregón, "Factors in the Historical Evolution of Mexico," *Hispanic American Historical Review* 2(2) (May 1919): 136; and Gloria Villegas Moreno, "Las armas de la historia," in *Memoria del Congreso Internacional sobre la Revolución Mexicana* (Mexico: Instituto Nacional de Estudios Históricos de la Revolución Mexicana, 1991), 133, and Villegas Moreno, "El viraje de la historiografía Mexicana frente a la crisis revolucionaria (1914–1916)," *Anuario de Historia* 11 (1983): 213–29.
21. See Robert McCaa, "Missing Millions: The Demographic Costs of the Mexican Revolution," *Mexican Studies/Estudios Mexicanos* 19(2) (2003): 367–400.
22. From "Manifiesto a la Nación," México, January 1920, quoted in Benjamin, *La Revolución*, 124.

23. Antonio Islas Bravo, *La sucesión presidencial de 1928* (Mexico, 1927), 64.
24. Spratling, quoted in Thomas Benjamin, "Regionalizing the Revolution: The Many Mexicos in Revolutionary Historiography," in Thomas Benjamin and Mark Wasserman, eds., *Provinces of the Revolution* (Albuquerque: University of New Mexico Press, 1991), 327.
25. Miguel Yepez Solórzano, *Mensaje al grupo revolucionario de México* (Mexico, 1924), 28.
26. Juan Sanchez Azcona, "Bifurcaciones de la Revolución," *El Universal*, 22 de junio de 1925.
27. See the Chamber of Deputies website, "Muro de Honor: Salón de Plenos de la H. Cámara de Diputados Letras de Oro," 2008, http://www.diputados.gob.mx/cedia/sia/re_muro.htm.
28. Dawn Ades, *Art in Latin America: The Modern Era, 1820–1980* (New Haven, Conn.: Yale University Press, 1989), 151.
29. Leopoldo Méndez and other graphic artists are discussed in Agustín Velazquez Chavez, *Contemporary Mexican Artists* (New York: Covici Friede, 1937). Also see Helga Prignitz, *El taller de gráfica popular en México, 1937–1977* (Mexico City: Instituto Nacional de Bellas Artes, 1992).
30. Anticlerical laws and policies provoked a popular rebellion in 1926–1929. See David C. Bailey, *Viva Cristo Rey! The Cristero Rebellion and the Church-State Conflict in Mexico* (Austin: University of Texas Press, 1974).
31. Ernest Gruening, *Mexico and Its Heritage* (New York: Century, 1928); Frank Tannenbaum, *The Mexican Agrarian Revolution* (New York: Columbia University Press, 1929); and Frank Tannenbaum, *Peace by Revolution* (New York: Columbia University Press, 1933). Also see Charles A. Hale, "Frank Tannenbaum and the Mexican Revolution," *Hispanic American Historical Review* 75(2) (1995): 215–46.
32. Carleton Beals, *Mexican Maze* (Philadelphia: Lippincott, 1931), and Stuart Chase, *Mexico: A Study of Two Americas* (New York: Macmillan, 1942).
33. See Alicia Azuela de la Cueva, "Peace by Revolution: Una aproximación léxico-visual al México revolucionario," *Historia Mexicana* 61(4) (2007): 1263–1307. Times quotation in Helen Delpar, *The Enormous Vogue of Things Mexican* (Tuscaloosa: University of Alabama Press, 1992), 56. Delpar notes that one hundred nonfiction books about Mexico were published in the United States from 1920 to 1935.
34. *La Democracia Social en México* (Mexico City, 1929), 102.
35. Emilio Portes Gil, *En memoria de Zapata* (Mexico: Partido Nacional Revolucionario, 1936), 5.
36. Calles, quoted in Max Parra, *Writing Pancho Villa's Revolution* (Austin: University of Texas Press, 79.
37. Jesús Corral, "La glorificación de los héroes revolucionarios," *El Nacional*, 8 de julio de 1931.
38. *El Monumento a la Revolución* (1933), quoted in Benjamin, "La Revolución hecha monumento," *Historia y Grafía* 6 (1996): 132.
39. Mariano Azuela, *The Underdogs* (New York: Signet Classic, 1963), 71.
40. Berta Gamboa de Camino, "The Novel of the Mexican Revolution," in *Renascent Mexico*, ed. Hubert Herring and Herbert Weinstock (New York: Covici Friede, 1935), 260.

41. See Elizabeth Henry, "Revolution as Mexican Novelists See It," *Hispania* 15(5/6) (1932): 423–36; Bernard Dulsey, "The Mexican Revolution as Mirrored in the Novels of Mariano Azuela," *Modern Language Journal* 35(5) (1951): 382–87; Beatrice Berler, "The Mexican Revolution as Reflected in the Novel," *Hispania* 47(1) (1964): 41–46; Donald Schmidt, "The Indigenista Novel and the Mexican Revolution," *Americas* 33(4) (1977): 652–60; and John D. Rutherford, *Mexican Society during the Revolution: A Literary Approach* (Oxford: Oxford University Press, 1971).
42. José Luis Martínez, "La literature mexicana y la revolución," *Combate* 13 (1960): 91.
43. John Mraz, "The Revolution Is History," *Filmhistoria* 9(2) (1999): 148.
44. Monsiváis, quoted in Joanne Hershfield, "Screening the Nation," in Mary Kay Vaughn and Steven Lewis, eds., *The Eagle and the Virgin: Nation and Cultural Revolution in Mexico, 1920–1940* (Durham, N.C.: Duke University Press, 2006), 275.
45. This book is discussed in length in Benjamin, *La Revolución*, 148–50.
46. Ramón Puente, 'Prólogo," in José T. Meléndez, ed., *Historia de la Revolución Mexicana* (Mexico: Talleres Gráficos de la Nación, 1936), 8.
47. Romero Flores, *Anales históricos de la Revolución Mexicana* (Mexico: Ediciones Encuadernables de el Nacional, 1939). Also see Romero Flores, *Discursos cívicos* (Mexico: Biblioteca del Instituto Nacional de Estudios Históricos de la Revolución Mexicana, 1956).
48. "Introducción," in *Documentos de la Revolución Mexicana*, ed. Isidro Fabela and Josefina Fabela (Mexico: Secretaría de Educación Pública, 1945).
49. Yvon Grenier makes this very interesting point in "Octavio Paz: An Intellectual and His Critics," *Mexican Studies/Estudios Mexicanos* 21(1) (2005): 253. Stanley Rypins compared this aspect of the Russian and Mexican revolutions in "Revolutions: Mexican and Russian," in Herring and Weinstock, *Renascent Mexico*, 152.
50. *El Nacional Revolucionario* referred to itself as "the newspaper adopted by the Revolution itself as the *vocero* of the principles raised by the people and their representatives."
51. José María Bonilla, *Individualismo y Socialismo* (Mexico: Herrero Hermanos Sucesores, 1944); *La Revolución Mexicana* (Mexico D.F.: Biblioteca del Instituto Nacional de Estudios Históricos de la Revolución Mexicana, 1954).
52. See *La Revolución Mexicana*.
53. See *Catálogo de Publicaciones del Instituto Nacional de Estudios Históricos de la Revolución Mexicana* (Mexico D.F.: Instituto Nacional de Estudios Históricos de la Revolución Mexicana, 1993). The INEHRM, however, published histories and anthologies of various points of view and reprinted books from the era of intense factionalism.
54. Daniel Cosío Villegas, "The Mexican Revolution, Then and Now," in *Change in Latin America*, ed. Cosío Villegas (Lincoln, Neb.: University of Nebraska Press, 1960), 24.
55. See Manuel González Ramírez, *Fuentes para la historia de la Revolución Mexicana*, 4 vols. (Mexico City: Fondo de la Cultura Económica, 1954–1957; Isídro Fabela and Josefina Fabela, eds., *Documentos históricos de la Revolución Mexicana*, 27 vols. (Mexico City: Fondo

de la Cultura Económica, 1960–1973); *Diario de los Debates del Congreso Constituyente, 1916–1917*, 2 vols. (Mexico City: Imprenta de la Camara Diputados, 1960); and Luis González, *Fuentes de la historia contemporánea de México*, 5 vols. (Mexico City: El Colegio de México, 1961–1967).

56. Jorge Gurría Lacroix y Miguel León-Portilla, "Las investigaciones históricas y sus aportaciones," in *Las humanidades en México, 1950–1970*, ed. Jorge Cardizo (Mexico: Universidad Nacional Autónoma de México, 1978), 7–92; and Xavier Tavera Alfaro, "La carrera de historia en México," *Historia Mexicana* 4(4) (1955): 624–36.
57. In his memoir, Valadés discusses his early life as an activist and how he first became a journalist and then a historian. See José T. Valadés, *Memorias de un joven rebelde* (Culiacán, Mexico: Universidad Autónoma de Sinaloa, 1985), 2 vols. The careers of Frank Tannenbaum and José T. Valadés are similar in this respect.
58. José T. Valadés, *El porfirismo: Historia de un regimen*, 3 vols. (Mexico, 1941–1947); *Imaginación y realidad de Francisco I. Madero*, 2 vols. (Mexico, 1960); and *Historia general de la Revolución Mexicana*, 10 vols. (Mexico, 1963–1967). Also see *José C. Valadés: Historiador y Político* (Mexico, 1992).
59. José T. Valadés, *Breviaro de historia de México* (Mexico, 1949), 176.
60. *Fuentes para la historia de la Revolución Mexicana*, vol. 4, vi.
61. Daniel Cosío Villegas, coord., *Historia moderna de México* (Mexico, 1955–1972). Also see Charles A. Hale, "The Liberal Impulse: Daniel Cosío Villegas and the *Historia moderna de México*," *Hispanic American Historical Review* 54 (August 1974): 479–98; and Thomas Benjamin and Marcial Ocasio-Meléndez, "Organizing the Memory of Modern Mexico: Porfirian Historiography in Perspective, 1880s–1980s," *Hispanic American Historical Review* 64 (1984): 323–64.
62. See Stanley R. Ross, "Historia Política: La Revolución Mexicana," Historia Mexicana 15(2/3) (1965–1966): 425–45; and Enrique Florescano, *Historia de las historias de la nación mexicana* (Mexico: Taurus, 2002).
63. See Stanley R. Ross, "Aportación norteamericana a la historiográfica de la Revolución Mexicana," *Historia Mexicana* 10(2) (1960): 282–308. For a thorough analysis of the work of one of the American historians, see Javier Garciadiego, "La obra de Charles E. Cumberland sobre la revolución mexicana, en español," *Historia Mexicana* 27(3) (1978): 501.
64. John Womack Jr., "Mexican Political Historiography, 1959–1969," in *Investigaciones contemporáneas sobre historia de México*, ed. Jorge Gurría Lacroix (Mexico, 1971), 468–92; and David Bailey, "Revisionism and the Recent Historiography of the Mexican Revolution," *Hispanic American Historical Review* 58(1) (1978): 62–79.
65. Bailey, "Revisionism and the Recent Historiography of the Mexican Revolution," 62.
66. The best short account of this development is Stanley R. Ross, "La protesta de los intelectuales ante México y su revolución," *Historia Mexicana* 26(3) (1977): 396–437. Also see Ricardo Pozas Horcasitas, "*La Revista Mexicana de Literatura*: Territorio de la

nueva elite intellectual, (1955–1965)," *Mexican Studies/Estudios Mexicanos* 24(1) (2008): 53–78.

67. We see this in the novels and essays of Carlos Fuentes, whose review of John Womack Jr.'s *Zapata and the Mexican Revolution* (New York: Vintage, 1968) is close to being the founding statement in English of the new revisionism. See "Viva Zapata," *New York Review of Books* 12(5) (1969).
68. *Proceso* 3 (March 5, 1979). Also see the cartoon collections of Rius (Eduardo del Río), *La revolucioncita mexicana* (Mexico: Editorial Posada, 1978) and *Su Majestad el PRI* (Mexico: Editorial Posada, 1982). For a broader assessment also see Victor Alba, "The Mexican Revolution and the Cartoon," *Comparative Studies in Society and History* 9(2) (1967): 121–36.
69. Arnaldo Córdova, *La formación del poder político en México* (Mexico: ERA, 1972) and *La ideología de la Revolución Mexicana: La formación del nuevo régimen* (Mexico: ERA, 1973). Luis Analya Merchant examines three Marxist histories in "La construcción de la memoria y la revisión de la Revolución," *Historia Mexicana* 44(4) (1995): 525–36. Also see Adolfo Gilly, *La revolución interrumpida* (Mexico: El Caballito, 1971); the essays in *Interpretaciones de la Revolución Mexicana*, ed. Adolfo Gilly (Mexico: UNAM, 1979); Ramón Eduardo Ruiz, *The Great Rebellion* (New York: Norton, 1980); and John Womack Jr., "The Mexican Revolution," in *Cambridge History of Latin America*, vol. 5 (Cambridge: Cambridge University Press, 1986), 84–149.
70. Tannenbaum, *Peace by Revolution*, 148.
71. See, for example, John Womack Jr., *Zapata and the Mexican Revolution* (New York: Vintage, 1968); Luis González y González, *Pueblo en vilo* (Mexico: El Colegio de México, 1972); Hector Aguilar Camín, *La frontera nómada* (Mexico: Siglo XXI Editores, 1977); Carlos Martínez Assad, *El laboratorio de la Revolución* (Mexico: Siglo XXI Editores, 1979); and Romana Falcón, *Revolución y caciquismo* (Mexico: El Colegio de México, 1984).
72. Allen Wells, "Oaxtepec Revisited: The Politics of Mexican Historiography, 1968–1988," *Mexican Studies/Estudios Mexicanos* 7(2) (1991): 342–43. For reviews of this regionalist historiography see Romana Falcón, "Las regiones en la Revolución. Un itinerario historiográfica," in Carlos Martínez Assad, ed., *Balance y perspectivas de los estudios regionales en México*, 61–89 (Mexico: UNAM, 1990).
73. See Douglas Richmond, *Venustiano Carranza's Nationalist Struggle, 1893–1920* (Lincoln: University of Nebraska Press, 1983); Samuel Brunk, *Emiliano Zapata: Revolution and Betrayal in Mexico* (Albuquerque: University of New Mexico Press, 1995); Odile Guilpain Peuliard, *Felipe Ángeles y los destinos de la Revolución mexicana* (México: Fondo de Cultura Económica, 1991); Linda B. Hall, *Álvaro Obregón: Power and Revolution in Mexico, 1911–1920* (College Station: Texas A&M University Press, 1981); Jürgen Buchenau, *Plutarco Elías Calles and the Mexican Revolution* (Lanham, Md.: Rowman and Littlefield, 2006); and Jürgen Buchenau, *The Last Caudillo: Alvaro Obregón and the Mexican Revolution* (Malden, Mass.: Wiley Blackwell, 2011).

74. Jean Meyer, *La Revolución Mejicana* (Barcelona, 1973); Ramón Eduardo Ruiz, The Great Rebellion (New York: Norton, 1980); John Womack Jr., "The Mexican Revolution, 1910–1920," in *The Cambridge History of Latin America*, vol. 5, ed. Leslie Bethell (Cambridge: Cambridge University Press, 1986), 81. For a broad synthesis of revisionism, see Enrique Florescano, *El Nuevo pasado mexicano* (Mexico: Cal y Arena, 1994).
75. The most comprehensive review of most of these volumes is found in the *Hispanic American Historical Review* 64(4) (1984): 767–85.
76. Pablo González Casanova, ed., *La clase obrera en la historia de Mexico* (Mexico: UNAM, 1980–1988); Enrique Semo, ed., *Historia de la cuestión agraria mexicana* (Mexico: Siglo XXI Editores, 1988–1992).
77. Guillermo Bonfil Batalla, *Mi pueblo durante la Revolución* (Mexico: Instituto Nacional de Antropología e Historia, 1985), 3 vols.
78. Friedrich Katz, *The Secret War in Mexico: Europe, the United States and the Mexican Revolution* (Chicago: University of Chicago Press, 1981); Han Werner Tobler, *La Revolución: Transformación social y cambio político, 1876–1940* (Mexico: Alianza Editorial, 1994), the first edition in German was published in 1984; François-Xavier Guerra, *De l'ancien regime a la revolution*, 2 vols. (Paris: Publications de la Sorbonne, 1985); Alan Knight, *The Mexican Revolution*, 2 vols. (Cambridge: Cambridge University Press, 1986); and John Mason Hart, *Revolutionary Mexico: The Coming and Process of the Mexican Revolution* (Berkeley: University of California Press, 1987).
79. In his review of Knight and Hart, John Foran noted that he found himself in substantial agreement with both historians. See "Reinventing the Mexican Revolution: The Competing Paradigms of Alan Knight and John Mason Hart," *Latin American Perspectives* 23(4) (1996): 115–31.
80. Benjamin, "Regionalizing the Revolution," 326–27; and Friedrich Katz, *Ensayos mexicanos* (Mexico: Alianza Editorial, 1994).
81. Friedrich Katz, *The Life and Times of Pancho Villa* (Stanford: Stanford University Press, 1998); see John Mason Hart's review in *The Americas* 55(4) (1999): 642.
82. Borges's short story was published in a collection of stories under the same title, *El jardín de senderos que se bifurcan* (Buenos Aires: Ficciones, 1941).
83. Dennis Gilbert, "Rewriting History: Salinas, Zedillo and the 1992 Textbook Controversy," *Mexican Studies/Estudios Mexicanos* 13(2) (1997): 271–97.
84. Thomas Benjamin, "A Time of Reconquest: History, the Maya Revival, and the Zapatista Rebellion in Chiapas," *American Historical Review* 105(2) (2000): 417–50.
85. See Alan Knight, "Subalterns, Signifiers, and Statistics: Perspectives on Mexican Historiography," *Latin American Research Review* 37(2) (2002): 136–58.
86. Mary Kay Vaughan, "Cultural Approaches to Peasant Politics in the Mexican Revolution," *Hispanic American Historical Review* 79(2) (1999): 269–305. Also see Claudio Lomnitz-Adler, *Exits from the Labyrinth: Culture and Ideology in the Mexican National Space* (Berkeley: University of California Press, 1992).

87. Benjamin, *La Revolución* (2000); Brunk, *Posthumous Career of Emiliano Zapata*; and Mraz, *Looking for Mexico*.

88. See the essays in William Beezley, Cheryl Martin, and William French, eds., *Rituals of Rule, Rituals of Resistance: Public Celebrations and Popular Culture in Mexico* (Wilmington, Del.: SR Books, 1994); and Vaughan and Lewis, *Eagle and the Virgin*.

About the Contributors

CARLOS MARTÍNEZ ASSAD is on the faculty of the Social and Political Sciences Department, Universidad Nacional Autónoma de México. He received his PhD in political sociology at the École des Hautes Études en Sciences Sociales, University of Paris, France. He was director of the journal Eslabones and completed "Tabasco, el experimento social: Un DVD relata la reducción nacionalista y el anticlericalismo que vivió en el estado con Garrido Canabal" in 2004. He also edited *Religiosidad* y *politica en Mexico* (Mexico City: Cuadernos de Cultura y Religion, 1992) and *Estadistas, caciques y caudillos* (Mexico City: UNAM, 1988), as well as *Balance y perspectivas de los estudios regionales en Mexico* (Mexico City: UNAM, 1990).

FRANCISCO E. BALDERRAMA is professor of Chicano studies and history at California State University–Los Angeles, where he was selected as Outstanding University Professor in 1997. Previously, he served as chair of Chicano studies. He has also held faculty and administrative appointments at Texas Tech University, Adams State College, and the Claremont Colleges. He is a noted Chicano historian with special interest in the American West, particularly California and Los Angeles. He received his doctorate from the University of California–Los Angeles. Most recently, Professor Balderrama is the coauthor of *Decade of Betrayal: Mexican Repatriation in the 1930s* (Albuquerque: University of New Mexico Press, 2006) and *Mexican-American Baseball in Los Angeles* (Charleston, S.C.: Arcadia, 2011).

THOMAS BENJAMIN is professor of history, Central Michigan University. He received his PhD from Michigan State University. His research focuses on Mexico and the Atlantic world. Recent publications by Professor Benjamin include *The Atlantic World: Europeans, Africans, Indians and Their Shared History, 1400–1900* (New York: Cambridge University Press, 2009). He is also the editor in chief of the three-volume work *Encyclopedia of Western Colonialism since 1450* (New York: Macmillan, 2007).

JÜRGEN BUCHENAU is professor of history and Latin American studies at the University of North Carolina–Charlotte. He obtained his PhD from the University of North Carolina–Chapel Hill. His areas of interest are nineteenth- and twentieth-century Mexico, its cultural, economic, and political aspects, immigration, Mexico in world affairs, and the Mexican Revolution. He is the coeditor of two books, *Aftershocks: Earthquakes and Popular Politics in Latin America* (Albuquerque: University of New Mexico Press, 2009), and *State Governors in the Mexican Revolution, 1910–1952: Portraits in Conflict, Courage, and Corruption* (Lanham, Md.: Rowman and Littlefield, 2009). He is also the author of *Mexican Mosaic: A Brief History of Mexico* (Wheeling, Ill.: Harlan Davidson, 2008).

DON M. COERVER is an associate dean and professor in the Department of History and Geography at Texas Christian University. He received his PhD in Latin American history from Tulane University. His areas of specialization include Modern Mexico, US–Latin American relations, militarism/foreign intervention in Latin America, and US business history (especially federal regulation and consumer fraud). His latest books are *Tangled Destinies: Latin America and the United States* (Albuquerque: University of New Mexico Press, 1999), and *Mexico* (Santa Barbara: ABC-CLIO, 2004).

MIGUEL ÁNGEL GONZÁLEZ-QUIROGA *is* a former state representative from the state of Nuevo León, México, and a former professor of history at the Universidad Autónoma de Nuevo León. He received his MA in Latin American history from the Universidad de las Américas in Puebla, Mexico. He has coauthored two books and coedited two others on the border region. One of his latest efforts has been as coeditor, with Timothy Bowman, of Melinda Rankin's *Twenty Years among the Mexicans: A Narrative of Missionary Labor* (Dallas: Library of Texas, 2008).

LINDA B. HALL is professor of Latin American history at the University of New Mexico, where she has also served as director of Latin American studies. She received her PhD in Latin American history from Columbia University. Her published work has focused principally on the Mexican Revolution and the US-Mexican border. Her scholarly interests also extend beyond Mexico, encompassing both US–Latin American relations and regional studies more broadly. Professor Hall is the author of *Mary, Mother and Warrior: The Virgin Mary in Spain and the Americas* (Austin: University of Texas Press, 2004). She is currently working on a biography of Dolores Del Rio titled *Dolores Del Rio: Icon of Beauty in Two Cultures*.

JOHN MASON HART is the John and Rebecca Moores Professor of History at the University of Houston and one of the nation's foremost scholars on Mexican history. He received his PhD in Latin American history from

UCLA. Dr. Hart has lectured in Mexico and has served as a Distinguished Visiting Professor at the Instituto Nacional de Antropología e Historia and the Escuela Nacional de Antropología e Historia in Mexico City. Professor Hart has authored several books, including *Empire and Revolution: The Americans in Mexico since the Civil War* (Berkeley: University of California Press, 2002), *Revolutionary Mexico: The Coming and Process of the Mexican Revolution* (Berkeley: University of California Press, 1987), and *The Silver of the Sierra Madre: John Robinson, Boss Shepherd, and the People of the Canyons* (Tucson: University of Arizona Press, 2008).

SAM W. HAYNES is professor of history and director of the Center for Greater Southwestern Studies at the University of Texas at Arlington. Specializing in the Jacksonian era and the American Southwest, Haynes is the author and coauthor of several books, including *James K. Polk and the Expansionist Impulse* (New York: Longman, 1997). His most recent work is *Unfinished Revolution: The American Republic in a British World, 1815–1850* (Charlottesville: University of Virginia Press, 2010). A member of the Texas Institute of Letters, he has served as a historical consultant for the History Channel and PBS, speaking on topics such as American continental expansionism and the presidency during the early national period. In 2008 he served as the lead consultant for the History Channel's two-hour documentary "The Mexican War."

STEPHEN E. LEWIS received his PhD from the University of California San Diego, where he is associate professor in history. Professor Lewis is author of *The Ambivalent Revolution: Forging State and Nation in Chiapas, Mexico, 1910–1945* (Albuquerque: University of New Mexico Press, 2005). With Mary Kay Vaughan, he coedited *The Eagle and the Virgin: National and Cultural Revolution in Mexico, 1920–1940* (Durham: Duke University Press, 2006). Most recently, he coedited and wrote the introduction to *Monopolio de aguardiente y alcoholismo en Chiapas: Un estudio 'incómodo' de Julio de la Fuente* (Mexico City: Comisión Nacional para el Desarrollo de los Pueblos Indígenas, 2009). His recent articles have appeared in *Anuario de Estudios Americanos*, *The Americas*, *Ethnohistory*, *Mesoamérica*, and *Latin American Perspectives*.

DOUGLAS W. RICHMOND is professor emeritus of history at the University of Texas at Arlington, where he received the Distinguished Record of Research in 2011 and was a Fellow of the Center for Greater Southwestern Studies. He received his PhD from the University of Washington and became involved with the US-Mexican War of 1846–1848 when he helped organize a conference on the theme in 1985 in the form of a Webb Lectures symposium. He is the author of *The Mexican Nation: Historical Continuity and Modern Change* (New York: Prentice Hall, 2001) and coeditor of *Dueling Eagles: Reinterpreting the US-Mexico War, 1846–1848* (Fort Worth: Texas Christian University Press, 2000). Richmond is best known for his *Venustiano Carranza's Nationalist Struggle, 1893–1920* (Lincoln: University of Nebraska Press, 1983).

NICHOLAS VILLANUEVA JR. is entering his final year as a doctoral candidate in history at Vanderbilt University. He is currently funded by the Excellence in West Texas History Fellowship through Angelo State University and will defend his dissertation in the spring of 2013.

Index

Selected Titles in the Walter Prescott Webb Memorial Lectures Series:

The African Diaspora, Jalloh and Maizlish
Manifest Destiny and Empire, Haynes and Morris
Creolization in the Americas, Buisseret and Reinhardt
Women and the Unstable State in Nineteenth-Century America, Parker and Cole
Sacrifice and National Belonging in Twentieth-Century Germany, Eghigian and Berg
Beyond Black and White: Race, Ethnicity, and Gender in the U.S. South and Southwest, Cole and Parker
Traveling between Worlds: German-American Encounters, Adam and Gross
Transatlantic History, Reinhardt and Reinhartz
Lights, Camera, History: Portraying the Past in Film, Francaviglia and Rodintzky
Catholicism in the American West, Treviño and Francaviglia
Baseball in America and America in Baseball, Kyle and Fairbanks
Assumed Identities: The Meanings of Race in the Atlantic World, Garrigus and Morris
Crossing the Atlantic: Travel and Travel Writing in Modern Times, Adam and Roemer
The Folly of Jim Crow: Rethinking the Segregated South, Cole and Ring